STARS FELL
ON ALABAMA

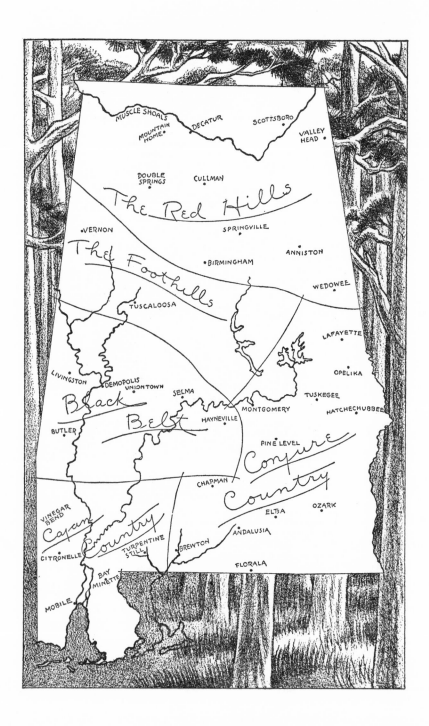

STARS FELL ON ALABAMA

CARL CARMER

Introduction by

J. Wayne Flynt

Illustrated by

Cyrus LeRoy Baldridge

The University of Alabama Press

Library of Congress Cataloging in Publication Data

Carmer, Carl Lamson, 1893–
   Stars fell on Alabama.

   1. Alabama—Social life and customs.   2. Alabama—
Description and travel.   3. Folklore—Alabama.
4. Afro-Americans—Alabama—Social life and customs.
1. Title.
F326.C275   1985   306'.09761   85-8107
ISBN 0-8173-0236-0 (alk. paper)
ISBN 0-8173-0235-2 (pbk. : alk. paper)

For

ELIZABETH BLACK

CONTENTS

Part VI. Cajan

INTRODUCTION

J. Wayne Flynt

C ARL LAMSON CARMER was a strange candidate to write a book about Alabama folkways. Born at Cortland in upstate New York on October 16, 1893, he was essentially a New Yorker, or as he preferred to be called, a "York State man" so as to escape any identification with New York City. His family moved early in his childhood to the ancestral home at Dryden, where Carmers had farmed since the time of his Dutch great-great-great-grandfather. As a boy he ran to fires beside the volunteer fire company, played baseball and tennis for his home town, and earned a fiddle by loading apples and selling them at a cider mill. He attended Hamilton College where most of his male ancestors had earned their degrees. There he was a half-miler on the track team and an avid tennis player, who also loved to dance, sing folk songs, and scratch out ballads on his fiddle. After graduation in 1914 he earned his M.A. at Harvard, then taught English briefly at Syracuse and the University of Rochester before taking leave to serve as a gunnery officer in France during the First World War.[1]

When he returned from Europe, he obtained a job teaching English at The University of Alabama. The six years he spent in Tuscaloosa would profoundly influence his life. He had already begun to write but had shown a decided preference for poetry over prose. As a professor at the University, he especially devoted his energies to English 13, a poetry class. Most Northerners would have fared poorly in a small Alabama town in the early 1920s but Carmer had special liabilities. The first night in Tuscaloosa he discovered that he did not like cornbread, okra, or collards. Shortly afterward University of Alabama students let him know that they did not appreciate a "missionary of Eastern culture," "one of those damn-Yankee professors who lectures on poetry and goes without a hat."[2]

But in time teacher and students warmed to each other. Although Carmer enjoyed observing such genial Alabama social diversions as golf, tennis, bridge, dancing, swimming, drinking, love-making and gossip, he discovered a world quite different from such familiar upper-class pastimes. While wandering backroads, listening to storytellers, sampling moonshine, and judging fiddle festivals, he discovered a different Alabama, one closer in spirit to the 1850s than to the 1950s. As he traveled during his Alabama sojourn (1921–1927), he penned copious notes in his journal, recording the color, peculiarities, and foibles of the people he met and the places they inhabited. He planned to turn his notes into a scholarly article on Southern folklore. It is the reader's good fortune that he turned them instead into *Stars Fell on Alabama*.

Carmer remained a protagonist to his students no longer than he remained a stranger to their land. In English 13 he required them to compose poetry. Each year the class conducted a meeting where students determined the person to whom they would dedicate their annual volume of poetry. Whatever sectional animosity that may have divided students and professor in 1921 had obviously vanished four years later when the class unanimously dedicated their volume of poems to Carl Carmer "Because he was able to see a Renascence in the South, and that nothing of the Arts is foreign to it."[3]

That special part of the arts from which the Southern renascence drew so much of its lifeblood was the region's folkways. At almost the same time that Howard Odum, the eminent sociologist, was exploring black folkways in Georgia, Carmer was recording them in Alabama. A few years earlier, across the state in Auburn, Newman I. White collected similar materials which he later used in a seminal book on American black folksongs. Alabama's poverty and backwardness proved its greatest asset, for currents of modernity had not yet swept across the state, erasing the rhythm and substance of its rural way of life.

Carmer's book, published in 1934, was an immediate success, selected by the Literary Guild and earning him a national reputation as folklorist and regionalist. Reviews were overwhelmingly favorable. Laurence Bell in *New Republic* concluded that Carmer "writes beautifully and his prose has a poetic quality." R. L. Duffus in *The New York Times* claimed that Carmer had "done well by Alabama": "He makes one love it and despair of it, just as he himself seems to do. . . . Mr. Carmer reveals himself here as a writer of more than ordinary perceptiveness and imagination, with the power of extracting from what he sees, hears and feels an essence which is fundamentally poetic."[4]

Two authors who knew the South better than Carmer and whose reputations would soon eclipse his, also reviewed the volume. Novelist T. S. Stribling wrote: "Mr. Carmer uses all three [dialects]: the Negro's, the hill-man's and the aristocrat's with satisfying precision. . . . When a reader gets up from the book he has not only a panoramic and vivid impression of all sorts and classes of folk in the State of Alabama, but he has an even keener impression of the author himself. . . . Mr. Carmer . . . has dramatized fields of Southern life with extraordinary success."[5]

In *The Yale Review*, Caroline Gordon praised Carmer's mixture of hyperbole and understatement and his faithful reproduction of the idiom of Alabama's people. Carmer's uncanny ear for a good story had allowed him "to penetrate as far as any stranger ever penetrates into the life of an alien community." She faults him only because he went beyond storytelling by exaggerating the strangeness of the tales and the habits of the people. She denied that Alabama was so different from other states. Most of the bizarre events Carmer described in Alabama had an equivalent in Passaic, New Jersey, or Mooresville, Indiana: "One wonders just what pattern of life it is against which Alabama looms so strange . . . and one concludes finally that it is a set of values that Mr. Carmer got perhaps in a newspaper office." But she liked the book anyway and predicted that stars would always rain for Carl Carmer.[6] And she was right!

By the time his book was published, Carmer had ended his peripatetic career as journalist in New Orleans and had settled into a house on 12th Street in the heart of Greenwich Village. After some years he took leave of the city, moving to Irvington-on-Hudson. There he resided in a landmark octagonal house known as the Armour-Stiner Octagon House, which was acquired in the 1970s by the National Trust for Historic Preservation.

In many ways his career remained close to his Alabama period. In *Deep South*, a book of poetry published in 1930, four years before *Stars Fell on Alabama* appeared, he located each poem in the state, even using Alabama place names for many of his pieces ("One Night in Calera," "Ballad of Steve Renfroe," "Sand Mountain," "Jackson's Gap").[7]

When he transferred settings to his beloved upstate New York, the specific names and places changed, but not Carmer's eye for a good tale well told. In a cycle of novels set in the region just after the American Revolution *(Listen For A Lonesome Drum: A Yank State Chronicle, Dark Trees to the Wind, Genese Fever)*, his descriptions of Shakers and sheepkillers contain the same keen eye for the exotic and the eccentric as his earlier work in Alabama. As editor of a series on the "Rivers of America," he wrote with particular affection about the Hudson and the Susquehanna.[8]

In some thirty-seven books, documentary films, scripts for his own radio program "Your Neck of the Woods," and as collector and editor of four albums of regional songs, he established himself as one of America's most popular writers during the 1940s and 1950s. His books for young people appeared as selections of the Children's Book Club, and he even adapted some of his folktales for Walt Disney's "Melody Time." His radio show dealt mainly with national folk heroes and myths, a dimension of his work which first appeared in *Stars Fell on Alabama*. Perhaps he was thinking of that first prose work when he said: "our folklore is the poetry of the composite American mind," and "it is a crop from American roots." And others said of him what he claimed of himself. Once at a dinner for visiting British publishers, he was introduced as "the completely American" writer.[9] Even his hobby of historic preservation and his ecological concern about pollution of the Hudson River reflected the same reverence for the natural roots of American culture.

Although Carmer never established himself as a preeminent novelist, poet, or folklorist, his peers honored him in numerous ways before his death in Bronxville, New York, on September 12, 1976. He served as president of the Author's Guild, of the Poetry Society of America, and of the American Center of P.E.N., the international society of writers and editors, and as a director of the American Civil Liberties Union. But his reputation never soared again to the heights reached in 1934.

Stars Fell on Alabama was both Carmer's first and most memorable prose work. Illustrated beautifully by LeRoy Baldridge, the book was first published by Farrar and Rinehart. Subsequently it was reprinted in 1952 by Doubleday and in 1961 by Hill and Wang.

The author wastes no time introducing his theme. The Congo was not more different from Massachusetts, Kansas, or California than was Alabama. He wrote of Alabama, not as part of the American nation, but as a "strange country," both eccentric and bizarre. With a marvelous eye for the colorful, he described Negro baptizings and Ku Klux Klan rallies, lynchings and Primitive Baptist foot washings, fiddling contests and quilting, moonshining and sacred harp singings. He recorded a treasure of surviving folklore, including B'rer Rabbit tales, lyrics of railroad songs and the names of four hundred fiddle tunes. At times his writing is clinically frank, as when he relates the fertility rituals told him by a conjure woman, or a black boy's seduction of a girl friend, or a bloody Black Belt lynching. A surprising number of the stories he collected in the Black Belt are filled with sex and violence.

He sometimes slips beyond journalistic limits, confusing fiction with fact. The streams of folklore and history flow together until the reader can no longer discern in the confluence which is which. He describes too many planters as descendents of Virginia aristo-crats who knew Lafayette or George Washington. Because most of his Black Belt informants knew he intended to include them in his writings, they exaggerated and he elaborated their exaggerations. Occasionally he warns the reader that he will relate a tale exactly as it was told to him, "preferring the truth that folk-say creates to the fiction of history." Usually he relates the tales as fact with no such cautionary warning. He is even casual with facts, identifying Mobile's Jesuit Spring Hill College as an Episcopal school.

But he also glimpses Black Belt plantation life in its last days, before the inexorable forces of history and technology swept away cotton choppers and dinner bells. He records the names of black farm workers on the plantations: Frog, Monkey, Mush, Cooter, John de Baptist, Fat-man, Pop Corn, Badluck, Cracker, Cat-fish, Rattler, Coon, Old Blue, and Jewsharp. The modern reader is mystified by such familiarity with nicknames so obviously the private possession of blacks or the denigrating descriptions of white informants. Carmer demonstrates little sensitivity to the nuances of race, even writing that in antebellum Alabama "slaves were plentiful and happy."[10] But perhaps to expect more from him is to expect too much. It was, after all, a different time and a different place. Read that way, *Stars Fell on Alabama* is an infor-mative and delightful book on black and white folkways during the 1920s.

And sometimes Carmer's imagery unmistakably conveys historical truth. He captures the enigma of Birmingham in the newly constructed Temple of Vesta on the crest of Shades Mountain. The private residence, a replica of the splendid Roman edifice, crowned the mountain with all its glory. But beneath the building in its base was a garage. Such was Birmingham, a city of the "nouveau riche," full of absurd pretension and of literary clubs, where Rotary and Kiwanis flourished, where even religion relied on advertising, where people were too busy to buy books or to read them. The city boasted many wealthy people who earned their fortunes by daring and unconventional means, then purchased only the most conservative and conventional art. Birmingham hardly belonged to Alabama's folk world, thus furnishing Carmer evidence for the incongruity and heterogeneity of the state.

At a superficial level *Stars Fell on Alabama* reminds one of another masterful period piece, *90° in the Shade* by Clarence Cason. Like Carmer, Cason was a professor at The University of Alabama during the 1920s. Both described Alabama folkways with a major emphasis on race. Both were appalled by the endemic violence and lynching of their times. Their books appeared only a year apart, Carmer's in 1934 and Cason's in 1935. Both authors employed a sprightly, popular style. Even their names led to confusion—Clarence Cason and Carl Carmer.

But there the resemblance ends. Cason's work is that of a native Alabamian, heartsick at the failings of his people, horrified by Alabama's visceral racism and mindless violence, and restless for change. Cason's book is reformist in tone, anxious to work out change within society. Carmer's Yankee detachment allows him a certain aloofness, as if he were describing natives of the Trobriand Islands or New Mexico aborigines. Like a highly verbal anthropologist analyzing subjects for a doctoral dissertation, he shares with the reader what he finds curious, bizarre, eccentric, folkish. Even those scenes which he movingly describes, he treats with a certain indifference. One never doubts that when his project is completed, he will pack his bags, purchase a ticket, and head back up North. But that very detachment sets his book apart from Cason's more serious and tortured work. In Carmer's mind not every foible is fatal, a grievous sin to be roundly condemned and repented. He is happier with the people he meets and lets them be themselves. Their flaws are to be observed, analyzed, and understood, accepted, and recounted. Unlike Cason, the purpose of Carmer's prose is to educate and entertain, not to convey social messages or promote reform. In the aftermath of the publication of *Stars Fell on Alabama*, Carl Carmer launched a prolific writing career. In the aftermath of the publication a year later of *90° in the Shade*, Clarence Cason committed suicide.

J. WAYNE FLYNT
Auburn University

Notes to Introduction

1. See obituary in *New York Times*, September 12, 1976, p. 42.

2. Carl L. Carmer, *Stars Fell on Alabama* (New York: Farrar and Rinehart, 1934), p. 11.

3. *Some University of Alabama Poets: Second Series*, edited by Carl Carmer (English Department, University of Alabama, 1925), p. 7.

4. *New Republic*, 79 (July 18, 1934), 272; *New York Times*, July 1, 1934, p. 1.

5. *Books*, July 1, 1934, p. 1.

6. *The Yale Review*, 24 (Autumn, 1934), 171–73.

7. Carl L. Carmer, *Deep South* (New York: Farrar and Rinehart, 1930).

8. *New York Times*, September 12, 1976, p. 42.

9. Ibid.

10. Carmer, *Stars Fell on Alabama*, p. 100.

FOREWORD

ALABAMA felt a magic descending, spreading, long ago. Since then it has been a land with a spell on it—not a good spell, always. Moons, red with the dust of barren hills, thin pine trunks barring horizons, festering swamps, restless yellow rivers, are all part of a feeling—a strange certainty that above and around them hovers enchantment—an emanation of malevolence that threatens to destroy men through dark ways of its own. It is difficult to translate this feeling into words, yet almost every visitor to this land has known it and felt in some degree what I felt with increasing wonder during the six years I lived there. Hill-billies and niggers, poor whites, and planters, Cajans and Lintheads are sometimes aware of the intangible net that encompasses them. But the stranger is more apt to realize that sorcery is at work on these people and know that the land on which they live is its apprentice.

What the strange influence is or when it began is a matter for debate. It is a legend that the great chief Tush-ka-lusa, upon the accidental death of his son at the hands of one of De Soto's men, drew himself up to his seven-foot height and, standing over his dead boy's body, called down upon all white invaders of this land the vengeance of the Great Spirit. And it is pointed out as one of many proofs of the power of his curse that from that day to this no year has passed in which the Black Warrior River (named for the giant redskin) has not claimed at least one victim.

Others say that the enchantment began in the year that two squaws in a Cherokee tribe, whose tepees were pitched near what is now the town of Oxford, Alabama, bore on the same day sons that were spotted as the leopard. The mothers were tried for witchcraft and sentenced to be burned—but when the flames licked about their bound feet the earth yawned and took them and all the tribe into itself. They lie now beneath the bottomless pit that is filled by the clear waters of Blue Pond. So the witch-mothers triumphed and they still rule Alabama.

But those who really know, the black conjure women in their weathered cabins along the Tombigbee, tell a different story. They say that on the memories of the oldest slaves their fathers knew there was one indelible imprint of an awful event—a shower of stars over Alabama. Many an Alabamian to this day reckons dates from "the year the stars fell"—though he and his neighbor frequently disagree as to what year of our Lord may be so designated. All are sure, however, that once upon a time stars fell on Alabama, changing the land's destiny. What had been written in eternal symbols was thus erased—and the region has existed ever since, unreal and fated, bound by a horoscope such as controls no other country.

Let those who scorn such irrationalities explain this state-that-is-another-land in ways they prefer. They may find causes economic and sociological quite as incredible as these fables and much less interesting. But few of those who know this ground and those who live on it will deny that the curious traveler will find his journeying amply repaid here. The Congo is not more different from Massachusetts or Kansas or California. So I have chosen to write of Alabama not as a state which is part of a nation, but as a strange country in which I once lived and from which I have now returned.

AUTHOR'S NOTE

ALL of the events related in this book happened substantially as I have recorded them. It has been necessary in a few instances to disguise characters to avoid causing them serious embarrassment (for instance my hosts during the lynching). I have also taken the liberty of telescoping time occasionally—since I have attempted to select significant occurrences which took place over a span of a half-dozen years.

The number of people who have helped me in the making of this book is legion. It must include a surprisingly large percentage of the inhabitants of Alabama. I should be graceless indeed, however, if I did not own my gratitude to Ruby Pickens Tartt and her daughter, Fannie Pickens Tartt, who made my Black Belt excursion possible; to Knox Ide and Robert Harwood who wandered the Red Hills with me; to the Honorable Earl McGowin and Francis Inge whose companionship throughout my life in Alabama and afterwards has been full of affectionate encouragement; to Clyde Robinson who has been an indefatigable scout for interesting material; to Marie Bankhead Owen of the Alabama State Department of Archives and History; and to all my Negro friends, unfailing in their warm-hearted assistance.

TUSCALOOSA NIGHTS

CHAPTER I

I Arrive

THE train had left the echoing passes in the high hills during the morning and now for some time had been rolling through vine-hung woods standing in yellow water. Suddenly it came out on a plain of red clay land sparsely overgrown with sedge grass. "Tuscaloosa, folks, Tuscaloosa," shouted the conductor.

As I came down the car steps, I felt a sudden burning gust. The train had been hot and still but this heat was alive and virulent. My tweed suit was oppressive and it made me a marked man. A dozen taxi drivers surrounded me. "Carry you to town, boss?" I gave up my bags and climbed in.

First some straggling low unpainted stores—a creaking wagon bearing one cotton bale and that bearing one old black man who slapped his reins over a slow mule—a few overpretentious bungalows, a lane of gaunt old elms, then a great blue-gray ghost of a house, dark and rambling. "Van de Graaf place," said my driver laconically. "Built before the war."

The shade of the elms ended. We were in the center of the low-lying town. A tall flagpole marked the junction of two wide streets. We swung around it.

"There's our skyscraper," said the driver, pointing to a tall office building—ugly promise of the future—rising into the hot sky. "And here's your hotel."

The heavy green carpet and the faded green walls of my room depressed me. I picked up the black Bible on the table and put it down. Through my window I could see into the street below. Men were strolling about in their shirt sleeves.

3

The sunlight was cruel on the gray pavement. A group of young black girls in brightly spotted cotton dresses had stopped outside a store from which came the sound of a phonograph. Their hearty laughter interrupted it pleasantly. I lay on my bed and tried to sleep.

About an hour later there was a rap at my door. "Here's a bunch of flowers for you, sir." They were roses of many kinds, wrapped in a newspaper, and there was card—"From some people who are glad you are here." I have never known who sent them. It might have been any one of the hundreds of families I later came to know, for it was a typical gesture. No people are more perfectly master of the unexpected and kindly.

I went down into the lobby, for it was dinner time. I saw the clerk jerk a thumb toward me as I passed and a pleasant short gentleman with a gray mustache and kindly gray eyes approached me.

"You're one of the new members of the university faculty, aren't you? I'm Howe, professor of history. Won't you join me at my table?"

At dinner, I learned soon enough that I did not like corn bread—it was heavy and unsweetened—not like the "johnny-cake" it resembled—nor could I eat okra, or collards. But the fried chicken made up for it. Professor Howe kindly volunteered much information about the town and the university but the more he said the more unreal and fantastic they seemed.

As we reëntered the lobby after dinner a group of men standing by the desk spoke to Howe and he stopped and introduced me to them. They spoke cordially—all but a short bald man with a white mustache. With no warning he began: "I've just met you and they say you're a college professor. I hope you're not the kind of a college professor who teaches that men are descended from long-tailed apes. That's the kind of blasphemy that is making our sons and daughters what they are today. The Bible expressly denies . . ."

Howe pulled me away bewildered as the other men tactfully interrupted the vehement speaker. "Don't mind him. He's a type down here. I used to argue with them when I came. That just drives them crazy. Now I avoid them. Let's take a walk."

The air had cooled a bit and the sun was setting in a crimson bank of clouds as we strolled down Greensboro Avenue—back to the old blue-gray ghost of the Van de Graaf place. Then we turned off on a side street and suddenly came upon a house whose white pillars rose high to its roof, their bases hidden by flowering bushes. The air was soft and very sweet with the blossoms.

"That's the back of the Washington Moody place," said Howe. "The other side is just like it." We walked around to the front to see again the clean white lift of the pillars. We saw, too, smoke curling up from the brick chimney of the little one-story wing at the left, evidently the kitchen. "This is what I thought Alabama would be," I said.

"It's part of it," said Howe.

We strolled back to the hotel. There was a note for me from an old friend—my only acquaintance in the state before my arrival:

"We are waiting for you in a car at the curb. Come join us. Knox."

I excused myself to Howe.

"Stop by my room when you come in," he said. "I'll be up."

It was a jovial party outside. Knox had brought a young married couple along—also a tall and beautiful lady who lamented in her soft contralto that her husband, Jim, was in Montgomery. She and Knox and I sat on the back seat.

"We've drunk up all the corn waitin' for you," said Knox.

"Now we'll have to go back home and get some more. We'd go there to have a drink but Grandmother's visitin' us and she's the woman who gave Alabama prohibition before its time."

We drove through the moonlit town, stopped at a house wherein Knox ran the gauntlet of Grandmother, and drove on. Suddenly the car began to lurch and toss. We were going down a steep incline and there was no road-bed save a few worn tracks through a dense wood. For half a mile the descent continued and then we were all at once in a flat open clearing.

"Dell's woods," said Knox. "I reckon the Klan won't find us here. Let's have a drink."

"Let's get out first and sit in the moonlight," said the soft contralto.

"Do you really mean," I said, "the Ku Klux might object to our being here?"

"They certainly would if they knew it. They've driven the parked cars out at Riverside and at the Country Club—off private property, too. That's what they were trying to protect in the seventies when my grandfather was high mucky-muck. —He'd turn over in his grave if he knew what poor white trash are wearing the sheets now. Oh, well, here's to 'em."

All about the little barren clearing the slim bare trunks of the pines rose like vertical bars to their tufted tops far up in the moonlight.

Knox turned to the husband and wife. "You've forgotten the baby," he said accusingly. "You've left him in the stuffy car when he could be enjoying this fresh air."

"I'll get him," said the husband and he took from the car a pillow on which rested a slumbering infant.

"But where was he?" I said, "I didn't see him."

"On the floor by my feet in front," said his mother, "where I could watch him. You see," she continued, "none of our

servants live in the house where they work. And they all insist on being at their own homes early in the evening. And so
if we have parties at night—well, the easiest way is to take
Baby along. He just sleeps through it all like an angel." She
bent over the child who slept placidly on in the moonlight.

"Have a drink," said Knox. "Let's sit down and enjoy ourselves." For six years I was destined to drink, on occasion,
corn whiskey. Friend after friend has assured me that *this* time
he had something "just as good as rye." Expert upon expert
has explained his method of treating it. It remains as vile and
as uglily potent a liquor as ever man has distilled. It is swift
and deadly—odious to the taste. And too often it ruins the
geniality it is meant to encourage.

I drank, coughed, sputtered. I said: "It's terrible." There
was a silence—long enough to be ominous. Knox saved the
day: "Y'all have to expect his sayin' things like that once in
a while—till he gets used to us. He's a damn Yankee—and
likely to tell the truth."

"But why should he—why should they—" said the soft contralto slowly. "It just sounds rude."

"They think there's a virtue in it," said Knox. "That's one
thing I learned at Harvard Law School."

"I'm sorry," I said miserably. "It was surprised out of me."

"It is never surprised out of us," said the contralto. "Don't
you mind, honey," she went on, "you're a friend of Knox's and
if you're as sweet as he is, we'll all like you—and if we do,
you'll be the first Yankee we ever *did* like."

"Forget it," said Knox. "Stop sweet-talkin' the new man
long enough to hear Mary Ellen tell what happened to my
cousin Tennant in Eutaw last week."

"I haven't heard anything else since she got back," said
Mary Ellen's husband. "But I reckon I can stand it once more."

We were all sitting on the ground in a little circle leaning forward eagerly.

"Well, Tennant was wantin' to go swimmin' in the river and Mary Louise had gone to Demopolis to see Cousin Augusta and Tennant couldn't find his bathin' suit. He says she always puts it in a different place. Anyway Tennant got so hot he decided he'd go anyway. He found an old middy blouse of Mary Louise's and an old short blue skirt of hers that didn't come down to his knees. He put 'em on and put his long raincoat on over 'em. He put on shoes and socks and got out the Buick and drove down to the river. He had his swim all right, but on his way back he decided to stop at the drug store for some cigars. He got out of the car at the corner—so he wouldn't have to turn around—and he was walkin' toward the store when something happened.

"Seems young Jim Batson, he's deputy sheriff over there, was talkin' to that new doctor that moved in from Linden; Acker's his name, he comes really from the Ackers down in Choctaw County. Jim was tryin' to get the doctor to join the Klan—but the doctor wouldn't do it and said somethin' about the Klan that made Jim mad. So he said: 'You can't say anythin' like that about me or my friends,' and the doctor said: 'I'll say what I so-and-so please,' and they both began shootin' at the same time, standin' out in the road in front of the courthouse square.

"Just then Tennant came along to go into the drug store and the first he knew about it, he was shot in the leg. The bullet made a hole right through the outside of his calf. It made him mighty mad and he let out a yell so loud that they stopped shootin'—they'd been too excited to aim well. Tennant saw Jim Batson standin' there with a smokin' gun—so he lit into him and he swore at him somethin' awful. Jim just stood there. I reckon he knew he was in the wrong. Finally Tennant got so mad he said: 'Just put down that gun and take off your coat for I'm goin' to whip you plenty.' Then he took off his raincoat and threw it on the ground and stood there in a dripping wet middy blouse and short old blue skirt—with the blood pouring out from his leg. His father says he looked like a piece of red, white and blue bunting.

"Jim Batson took one look and began to laugh and that made Tennant madder than ever and he stepped up to whale Jim when some men stepped in and stopped it all and got Tennant to put on his coat and go home. They've 'most had trouble down there ever since, for both Tennant and Jim are kin to half the county and every day some menfolks would ride in with their guns. They said they'd heard a feud was startin' and they wanted to do their part."

We all laughed and the corn liquor emboldened me:

"Please don't be offended if I ask about these people you've told about. Do you people know them well and who and what are they?"

Knox spoke up quickly.

"They probably do sound fantastic to you. They won't seem strange when you meet them—you will when we all go down to the Greene County Rally next spring. They are all charming civilized people—I reckon Alabama's about the only place left where exciting things can happen to the gentility."

"Don't boast, Knox," said the contralto. "Tennant is kin to you, you know. And speakin' of kin, my husband's goin' to call me up at midnight—so let's go back."

On the way back, Mary Ellen said: "You're the first Yankee who hasn't told us how fascinating and exciting New York is. Maybe you'll do."

"I hope so," I said. I certainly felt disposed to "do."

As I passed an open door in the stuffy hotel corridor that led to my room, I heard Howe call me.

"Come in," he said. "I want you to meet Saffold of my department."

A courtly bald gentleman in a spotless white suit greeted me. His tone was friendly and his manner gracious. I liked him at once.

"We are having a little scuppernong wine," he said. "Won't you join us?" I thought of the corn whiskey I had consumed and hesitated—but a glass was pressed into my hand and I found myself tasting as mellow and palatable a drink as the former had been raw and distasteful.

We sat up late talking shop, while two electric fans moved the hot air about us.

About two, a cool breath came from the window. Saffold rose to go and I left with him. In the corridor he said: "I am glad to know you and I hope you're going to like your work and the place." He paused. "On second thought," he said, "I'll withdraw that last clause—for if I knew you well enough to advise you, I'd say 'For God's sake, get out of here before it's too late.'" He turned abruptly and walked away, his footsteps echoing in the silent corridor.

CHAPTER II

Tuscaloosa

I WAS to live in Tuscaloosa six years before I fully realized what Saffold had meant and left Alabama. Whether it was "too late" then is a matter of opinion. Certainly the virus against which he had warned me was by that time in my veins and I had learned to live the Alabama way. I knew what to expect of the people and what they expected of me. I believe that many had even forgotten I was a Yankee.

There were differences at first. I remember that once before a large class I had become enthusiastic over the picturesque quality of Tuscaloosa on a Saturday afternoon. I spoke of the crowds of negroes come to town to shop, their husky deep laughter, their ceaseless high-pitched chatter, the red, green, yellow brilliance of the clothes of the women, the careless graceful nonchalance of the men. They formed a strange contrast, I said, with the taciturn, lean white farmers and their soberly clad wives, and I could think of no streets in the world that provided so fascinating and variegated a human mixture save those of the cities on the north coast of North Africa. On the next day six serious young men waited upon me with a petition asking me to retract the statements I had made with regard to their native city whose inhabitants I had made out to be "no better than a bunch of foreigners."

For a year or so I was suspected of being a "missionary of Eastern culture" as one student dubbed me. I was described on one occasion as "one of those damn-Yankee professors who lectures on poetry and goes without a hat." But gradually suspicion of me lessened and I found myself, if not a born South-

erner, born to be a Southerner. My lectures were all scheduled
for the morning, leaving the long afternoons for tennis and
swimming. My evenings were spent in bridge and dancing and
swimming and drinking. And while I was enjoying the diversions of Alabama life I slowly became aware of the fact that
they are a frivolous film covering deep waters. Living was always too bright or too dark. There was no middle way of
normality. Strong contrasts followed each other in startling
sequences.

No people of the world give more thought to social enjoy-
ment than the Alabamians. The early afternoon finds most of
Tuscaloosa's business men on golf courses and tennis courts,
even when business might be improved by closer attention. In
the evening the town is alive with small impromptu parties
except on the nights of larger, more formal affairs.

During the hot months social activities do not decrease.
Moonlight swimming parties in the Black Warrior River are
frequent. There is dancing on the "front gallery" to radio and
phonograph, the men looking very tanned and fit in their white
starched suits, the women very feminine in the ruffled dresses
that are the despair of their New York relatives when they
come north to visit on Manhattan Island.

Aside from these the main diversions of the Alabamians are
love-making and gossip. The constant social chatter dealing in
personalities at first annoys and bores the stranger. Gradually,
however, as he picks up the threads of the relationships
through which it sometimes seems that the entire state is bound
into one family, he becomes not only tolerant but an eager
participant. The proportion of malice in this talk is not greater
than in other communities. There are the usual Mrs. Grundys
and meddlesome scandalmongers. But the majority of Alabamian gentlefolk take a strong interest in people that is not
unlike that of a novelist. They are entertained and instructed

by the antics of their fellow beings—they like to speculate on motivations. And talk about an individual takes on added zest when (as frequently happens) he is a cousin in whom flows the blood of a common ancestor.

As for love-making, it is the accepted basis of all social activity. Even very little boys are trained to be gallant and the ambition of every daughter's mother is that her girl shall be a belle. Trained by negro mammies who know gentle ways better than the gentry themselves, the young in Alabama always seem precociously well mannered. The girls begin going to their first grown-up parties at thirteen and fourteen, the boys sometimes earlier. Pairing off is frowned upon. The Eastern miss counts herself fortunate to have one beau, the Southern is not content with a dozen. Her Christmas gift display table is laden with presents from many admirers. Fortunately Alabamian fathers are indulgent, for sons at Christmas time feel that they must remember at least a half-dozen sweethearts.

A dance in the summertime will bring all the young people within a fifty-mile radius to crowd the floor. University students pay fabulous prices running into thousands of dollars to bring second-rate Northern bands, groups of sleek-haired substitutes in famous dance orchestras, to Tuscaloosa. At commencement time there are afternoon dances, evening dances, morning dances, the latest innovation being "early morning" dances from six to eight.

The dancing itself is extraordinary, particularly among the younger and college groups. It is violent and full of strange and fanciful variations. An Eastern collegian, sedately accustomed to dignified stepping to the music of New York hotel orchestras is completely baffled here. I said something like that to a Tuscaloosa girl once. She replied that Alabama stepping was tame compared to that of Mississippi and offered to pick out by their dancing from the mass of whirling, strutting couples, the girls who came from the neighboring state. She was right in every instance.

Perhaps because of close blood relationships and the dearth of large cities, "visiting" is a happy recreation in Alabama. Visits usually last indefinitely, sometimes for months. And the hosts take their responsibilities very seriously. A girl from the Black Belt, recently returned from a stay in New York, complained that her Northern hostess had brought no beaus to the Pennsylvania Station to meet her. Had she been arriving in Selma she knew she would have been greeted at the train by a half-dozen young men, herded by her girl cousin, all of whom would have besieged her for "dates" throughout the coming week.

"Dating" is an important problem. Since a popular young lady finds that custom requires her to be catholic in her tastes, her schedule is frequently as full and as complicated as a time-table. There are lunch dates and afternoon dates and supper dates, and in the evening there are early dates and regular dates, and late dates, the last of these beginning sometimes after midnight.

While it is evident that Southern mothers are inclined to be lenient and to differ in their attitude from their Northern sisters toward a daughter's quest for popularity, conventional morality is a much more generally accepted standard in the deep South than in other sections of the country. The revolt of youth against orthodox moral attitudes during the 1920's did not kindle much of a flame in Alabama. Indeed, the traditional chivalric code of the Southern Gentleman is still given lip reverence. One of the rituals of the university dances is that of a fraternity of young blades entitled The Key-Ice. During an intermission the lights are turned out and these young men march in carrying flaming brands. At the end of the procession four acolytes attend a long cake of ice. Wheeled in on a cart it glimmers in the torches' flare. Then the leader, mounted on a table in the center of the big gymnasium, lifts a glass cup of water and begins a toast that runs: "To Woman, lovely woman of the Southland, as pure and chaste as this sparkling water, as cold as this gleaming ice, we lift this cup, and we pledge our hearts and our lives to the protection of her virtue and chastity."

Frequently the young man is slightly inebriated and the probability is that he and his cohorts are among the better known seducers of the campus, but no one sees any incongruity in this. The hall resounds with hearty applause as he drains the cup and the picturesque procession returns to the locker rooms whence it emerged.

These are only a few of the obvious superficialities of social life in Tuscaloosa. They are not without their significance, however, and they provide an amazing contrast to what lies beneath the surface. For Alabama is a land of quick reactions, of sudden and stunning violences. Frontier life and constant war with revenuers have made the mountain people of the north a gun-toting, quick-shooting lot. Pride and maintenance of their dominance over the negro has done the same for the planters in the south. Birmingham, which is between the two, has pretty consistently been at or near the top of the annually computed record of homicides per capita in the city populations of the United States. The civilizing influence of the state university fails to render Tuscaloosa an exception to the general attitude. Differences of opinion there are frequently settled by physical combat, even among the most cultured and distinguished people. Two of my good friends surprised me considerably by indulging in fisticuffs during a bank directors' meeting. I saw little boys who had clambered over the fence at a ball game racing for seats on the bleachers while an enraged policeman chased them with leveled gun. Officers raided fraternity houses for liquor with drawn revolvers. A crowd of Alabama college boys attempted to mob a few Italian students from New York City who had hazed a Southern freshman. The Italians were rescued in the nick of time by police waving firearms, were given refuge in the jail and sent home to New York. Fraternities received threatening letters—"One of your members will be killed." Shortly afterwards a negro butler found a freshman at midnight, bound and gagged, clad in pajamas, lying in the middle of a fraternity living room, his skull fractured. He recovered, but his memory of the last year had been completely destroyed. A series of Ku Klux floggings began. It was said that one of the leaders of the night-riders had had a prosperous negro flogged into selling his $10,000 farm to him for $500. The courageous editor of a Montgomery newspaper won a Pulitzer Prize by his attacks on the masked cowards, but it was not a long while ago that I saw a little group of white-hooded men moving swiftly and secretly about in a negro section terrorizing its inhabitants. A favorite student failed to appear in my class one morning. He had committed suicide for love of a girl. An elderly maiden killed herself for love of a student. A schoolboy shot himself because his teacher had made him apologize before his schoolmates to a little maiden whose skirts, he had said, were noticeably short.

Everywhere in the state, as in Tuscaloosa whose inhabitants represent most of the well-defined sections, the inevitable reaction to any unusual stimulus was to do something about it, something physical and violent. Throughout Alabama life is a hard-lived melodrama, made the more startling because it exists against a background of lazy serenity, of happy-go-lucky ease. Emotions are on hair triggers beneath the smooth veneer of charm and gentility. No one knows what storms are brewing in the soul of his jovial golf partner, his sedate colleague on the university faculty, the lanky sallow-faced farmer at the street market, the black cook singing at her work in the kitchen. Tomorrow any one of them may have committed a *crime passionel.*

But it was more than violence and melodrama that provoked Saffold to his outburst. He is a scholar living in a community that prides itself on its culture. But culture in Tuscaloosa is generally rather a tradition than an actuality. The prevailing sentiment seems to be that it is a quality that one inherits from distinguished ancestors. Saffold had been professor of Greek and Latin. And he had seen the sons of the old aristocrats, those virile, energetic, bearded quoters of Homer and of Horace, turn from the classics to courses in modern drama or business administration. He had seen his classes dwindle until they no longer existed and he had been transferred to the department of American history. And he had seen life so arranging itself in the state that the culture of which he was a delightful example was excluded. Gossip, dancing, swimming, drinking, love-making, even religious observance, each has its niche in the structure of a day. But not reading and contemplation. Gradually life in Tuscaloosa comes to follow a formula that anæsthetizes. More virulent than the germs of violence are those that make their victim unaware of the passing of time. Weeks, months, years go by and no one wakes up to discover that they are gone. Like the little lost town of Germelshausen, that Gerstäcker wrote of, Tuscaloosa lives a life of its own— an enchanted life in an age other than ours. Mountains lowering from the north, stagnant marshes sleeping in the south shut it from the world. A malevolent landscape—lush and foreboding—broods over it bending its people to strange purposes.

CHAPTER III

Black Rituals

I. GOLF COURSE CABIN

THE seventh hole of the Tuscaloosa Country Club golf course is at the top of a steep little hill. A good player drives from the sixth tee across the little brook at the foot of the rise and then lifts a mashie shot onto the green which is just out of sight on the flattened summit. Less than twenty yards to the left of the fairway on the hillside is a negro cabin. It is partially concealed by high sedge grass, by underbrush, by a few long-leaf pines. Players are constantly passing it in the daytime but they are so intent on their game that they are hardly aware of the weathered low structure with its mud and stone chimney. I do not remember when I first became conscious of it, but the incongruity of its presence on the land of a country club did finally make an impression on me and I once asked if it was occupied. Nobody seemed to know.

The question answered itself one soft May night. I had been playing in a late foursome. We were doing an extra round, for ladies were to meet us at the club afterwards and there was to be a picnic supper beside the pool and swimming by moonlight later. The sun had set and even the supernaturally keen eyes of our little black caddies had difficulty in following the white balls. My drive had been short and my second shot had gone to the left and halfway up the hill.

As I approached my ball which lay in the rough I heard a soft rhythmic beating, regular and insistent, hardly more than a pulsing of the dusk.

"What's that noise, Henry?" I said to my caddy.

"Dunno, sir," said Henry. "Reckon they got a drum over in that cabin."

"Who lives over there?"

"Some colored folks, I reckon, I dunno."

I played my shot and went on. For a while I forgot the drum.

After supper and a long swim in the warm pool lighted by a full reddish moon, I dressed and came out of the locker room to stand alone at the first tee and look down on the flats that suddenly terminated in the gleaming channel of the Black Warrior River. There was the drumming again—so faint that I thought I might be imagining it. I went back to the locker room. The other men were arguing briskly, waving long high-ball glasses.

"If I'm not around when it's time to go, blow the horn on my car, will you?" I said.

"You and who else?"

"An assignation, by God!"

"What girl got dressed *that* fast?"

I walked up the road a little way, turned to the left past a cairn of bricks known for some romantic reason as "The Pirate's Grave" and made my way slowly down through the pines and brush. As I drew near the cabin the drumming grew louder. Like yellow eyes two windows opened on the cabin gallery. I know I dared not go up the steps and peer into one of them and fearfully I bore off to the right, to the end opposite the chimney. A beam of light on the trunk of a slim pine reassured me; there was a window on that side and I could approach it. I walked softly down until I was beside the window. Then I ventured a quick glance inside. I need not have worried about being detected. Everyone in the cabin was too much taken up with what he was doing even to imagine an uninvited audience.

Beside the chimney on a cot covered by a white spread sat a black crone in a black dress and on the floor in front of her was a bass drum, a small one with large red letters on it which I could not quite read. She held a drumstick in her right hand and her eyes blazed as she raised it and let it fall at short regular intervals. In the middle of the narrow room four black boys and four black girls pranced to the sensuous rhythm. A boy with gleaming teeth and protruding black eyes stepped lithely about twisting his hips sharply within a ring the others had formed by joining hands. As he danced he chanted in a monotone to his companions who circled about him and they replied in an answering chorus:

> See more, babe, satisfy,
> (*All*) Satisfy!

> See more, babe, satisfy,
> (*All*) Satisfy!

> Got my woman by my side
> Ise satisfied, Ise satisfied
> (*All*) Satisfied, Lor', satisfied.

> See Corrinna tell her I say hurry home
> Ain't had my rice since she been gone
> What I mean when I say my rice
> Three meals a day an' jelly at night
> (*All*) Satisfy, Satisfy.

> If I had a ten dollar bill
> (*All*) Satisfy, Satisfy.
> Buy me a rockin' cheer
> An' rock from here.
> If you ain't satisfied, nigger,
> Doncha sing satisfied.
> (*All*) Satisfy!

As he chanted the lewd lines about the rice the boy stopped moving about the ring and his hips rolled in sinuous sexual gestures. The old crone on the bed laughed loud and long at this and essayed a roll on the bass drum—making it sound like distant thunder. Then the dancer suddenly burst into a storm of activity, flinging his feet about in an ecstasy of rhythmic motion. And as he chanted "Doncha sing satisfied" a lean yellow finger pointed to a young buck, tall and supple and loose of joint who promptly jumped into the middle of the ring. The first dancer backed into the new leader's place and the drum began to beat faster.

"Hey holy, hey holy," chanted the young buck and the rest replied, "Holy Rider!"

> Lor' I wonder what de matter
> Can't git no answer from my rider
> Went to de window clean my fishes
> Fell out de window, broke my dishes
> Mama gwine whip me drinkin' whiskey
> (*All*) Mama doncha whip her, doncha whip her,
> doncha whip her
> Train is comin' to the station
> (*All*) Heavy loaded, whoopin' holy!

As these words were being chanted the circling chorus provided startling variations. Some of them imitated the choo-choo of a train, others the long wail of a train whistle, the "doncha whip her" section was given perfectly to represent the rhythm of railroad cars passing a crossing, and the last line was chanted slowly to the accompaniment of groaning brakes and the release of steam. As his train stopped the leader pointed to a fat, good-natured boy, grabbed the hand of a yellowish girl in a brilliant green dress and whispered something in her ear. She nodded and they both left the ring. The others closed in on the leader who began at once. I suddenly realized that the couple were coming out and in a panic I pressed close to the side of the house. They passed within a few yards of me, intent on each other, laughing boisterously as they walked towards the thick woods beyond the clearing. Inside the fat boy was chanting, moving with surprising lightness and grace around the decreased circle.

> I went to the river, Hop Fly,
> Set down under a willow tree,
> Willow leaves roll down on me
> (*All*) Roll down on me, Hop Fly, roll down on me.
>
> Is that your man, Hop Fly,
> Pin him to your side
> He done flagged my train an' he got to ride
> See dat man wid de blue serge on,
> Ain't got no money, better let him alone
> (*All*) Better let him alone, let him alone.
>
> Didn't come here, Hop Fly, to raise no san'
> Just come here to git my man
> Fifteen cents to buy me a pan
> Dollar an' a quarter to git to my man.
> If I had, Hop Fly, mouth full o' gol'
> I'd put these niggers under my control—
> (*All*) Under my control, Hop Fly, under my control.

The fat boy fairly outdid himself as his chant ended. His feet flashed in a lightning "Charleston" step, his rounded body shook, his mouth flew open, taking in air in great gasps. As he finished he dashed from the circle and fell on the cot beside the old woman who laughed again, raising her voice in a high cackle, and then threw the drumstick on the floor. There was a silence broken by the heavy breathing of the fat boy. The three girls sat down in chairs primly and the boys stood by the fireplace together, looking a little embarrassed. Suddenly in the woods, it could have been only a few rods away, a woman screamed. I was frightened. I wondered what I ought to do. But all was calm inside the cabin. The embarrassment seemed to be increasing, though. The boys looked at each other furtively and the girls looked down at their hands in their laps. Perhaps they did not hear the scream, I thought. Then it sounded again, longer and louder than before. A boy chuckled. In a twinkling the cabin was resounding, every boy and girl in a roaring gale of laughter. The fat boy rushed toward my window and I ducked beneath it. His head was close to mine as he leaned out and shouted in a derisive chant:

"An' my jelly at night!"

As he drew back, I ran for the road. When I got to my car I saw that it was full.

"We blew and blew for you. Where in the merry hell have you been?"

"I'll tell you some time," I said.

The next morning after breakfast:

"Lula, did you ever hear a song that begins 'Hey holy, hey holy, holy rider'?"

"I've heerd *about* it," said Lula, stopping in the kitchen doorway, "but that's a bad railroad song that colored folks dance to. I belongs to the Babtists and we don't dance."

"What's a railroad song?"

"It makes a noise like a train—like this—hey holy, hey holy, holy rider." Lula's hips twitched in the rhythm and she took a few abandoned steps that put the previous night's lewd performance to shame.

"Lula," I said, "remember you're a Babtist."

"I just pranks a bit," said Lula pridefully, "I don't do no real dancin'."

"God forbid," said I, "if that's just prankin'."

"It's just the secular niggers that sings those songs and dances 'em," said Lula. "Have another waffle, Mist' Carl?"

2. SHOUTIN' IN MOONLIGHT

"My twin daughters come through at the last 'tracted meetin'," said Lula, "and they's goin' come to Jesus for good in Cribbs Creek 'round nine o'clock tonight at the moonlight babtizin'."

"I'd like to go," I said, and a satisfied gleam appeared in Lula's black eyes. "I reckon it'll be a big night for you. I wouldn't be surprised if you got to shoutin' with the rest of 'em."

"No, sir, Mist' Carl," said Lula emphatically, "I don't hold with no such goin's-on. That's just old-fashioned 'ligion an' it ain't right an' it ain't dignified. Nobody'll ever catch *me* shoutin'."

"It's a good thing I'm having supper at Dr. Moody's tonight," I said; "that'll give you time to dress up the way a mother should when her twin daughters are coming to Jesus for good."

Lula giggled. "Yes, sir, Mist' Carl. Sure will—an' don't forgit about the time an' not come."

"I'll be there," I said.

It was nine-thirty when our headlights picked out the wooden bridge over Cribbs Creek. A little road swept downward to the right and we turned off on it into a stubble field crowded with dusty ancient Fords and patiently drooping mules. The service had already begun, for we could hear the regular beat of a spiritual sung by hundreds of voices, the singers concealed by dark water oaks and white sycamores that lined a bend in the stream. A path led toward them and in a few moments we stood on the creek bank: the babtizin' was before us.

Two dark spots punctuated the gleaming silver of the water. As my eyes became accustomed to the soft white light of the moon I saw they were two men, standing waist-deep in midstream. One of them was waving an arm in time to the music, a stub of an arm so short that it lacked an elbow.

"That's the one-armed preacher they're all crazy about," said Dr. Moody.

> I want to be in that number
> When the saints go marching home,

sang the long dark mass of men and women that lined each side of Cribbs Creek. In the center of the curve opposite us stood a semicircle of twenty silent sheeted figures—blankly white—waiting—while the song throbbed on and on.

Suddenly the preacher's voice rang out high above the singing:

. . "*And*—when I gets to my moanin' dyin' room and they close the do' an' they pull down the shade—*and* it's dark in there, and the muddy water of death is in my eyes, and the preacher comes and my family sits beside me a-prayin', *then*, Lord, Lord, make that crossin' over Jordan an easy one fo' me. I don't want to get bowled over by no swift an' splashin' stream. I wants to cross in the mud like Jesus did, easy-like, and not git wet. I wants to tromp over on the sticky flats to where the chariot's waitin' fo' me. Lord, if Jesus was a mudcat, I don't mind bein' a mud-kitten."

Sharp cries came from the bank interrupting the long minor chanting. "Ha! mercy, Jesus," "Yes, Lord, yes," "Ain't it the truth?"

Now the preacher held out both his arms, one absurdly

longer than the other, toward the white arc of figures on the bank.

"If you wants to cross the Jordan safe come here to me," he said. "Come down, sister, an' be saved."

Two black men approached the sheeted figures, took one of them into their arms, half led, half forced her down the bank and into the water. The preacher's companion, a tall powerful negro in a coat that from its upper portions seemed to be a Prince Albert went to meet her. Tenderly he took her from the deacons and, almost carrying her, advanced with her into the water. She stood stock-still now, her eyes fixed on those of the one-armed preacher. Suddenly the gorilla-like arms of the man behind her spun her about, the hand of the preacher was at the back of her neck, over backwards she went, her head below the surface. As the preacher shot her back up out the stream the big man grabbed her again and started for the bank. But all his strength could not control her. Convulsively her arms lifted over her head and she leaped almost out of the water. Her face was wrenched into agony.

"I see Jesus!" she screamed and began beating the shining surface of the stream with flailing strokes of her long arms. She plunged about and would have fallen if the big black man's arms had not been about her. The two deacons who had led her to the bank, entered the water and helped bring her to the land where she threw herself down and flopped about like a big silver fish, her wet robe gleaming in the moonlight.

> When the stars begin to fall,
> When the stars begin to fall.

There was no break in the steady surge of the music as the singers saw emotion sweep their converted sister into an hysterical mass of twitching limbs. "Come down, sisters, come down.

Jordan'll be jes' a muddy branch for those that's saved in Jesus."

Lord, I wants to be in that number.

On the bank stood two girls, curly headed, spindly little creatures, their eyes starting from their heads in fear—the whites of their eyeballs painfully distinct in the soft light. I realized that they were the reason for my presence, and I looked about for Lula, but I could not identify her in the great crowd along the banks. The deacons were herding the young-sters into the creek. Docilely, hand in hand, they walked through the water. Then the big black man tore their clasp apart and the first of them went under, and the second. Both came up choking in speechless panic. They moved toward the land again rigidly like figures in a nightmare—incapable of escaping a pursuing horror. A sudden high shriek from the bank—then a woman's voice babbling wild indescribable sounds. I saw men converging on a tall writhing figure. As they grasped it I saw it was Lula. Her long body jerked spas-modically and with terrific force—breaking the hold of the men again and again. Her eyes rolled wildly, and from her mouth came sounds so incoherent and strange that I felt cold shud-ders. For months on months I had been served by this gentle, amusing, loyal woman. For the first time I was seeing what lay beneath the easy, pleasant stream of her consciousness. When the convulsions of her body lessened, her two daugh-ters came to her and the men laid her on the ground where she lay moaning softly. As the wet white sheets bent in double arc above her I turned away and walked back to the car in which we had come. I never spoke of the moonlight babtizin' to Lula again.

CHAPTER IV

Flaming Cross

W E heard them coming long before we saw them—three distant high blasts of a bugle, then a drop of a minor third on a long wailing note.

"It's the Ku Klux," said Knox. "They're havin' a parade tonight. Goin' to burn a cross out at Riverside." He settled back in his porch chair and sipped his julep.

"I want to go," I said, teetering dangerously on the porch rail. "Can anybody go—even Yankees?"

"Anybody can go. But why anybody would want to—"

"I'm surprised you ain't out there with 'em," said the judge chuckling, his white head bobbing up and down. "Didn't they get your sheets washed in time?"

"You know damn well why I'm not with 'em, judge." The ice in Knox's glass tinkled violently. "When they came to me I said: 'My grandfather was the boss of the real Ku Klux in this section when there was some reason for it. This club you've got here hasn't got as much relation to it as the Boy Scouts. Besides I may get mad enough some day to want to hurt somebody and if I do I want to do it like a man and not with my face hid behind a mask.' I haven't heard from 'em since."

"Better watch your step," said the judge. "They may catch you out tryin' to kiss a pretty co-ed some night."

"I'd try to kill some of 'em before I'd let 'em touch me. The sight of those white sheets does somethin' to me—gets my blood boilin'." Knox stood up and walked to the end of the gallery. "Look at the bastards," he said.

Beneath the tall elms on Queen City Avenue rode three

horsemen robed in white. As they passed the black background of the big tree trunks the moonlight picked them out distinctly. One of them raised a bugle and again the minor four-note call sounded. Behind the mounted trio stretched a long column of marching white figures, two and two, like an army of coupled ghosts, their shapeless flopping garments tossing up and down in the still night air.

An automobile drove up and backed into the drive, throwing its headlights on the rhythmically swaying lines.

"Come along to the street," said Knox, "I want to show you something." We went down the steps and out the walk.

"Look," he said, "can you see their shoes? They tell a lot."

Moving under the edges of the white robes were pants-leg ends and shoes, hundreds of them. A pair that buttoned and had cloth tops, a heavy laced pair splashed with mud, canvas sneakers, congress gaiters—a yellow pair with knobby toes swung past. At the very end a lone figure in sturdy grained oxfords, his sheet twisted awry, stepped gingerly—a little uncertainly. Knox laughed.

"I reckon I know who that is," he said, "poor devil. Let's go finish our drinks and then, if you're still insistin', we'll have a look at their damned cross."

An hour later we drove out past the university, turned left at the insane asylum—and right again toward a glow that was growing in the sky to the north of us. Then through a woods-lined road and suddenly we were in a wide cleared area beside the river. Down on the bank a huge willow bent over into the stream. A mound of earth had been thrown up in front of it and from that mound the tall cross streamed upwards in orange flame. Before the cross and a few yards from it was a small platform which bore a single hooded figure. And in a great arc, closed by the platform, stood the white-robed men who called themselves "The Knights of the Ku Klux Klan." Hundreds of cars had already been parked in the rear of the clearing and their occupants, crowded down close to the arc of sheeted figures, were black silhouettes against the white cloth and the orange light. Before we turned off our engine we could hear the steady booming of the speaker's voice, rich, powerful, bass. We could have understood every word from where we sat but we moved near to the figures with the grotesque deep black holes for eyes. I was spellbound by the scene—hooded army, white-robed central figure, burning cross, dark crowd—all against the soft green of the drooping willow branches or the black cavern beyond it where the yellow water of the river fitfully caught light from the flames.

Suddenly the speaker lifted an arm, throwing his robe into sharp oblique lines.

"Why?" he shouted, and the woods before him and the river behind answered with plaintive distant echoes. "Why? Why?"

"Because the Pope believes himself to be all-powerful. Because he and his minions here, right here in these United States, are at this minute planning the overthrow of our democratic government. Do you want to wake up one morning and find a dago priest in the White House a-givin' orders to white folks? Do you know what he plans to do right here in Alabama—he's got it all worked out—he's goin' to give Alabama over to be ruled by a nigger cardinal!"

There was a low growling murmur from under the white masks.

"Are the people of Alabama—in whom flows the purest Anglo-Saxon blood of any state in this great and glorious Union —goin' to stand for *that?* The curse of Roman Catholicism has threatened white supremacy and how are we goin' to meet that challenge? By *organization,* ladies and gentlemen, by banding together in such noble communion as we have here to fight to the last drop if need be for the rights of Protestant white folks, for the honor and virtue of Southern womanhood, for freedom from oppression—all of which are endangered by the devilish plots of a foreign potentate."

I looked at Knox.

"I don't believe it," I said.

"About the Pope?"

"You know what I mean. And you'd better get me out of here."

"You wanted to come. Listen to some more of it."

"Stamp it out!" roared the speaker. "Stamp out the worship of graven images just like we have stamped out immorality and licentiousness in parked automobiles along our country roads, and shameless nude bathing in this lovely spot and at the country club pool."

"I think I'm getting a little sick," I said, "*please* let's go home."

"All right," said Knox. "I just thought you might like to wait until he starts on teachin' biology at the university."

On the road back I said:

"Aren't there any Roman Catholics in Tuscaloosa?"

"Sure. A hundred or so. They have a church."

"And don't they suffer from mobs like these?"

"Never heard of it. Come to think I don't believe these fellows ever connect 'em up with the Pope."

"But what's it all about then?"

"Well, they're jealous of the young folks having their fun in the parked automobiles. And they like to scare niggers—it gives 'em a sense of power and they think a scared nigger is funny. As for the Catholics—that's just a way to get votes; it's like Wall Street tryin' to lower the price of cotton. The only obstacle in the way of the Pope and Wall Street is the politician. You'd be surprised—if you don't know already—who that speaker was tonight. He was no small-time vote-grabber."

"But are people really as ignorant as that around here? I don't see how he dare talk such damned nonsense in a university town and with lots of people around who know he's lying."

"Get away with it in Tuscaloosa?" said Knox. "I guess you aren't acquainted with the back files of an amusing journal published in the capital of these United States and entitled *The Congressional Record*."

We rode on in silence. The lights of town seemed friendlier than the flames we had left behind on the river bank. I said:

"Speaking of vote-grabbing, I hear you're going to do a little for yourself in the mountains next week."

"Get a few days off and come with me."

"I hoped you'd say that."

"I'll be in Montgomery over the week-end," said Knox, "but I'll meet you in front of the post office at Springville around five o'clock Monday afternoon. Reckon you can make it?"

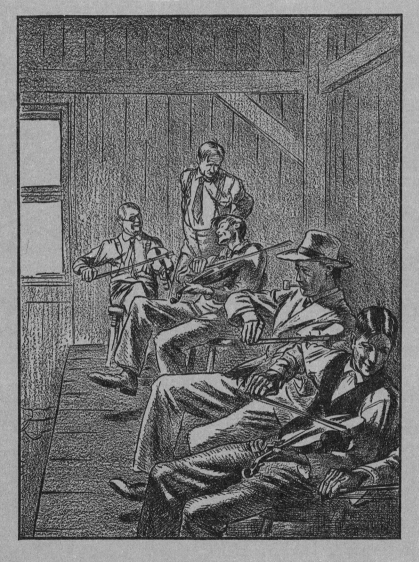

CHAPTER I

Ladies Bow, Gents Know How

KNOX met me at Springville. The trip from Birmingham had been dusty, but a shower had reddened the clay road just outside of Springville and my tired eyes were refreshed with the white gleam of the dogwood trees in the greening woods along the way—like foam in falling green water. We passed a clump of honeysuckle—a pink cloud hovering close to the ground—and we caught a fragrance too sweet for a Yankee to smell—too lacking in subtlety and restraint. I drove faster, gazing eagerly down the straight road to the point where it lost itself beneath the curving slopes of the mountains. Somewhere among those purple acres against the late afternoon sky we would find Knox's friends awaiting us.

"I reckon we'll get there before sundown," said Knox slowly, and he was again obligingly silent. When he spoke once more we were rolling along between two mountains following the pass made by a sturdy yellow river and the only evidence of sun was a crimson cloud silhouetting the pines far above our heads.

"We turn off here for the ferry." We bumped down a ragged track that wound among the trees and suddenly we were beside the river. On the bare clay incline stood a shack. In New England weathered boards turn dark gray, but unpainted homes in North Alabama, taking color from the red soil and the yellow sedge, are mellowed into soft deep browns. The crimson cloud had set ablaze the glass panes of the one window we could see. Out on the water a few yards from shore a small rectangular raft was moving toward us. A tall man in blue overalls, khaki flannel shirt and black felt hat was pulling on a cable that had been stretched from one tree trunk to another across the stream.

"Be there toreckly," he called. "Howdy, Mist' Knox. Howdy, perfesser."

"How does he know who I am?" I said to Knox.

"I told Jim we were coming in when I saw him in Anniston. Isn't a family in these mountains doesn't know who we are and why we've come. If there is we'd better not meet 'em. Strangers are revenuers in these parts. But word gets around the mountains faster than you'd think, so we needn't worry."

The ferry grated on the shore and with many shouted admonitions from the ferryman I drove aboard.

"Let me make you acquainted with Mr. Hightower," said Knox. "I reckon you heard we was comin' through, Mr. Hightower."

"Howdy, perfesser," said Mr. Hightower again. "Yes, I heerd you was on your way up to Henry's." He began heaving at regular intervals on the cable and the water gurgled protestingly against the logs of the raft.

"We'll be seein' you at the singing tomorrow," said Knox.

"I reckon not," said Mr. Hightower grimly. "My wife, she ain't so good right now. Not but what I could leave her for a while except for somebody come up to the door night afore last while I was cross the river. She heerd him movin' around outside and he tried the door. Ain't nobody we know been here. I been askin' round, so I give her my pistol and I got my shotgun right here." He pointed to where it rested on a square beam laid by the log surface. "I reckon one of us 'll kill him next time he comes."

"Maybe he ain't comin' back," said Knox.

"He'll come," said Mr. Hightower with a sort of disinterested certainty. "What'd he come the first time for? Well, he didn't get it."

"Maybe it was just a neighbor."

"I don't have neighbors," said Mr. Hightower, and I looked back at the little deep brown dwelling and saw it standing very lonely.

I drove the car off the raft and Knox paid Mr. Hightower a quarter.

"We'll be seein' you," said Knox.

"They's a fiddlers' convention at Valleyhead," said Mr. Hightower. "I reckon Henry'll be carryin' you to that. Wisht I might could go, too. But my wife, she ain't so good."

"I hope she'll be better soon," said Knox, "and I trust you'll extend to her my sincere good wishes."

"Now that's right polite of you," said Mr. Hightower, moved by the courtliness of the speech. "I'll try to remember to tell her what you said."

Twilight was beginning. The narrow mountain road dipped, then climbed upwards. Near the top of the rise Knox saw the fork he was expecting.

"Right," he said.

I turned right and the car climbed a moment desperately in a shower of stones. Then we were in a clearing. In its center stood a "saddlebag" house. A Ford car stood in the clearing, its back to us. Knox and I climbed out and walked toward it. Just as we reached it I realized that a man was sitting in the driver's seat. And I was painfully aware that I was looking into the barrel of a gun. A long revolver lay across the steering wheel. It was held, carelessly, it seemed to me, in a bony hand. I felt a hard close scrutiny from dark eyes under a black felt hat. Suddenly the eyes softened and the man chuckled.

"Damned if I didn't take yuh fer a couple o' revenuers. Howdy, Knox, how's your pap? Howdy, perfesser?" He put the revolver down on the seat beside him and slowly climbed out of his seat and down.

"Didn't expect you quite so soon. Hey, Mattie Sue. Here's Knox and the perfesser—lookin' mighty hongry. Reckon we better feed 'em 'fore they git so empty we'll hev to shoot a hawg." A pleasant-looking girl of about twenty-five appeared from the doorway and stood silhouetted in the wooden frame of the house. She wore a clean red and white checked gingham dress but no shoes.

Some day I hope an American painter will do justice to the loveliness of the masterpieces of the backwoods architects of Alabama. A long roof line slopes in a gentle undulating curve from the ridge-pole down, down until it is finally met by the upright pillars of the porch. The stone chimney rises in uneven outline from the center at an end wall. The right wing, usually one room, is a complete unit. So is the left wing—which usually contains the kitchen and chimney. Between the two wings—with the roof above and the porch floor below—is nothing. A big square hole through the center of the house, sometimes called the "dog-trot." To the passer-by the house seems a wooden frame set about a landscape. Sometimes it rims a view of tossing green corn leaves; sometimes, when the house is on a ridge, there is a perspective of a distant hill and the tufted tops of lolly pines—such as we looked on now.

"Howdy, perfesser. Howdy, Mr. Knox. I reckon you caught me 'fore I had a chance to red up a bit. Supper's most ready, though. Come right in."

We walked up two steps to the porch and Mattie Sue led us into the left room. Salt pork was making a great to-do in a pot on the box stove. And the odor of corn bread came from the oven.

"You'll sleep t'other side of the dog-trot," said Mattie

Sue, "though I reckon they won't be so much sleepin' tonight. You might come look at your bed."

We crossed the dog-trot to the right wing. It was a long low room. In a corner lay a great rectangular burlap bag. A patchwork quilt partially covered it. Beside it was a pile of quilts. Beside that pile was another. The whole wall was lined with them. There were at least a hundred. I gasped. Knox laughed.

"Do you reckon we'll have enough cover?"

He turned to me: "Henry married Mattie Sue to get these quilts."

Henry laughed self-consciously.

"Don't let Mr. Knox deceive yuh, perfesser. Mattie Sue's pap and mammy, they made each one o' their gals (they had three) make a hundred 'fore she could get married. They was quite a few waitin' 'round for Mattie Sue to finish. The preacher was visitin' her pap when she took the last stitch. He was expectin' to stay another week but the old man told him he better go his way a-preachin' of the word. Reckon he ain't never had the word gobbled up more eager. First house he stopped at was my pap's. 'How's Miss Mattie Sue gittin' on with her sewin'?' I says. 'She jest stitched her last quilt,' he says and I hit out."

Mattie Sue giggled. " 'T was your pap's liquor did it. We sent that preacher off in t'other direction but he heerd your pap had some corn in the charred keg."

"Well, I got the quilts," said Henry; "here they is."

"They're beautiful," I said, "and the patterns are all different."

"They're piled up accordin' to patterns," said Mattie Sue. "This pile's all from the Bible. Here's Garden of Eden and Star of Bethlehem and Tree of Paradise. Then there's Golden

Gates and Solomon's Temple and Forbidden Fruit and Joseph's Coat."

"What's this pile?" I said.

"Them's all politics," said Mattie Sue. "Hobson's Kiss and Lincoln's Platform and Whig Rose and a lot more."

"What's the one on the bed?"

"Hearts an' Gizzards, an' right beside it is Hairpin Catcher an' Tangled Garters, Drunkard's Path, Devil's Claws, Crosses an' Losses, Odds an' Ends, Air Castles, Wonder of the World, an' Aunt Sulky's Patch. They's lots more but we better eat if we're goin' to carry you to the fiddlers' convention."

We went back to the kitchen and sat down to a steaming mess of salt pork, collard greens, cowpeas and corn bread.

"Where's the convention?" said Knox.

"Valleyhead," said Henry, piloting a well-forked bale of greens into his mouth.

"Biggest this year," he continued. "Fiddlers from all over the state. Ez Cowart and his boys—'Cowart's Hell-Raisin' Quintet' they call 'emselves—be comin' through the country from Lawrence County. They say Bob Taylor is comin' by train from Tennessee. Then there's Monkey Brown from Tuscaloosa County and the Rice Brothers an' Chun Gizzard an' a heap more. Let's get movin'. I'm as nervous as an old woman in a Mother Hubbard standin' on an anthill." He rose and went into the other room, returning soon in a blue suit and stiff white collar with a black tie.

A very round and incredibly red moon seemed to be rolling along the top of the ridge beside us as we four rattled along toward Valleyhead. The air was cool and full of mist that smelled of sweet woodlands. Henry brought out a bottle from the hip pocket of his suit. Knox tilted it upward.

"Reckon you inherited that charred keg," he said.

"Been in there three months," said Henry. "My own run. Have one, perfesser?"

I tilted the bottle but, alas, I was too unaccustomed to white lightnin' to treat it so cavalierly. I choked and gasped. My throat was burning. I could not speak and Knox laughed at me. But a pleasant heat had attacked my stomach and I laughed, too. Mattie Sue giggled delightedly, but she did not touch the bottle.

"Most there," said Henry as a cluster of four bright lights in the distance indicated Valleyhead.

Three of the cluster illuminated the shiny filling station. The fourth hung over a doorway just beyond it, the entrance to a long boxlike frame building. "Undertaker's Parlors" was the sign on the glass window of the ground floor. The parlors were entered by another and grander door. Beside the building was a wide stretch of barren red-clay ground and almost every inch of it was occupied by mules and wagons and Fords. We left our Ford farther down the street and returned to the lighted door. It led to a narrow straight staircase. As we climbed it, Mattie Sue in the lead, we could hear a man talking. Henry turned to me.

"That'll be ol' fatback Shelton. Hope he's got through his Ford jokes an' started on the women. Maybe he's got 's fur 's the Bible."

Apparently he hadn't, for as we came to the top of the stairs and could see his ungainly burly figure on the platform at the end o' the room we heard him saying: "I sure like to do the speakin' at meetin's like this 'un. It's about the only chance I git tuh say suthin 'thout bein' broke in on. Not that my good wife talks any more than the next one. Why, I remember a fellow that didn't say nothin' for six years 'cause he was raised polite and didn't think he ought to interrupt."

A guffaw came from the front row. A wave of tittering swept

over the audience. The long room was crowded and hot. Men and women sat on chairs brought from the rooms below. As we turned to go toward the back a lanky youth rose and sidled to the wall not apparently aware of Mattie Sue's look of gratitude. Knox and Henry and I took our places beside him as Fatback went on:

"Now just afore this convention gits started I want to urge you all to read the Good Book." He talked faster now as if reciting and wanting to get through. "I reckon if we all'll do that an' keep on a readin' of it most ever'thin' 'll come out all right. And now—ladies and gentlemen—I wish to announce two of the prizes that's already won. The fruitcake baked by Miz Turnipseed fer the biggest number comin' in any conveyance goes as usual to Mr. and Miz Ventress and their family, all twelve of 'em havin' come in a 1925 Model T Ford. The other prize is a box of seegars for the person comin' the longest distance, and goes to Monkey Brown who's brought his fiddle all way from Tuscaloosa County. Now jest as soon as these fiddlers can tune up we'll have the first number, which will be *Hell After Yearlin'* by the entire lot of 'em."

With a loud scraping of chairs about a dozen men rose and walked to the platform. Some carried their fiddles in cloth bags under their arms, others had attained the dignity of violin cases held by handles. Fatback was pounding an insistent A on a battered piano. There was a great squeaking of pegs in resined holes—now and then a snatch of melody. Eager supporters were placing chairs on the platform for their favorites.

"Now, boys," said Fatback, "ever'body start together when I say go. *Hell After Yearlin,* 'member." Each fiddler tucked his fiddle against his upper arm (no real fiddler places his instrument under his chin), settled back in his chair, freed his right foot ready to pat the rhythm.

"Go!" said Fatback.

It was evident after the first few bars that unison was not contemplated. Each fiddler was playing his own way, the only right way. Every foot was patting a different rhythm and the notes were leaping from each fiddle in separate cascades. It was a bedlam and like all bedlams permeated with a tremendous vitality.

"Whoo-oo-p." Somebody in the audience was lickered and lettin' go. "You show 'em—Monkey—show 'em yuh kin play better 'n they kin behind yo' back."

One of the fiddlers flipped his fiddle behind the back of his chair and sawed away. The crowd laughed and the lickered one shouted again. "Play that fiddle all over the lot, Monkey. Show 'em you kin." Monkey raised the fiddle above his head and went on playing. Then he lifted his left leg, put the fiddle under it and still his fingers flitted on the strings, his bow kept moving. Suddenly the beating feet sounded a swifter tattoo. The bows and fingers moved faster—and then one by one the fiddlers ceased to play. One started on as if to begin a new movement, then thought better of it and stopped.

"That starts us off in great shape," said Fatback. "The judges goin' to have a hard time decidin' *this* contest. Chun Gizzard'll do the first fiddlin' for the prize. Set out here, Chun. What ye goin' to give us? Chun's reg'lar *guit*ar picker couldn't come, so old man Ventress'll beat the straw fer him."

A grizzled veteran of a thousand contests brought his chair forward, placed it carefully, sat back in it until its front legs left the floor.

"*Devil's Hiccup*," he said shortly, patted his right foot and was off. As the first notes raced from his fiddle, old man Ventress stepped up to him. In his left hand he bore what was apparently a broom straw. This he placed across the strings of the singing fiddle. Then with the straw between the second and third fingers of his right hand he began to bounce it up and down on the strings. He was drumming out an accompaniment on the same instrument that carried the melody. Chun was in full swing now, the notes flying from his fingers. But the swifter his pace, the swifter and merrier rose the jigging accompaniment. Loud whoops sounded from the audience. Everybody was getting warmed up. Then a tall man rose in the aisle and very solemnly did a shuffle, his big brogans banging on the wide-plank floor.

Suddenly the tune stopped—as if broken off in the middle—and Chun and his accompanist retired. The audience applauded loudly, clapping and stamping with their feet.

"Next'll be Monkey Brown, champeen of Tuscaloosa County," said Fatback. "Monkey's brother is his *guit*ar picker. Monkey kin play that fiddle o' his'n in any conceivable position o' the body. We look to see him try. What'll it be, Monkey?"

Monkey, an angular young man, brought his chair to the platform. His brother, obviously younger, followed.

"*Old Cow Died in the Forks of the Branch,*" said Monkey.

For almost two hours the convention went on. Glasscock and Norris and Dunnaway and Houze, Taylor and Atkinson, and McClesky and Bowers—all had their turn. And the five Cowarts, playing like one man, brought the program to an end quite different from the dispersed melodies of its beginning.

We heard *Wolves A-Howlin'*; *Jim Along Josy*; *Chaw Roast Beef*; *Circus Rider*; *Old Time Sorghum Mill*. Then came the old favorites *Leather Breeches* and *Mississippi Sawyer*. Then *Who Bit the Tater*; *Uncle Wash Washed His Corn*; *Mustard Plaster Hurts*; *Whole Hog or None*; *I'll Never Get Drunk Any More*; *Alabama Gals*; *Bobbed-Tail Buzzard*; *Bucking Mule*; *Billy in the Low Ground*; *Cotton Choppin' Dick*; *Black Bess* (the name of a famous train);

Dead Up the Stump; Danny in the Cotton Patch; Double-Headed Train; Horse Shoeing; Mountaintop Cabin; Methodist Preacher; Rabbit Plowed the Possum; Shout Lula; Corn Shucking; Three Nights in the Piney Woods; Throw My Fiddle over the Fence; River Bridge; Sugar in the Coffee; Rocky Hollow Hard Times; Wooden-Leg Diana; Third Party; Waggoners; Went Down to the New Ground; Wild Horse in the Canebrake; The Old Water Wheel; Wild Goose; Old Mollie, Here What You Doin' There; Such a Gettin' Upstairs; Mister Chicken; Set My Trap in the Old Straw Field; Black B'ar'll Git You, Honey.

"Time for the judges to retire an' consider their *de*-cision," said Fatback. "Let's clear this floor and get ready for a little dance."

The fiddlers of the Alabama hills have translated the life they and their neighbors live into notes. Fiddle songs are the folk music of their generation, ballads the relic of the past. From the names of these rollicking tunes much of the course of the mountain living may be read. To the uninitiated ear the melodies sound very much alike. There is the same breathless, tumbling pace in all. But the mountaineer dancer can recognize each one by a phrase. He hears in them the cries of the wild beasts in the woods, the creaking of axles, the sounds of work, the crescendo and diminuendo of the express train roaring through the pass.

"The judges have decided," said Fatback ponderously, "that it was a purty close contest—best we ever had in these parts. Ever'body played good but on account of havin' had a *little* more experience and playin' *extry* good, Old Man Ventress gits the five-dollar gold piece." There was perfunctory clapping from the audience now standing about the walls of the long room—their chairs having been removed to the parlors below.

"He needed it wuss," said Henry to me softly.

"Let's play," yelled Fatback. "Start it off agin, Chun. Fust couple on the floor."

There was excited pairing. Couples walked about self-consciously, impatiently. Suddenly Chun struck up fiddling and singing at the same time.

> "Tune up your fiddle
> Resin up your bow
> We'll knock the devil
> Out'n Cotton-Eyed Joe."

"Swing four," chanted Fatback in a high voice.

> "Swing your partners one and all
> Swing that lady in the checkered shawl."

The room was a checkerboard of moving squares made by dancing couples, four couples to a square. The men were stepping in perfect time but dragging their feet a bit in a syncopated shuffle. They "promenaded" with sidling gait, proud of their skill. The girls stepped briskly. Fatback's voice rose high above the fiddler and the noise of feet:

> "Gents, hands in your pockets, backs to the wall
> Take a chaw of terbacker and balance all."

Swinging the ladies was becoming more and more exciting. Now and then feet left the floor in a flutter of skirts to the accompaniment of hearty shrieks.

> "Quit that huggin'. Ain't you shamed?
> Promenade, O, Promenade.
> Chicken in the bread pan peckin' out dough
> Monkey on a fence rail, here we go

Promenade, O, Promenade.
If it hadn't been fer Cotton-Eyed Joe
I'd 'a' been married long ago
Promenade, O, Promenade.
Walk and talk
Partners swing
Chicken in the bread tray peckin' out dough
Sally, will your dog bite, no child no,
Dance the Ocean Wave,
Swing your partner
Ladies bow
And Gents know how—
All run away."

The dancers were skipping merrily. Now and then a gent got so lickered up that he had to express himself in a superfluous "Pigeon-wing"—while other dancers waited patiently for him to wear down. Chun stopped playing. Immediately Fatback began promoting the next dance. "Monkey Brown'll fiddle this 'un."

Mattie Sue stood before me. She was smiling and Henry was standing beside her smiling, too.

"Come on 'nd play, perfesser. You know how to play."

I shook my head.

"I can't fiddle."

They shouted with laughter.

"Ain't what she means play," said Henry. "She means dance with her."

"I couldn't," I said—but I felt myself being propelled toward the middle of the floor.

"Rufus stoled a pumpkin, he took it down to town.
Policeman said, Hey, Rufus, just lay that punkin down."

Monkey was in full swing. I felt awkward and fearfully self-conscious. I bowed and swung my partner as I had seen the others do.

"Promenade, O, Promenade," sang Fatback. Suddenly I was aware of the irresistible rhythm of the music and of the people. I could feel something of it in me. I took courage and danced boldly. I made mistakes but I muddled through. The perfesser was a proud man when he led Mattie Sue back to her husband after the music had stopped.

"Reckon we better start back," said Henry. "Goin' to be All-Day Singin' tomorrer."

We dragged Knox away from a pale little girl who resented his departure cordially.

Then we were out in the soft night. The moon was higher now and whiter. We were rolling towards home in the Ford.

"You done pretty good, perfesser," said Mattie Sue. "I reckon you could learn it fine in a while."

"Henry," said Knox, "you've got to watch that wife of yours. She's the sweet talkinest little ol' gal."

"She don't mean nothin' by it," said Henry stolidly. "Don't mind her, perfesser."

But the perfesser was still happily minding her when he dropped off to sleep—with the quilt called the Road to California resting lightly above him.

CHAPTER II

All-Day Singing

Sacred Harp Singin'
Dinner-on-the-grounds
Whiskey in the woods
An' the devil all around.
—*Alabama Mountain Song.*

KNOX waked me at four.

"Here's a black tie," he said. "Wear a white shirt and your blue suit and leave off the vest. I can't have you losing votes for me."

When we were eating our grits and bacon a few minutes later he looked me over critically.

"If you'd shaved the back of your neck you might be one of 'em."

We heard a long whoop outside.

"That'll be Tom Somerville," said Henry. "We'll be goin' in his Ford. He knows your pap and he's the vote-gettin'est man in Alabama. Mattie Sue, put plenty grease on his grits."

He unbarred the door and Tom came in. He was short, thickset, and his grin, lining his sun-browned face, showed tobacco-stained teeth. He came straight to me.

"Mighty proud to make your acquaintance, perfesser. Howdy, folks. Knox, how's your pap? Ain't seen him since the singin' down at Samanthy. Thank yuh, Miss Mattie Sue. Sure is good grits an' bacon."

Down near the road, under the sweet-gum tree, we climbed into Tom's Ford. Mattie Sue came last, almost hidden by a pile of shoe boxes balanced expertly in her arms. Tom laughed.

"Don't let nobody git near them boxes o' yourn, Miss Mattie Sue. I figure on eatin' 'em as empty as a jackass's head." Mattie Sue grinned, and Henry said: "Better try that vote-gettin' on some o' them Sand Mountain ladies. You've got her'n."

Tom cranked the Ford. "I sent all my tin cans to the factory in Dee-troit and they sent me back this. Said they hoped I wouldn't have no more accidents." He threw back his head and guffawed.

"Tom knows more Ford jokes than anybody in the county," said Henry. "Helps him get votes."

We could see the sunrise barred by the straight thin trunks of the lolly pines as the car traveled the narrow red road. In a dip we crossed a clear-water branch, the slipping wheels stirring up rust-colored clouds that drifted downstream. Sometimes we passed a saddlebag house like Henry's and once we met a plodding ox-team dragging a long tree lopped of its branches, and there was much geeing and hawing before we got by. Tom leaned out:

"Ain't yuh comin' to the sing, Bije?"

"Reckon. Soon's I tote this down by Deep Branch."

Reckon you'll git there for dinner-on-the-grounds," yelled Tom. The road began to climb.

"Up Sand Mountain," said Henry.

The car struggled desperately and once we stopped to let the motor cool and to fill the radiator with branch water by means of a tin can. One last steep grade and suddenly we were on flat land, in the midst of tall green corn. As far as we could see the road kept one level.

"Just like a table," said Knox, "and it grows fine crops."

We overtook a lumber wagon drawn by a pair of drooping mules. Behind the driver's bench six sturdy ladderback chairs held children, all sitting very straight and looking very shiny —the little girls brilliant in their checked ginghams.

"Reckon Missis Albrest couldn't come," said Tom. "She's been expectin' some time. 'Scuse me, Miss Mattie Sue."

The road was suddenly full of cars and wagons and we could see the little wooden tower of Sand Mountain Church rising above the corn. When we reached the big open space in front, it was already lined with cars and the pine grove beside it was dotted with horses, mules and wagons. Tom drove the Ford full-tilt into the grove and stopped. We climbed out and strolled toward the church, faithlessly bringing Mattie Sue's boxes along.

Alabama sun and storm had stained the unpainted church a lusterless deep brown. Some piles of worn bricks held it a scant yard above the sandy earth. Built like a box except for its roof which sloped slightly down on each side from its center elevation, it boasted no adornment save a tower obviously meant to culminate in a spire. A few cross pieces hanging disconsolately from the tower testified the builder's discouragement.

As we trooped in everybody already seated turned to look. Tom saved the rest of us from embarrassment by taking upon himself the onus of attention.

"Howdy, Joe. Hi, Miss Ellie. Countin' on eatin' out'n your box today. Howdy, Aleck, how's craps?"

We sat on wooden benches with single plank backs. A center aisle led down to the platform which was surrounded by benches on three sides. A tall man stood on the platform.

"Trebles on the left. Basses on the right. Tenors in the center."

"What about altos?" I whispered to Knox.

"Don't mention the word," he said. "The real Sacred Harpers think it's a newfangled and wicked affectation. They've been having a big fight with the Christian Harmony folks about it."

The tenors, I noticed, were of both sexes. The seats of the trebles were crowded with women. Opposite them sat the basses, all men.

Henry passed me a thick rectangular book.

"I borrowed an extry notebook for you and Mist' Knox," he said. "That's Perfesser Hinton histin' the rhyme. He had a singin' school over in Winston County last month."

I read on the title-page: "Original Sacred Harp, The Best and Most Valuable Sacred Tune and Hymn Book. From the pens of authors of unquestioned reputation and ability to be found in America and many other countries. With complete sketch of the authors of tunes and hymns connected with each tune, all founded on Scripture Text, Quotations and Citations from the Bible."

During the long opening prayer led by a worn-looking man announced as "the Reverend Boone" I irreverently turned a page to the preface: "To a considerable extent the sacred song books of this section is badly tainted with operatic, secular and ragtime strains of music forms. Such compositions drive away, in place of promoting, religion and religious feeling. . . . In these compositions there are but few of the twisted rills and frills of the unnatural snaking of the voice, in unbounded proportions, which have in the last decade so demoralized and disturbed the church music of the present age."

The tall man was speaking:

"We'll begin with a short one—*The Bride's Farewell.* Some o' you gals goin' to git married soon ought to sing this pretty good."

The gals giggled. I wondered what Text, Quotation or Citation from the Bible could have inspired this "Sacred Tune and Hymn." Knox found the page for me just as the perfesser said:

"Perfesser Stringfellow ain't come with his tunin' fork yet, so I reckon we'll have to pitch it the old way. Sister Dendy, you got mighty nigh the highest treble in the county. Sound a note, please, ma'am."

A wild, high screech from the midst of the trebles.

"Tom Rice—git down below with that bear's growl o' yourn."

A deep rumble from somewhere among the basses.

"Ought t' be easy to git in between 'em," said Perfesser Hinton, and sounded a nasal barytone *mi.*

"That'll be the pitch," he said. "We'll sing the music first. Are you ready?" He raised his arm, pencil in hand, and brought it down.

Tom and Henry took in great breaths and let out staccato yells. So did everyone else except Knox and me. A fearsome hodgepodge of sound arose. They were singing an outlandish gibberish—great sharp bursts of sound. Knox shouted in my ear:

"They're singing the notes."

I did not understand, but gradually, as I listened, I made out a tune, a wailing minor, and I discovered that Henry and Tom were singing *mi, fa, sol, la.* I looked at the book and for the first time saw that the notes, though placed on the familiar scale, were printed in different shapes. *Mi* was a diamond, and I found by careful comparison of the book and the singing: *fa* was triangular; *sol* was round; *la* was square. Weeks later by study of the book I learned how these notes are repeated in the scale.

Exact as a metronome and with as much expression, Perfesser Hinton beat time. Everyone sang as loud as he could and kept on the beat. Suddenly as it began the great noise stopped.

"Now we'll take the poetry," said the perfesser. Still staccato and with all the breath they could summon they sang:

> Farewell, mother, tears are beaming
> Down thy pale and tender cheek
> I in gems and roses gleaming
> Scarce this sad farewell can speak.
>
> Farewell, mother, now I leave you
> Griefs and hopes my bosom swell
> One to trust who may deceive me
> Farewell, mother, fare thee well.

As the last note died the perfesser began again:

"That's a good start. Now let's take number one-eighteen. That's a good religious tune. Music first."

Again the hubbub.

"Now the poetry."

> Young ladies, all attention give
> You that in wicked pleasures live
> One of your sex the other day
> Was called by death's cold hand away.

The church was full now. People stood along the walls and the doorway was packed. Crowds were huddled outside each window singing lustily. I remembered being incredulous of the great numbers Knox had told me that these sings brought out. Yet there were surely more than two thousand people in and around the church at this "right small meetin' at a bad time o' year." And they were all doing their best. Hard blows of sound beat upon the walls and rafters with inexorable regularity. All in a moment the constant beat took hold. There was a swift crescendo. Muscles were tensing, eyes brightening. The perfesser stepped quickly toward the basses. Deep roars answered him. He wheeled, almost ran to the tenors. Nasal and high they responded. The trebles, screaming, rode above. In the front row a slim brown-eyed girl in an orange dress was throwing her head from side to side in the rhythm. Her black hair had fallen from a knot at the back of her neck, and flew about her face. She was gasping for breath. The silence that followed was restless. No one spoke, but there was much turning of pages—as if they were avoiding looking at each other. Relentlessly the perfesser drove them into the next song. Beads of sweat rolled down his cheeks. As the last explosive chord sounded he drew a sleeve across his forehead.

"Perfesser Stringfellow from Lamar County just come in. He'll hist 'em for a while. I'm goin' out 'n' wet my whistle."

A short wiry bespectacled man arose and took off his coat, displaying flowered suspenders.

"As the feller says, a mule runs faster out'n harness. Let's git up some noise on *The Dying Californian*."

It was almost two hours later when he raised his hand at the end of a song:

"I reckon y'all got a hankerin' to find out what's on th' inside o' them boxes. Well, it's time for dinner-on-the-grounds."

The men and women who crowded out of the door were not the grim taciturn lot who had entered it. A note almost of hysteria sounded in their laughter. They seemed to be glad of escape—still a little fearful.

We bore Mattie Sue's boxes back to the grove. Here each family took its position, flanked by boxes, and proudly prepared to meet all comers. Tom Somerville grasped Knox by the arm.

"Come along, boy. I'll talk and you just keep feedin'. Every box y' eat out'n counts a vote."

The tops were off the boxes now, revealing great quantities of fried chicken, beaten biscuit, corn bread, pickles, preserves, white frosted cakes. No one dared wander far from his own boxes for fear of being gorged by friends who would be hurt by a refusal. Back-slapping and deep laughter, excited squeals and giggles accompanied all the hearty old jokes about human capacity.

Down in the gully behind the church was a spring. Young girls in bands of four or five strolled toward it, loitered on the way back. Disorganized groups of embarrassed boys followed. The girls seemed not to notice but their laughter was shrill.

A bell-note sounded from the unfinished tower. There was a repacking of boxes and a movement toward the church. Knox and Tom returned to us looking very genial. As we were re-entering I looked back. Girls still wandered to and from the spring and boys still followed. Inside, the singing began with increased vigor. The informality of dinner-on-the-grounds had had its effect. Under Perfesser Hinton's adjurations the singers reached a greater volume than before. More and more leaders were called on. The restless feeling, the suppressed excitement returned. But I noticed that the girl in the orange dress was no longer in the front row.

"Now we'll sing *Edmunds*," said the perfesser. A stir ran through the church—as of pleasant anticipation. In the first stanza I heard something about Adam. I listened:

> He had no consolation
> But seemed as one alone
> Till to his admiration
> He found he'd lost a bone.

> Great was his exultation
> To see her by his side,
> Great was his elevation
> To have a loving bride.

I lost the words in the volume of sound. The song seemed endless. When I again caught on, it had turned moralistic. I heard something about "the solemn duties of every man and wife":

> This woman was not taken
> From Adam's head we know;
> And she must not rule o'er him,
> It's evidently so.

At last *Edmunds* reached its close.

"It's been a great day," said Perfesser Hinton, "and let's end it by singin' *The Great Day.*"

A haunting melody rose, minor and plangent, a tune that lent itself in some strange way to the reedy, metallic quality of this strange chorus. The words were peculiarly distinct.

> I've a long time heard that the sun will be darkened
> That the sun will be darkened in that day,
> O sinner, where will you stand in that day?

There was a long pause and then the song lifted again:

> I've a long time heard that the moon will be bleeding

On it went.

> I've a long time heard that the stars will be falling—
> I've a long time heard that the earth will be burning . . .

As the last stanza started the singers, still singing, began moving to the door. When the last note died the church was empty.

Then the grove and the roadside came alive with wagons and automobiles. There was a calling of good-bys. We left late—Tom was still vote-gettin' for Knox—but there were still cars and horses in the grove when we rolled away. I glanced back toward the spring. An orange dress burned through the gathering dusk. Beside it towered a dark figure. Behind them stretched a long line of couples, girls no longer shrill and boys no longer shy.

CHAPTER III

Footwashing

"HARDSHELL is what most folks call 'em," said Henry, "but you better not let *them* hear it. It makes 'em mad an' a mad hardshell is as ornery as a grown wildcat."

"Tell me more about them," I said, "so I won't make any mistakes when we get there."

"Plenty of time to tell yuh. We ain't to Cullman yet."

"And we ain't goin' to be," said Mattie Sue's voice from the back seat, "less'n you drive faster. What I don't like about hardshells, they think everybody but them is goin' t' hell— even the little dead babies."

"They're gittin' over that a bit," said Henry. "Ol' Missis Venable tol' me last year the Lord makes special arrangements for babies an' idiots. She's been claimin' her Ezra's half-baked ever since he j'ined the Missionary Baptists."

"Sounds like Calvinism," I said.

"May be," said Henry, "all I know is the hardshells call 'emselves Primitives. They pay their debts, they vote Republican, and they take their whiskey straight, as the feller says. My old man was one of 'em till he took to pickin' on the *gui*tar an' they thrown him out."

"The real old-fashioned ones won't even have no organ or piano in their church," said Mattie Sue, "they think it's wicked."

"Here's Cullman," said Henry as we swung round a bend in the pike and rolled past a series of brick houses so neat and clean that they might have been part of a New England landscape.

"This is a German town," said Henry. "Some of 'em can't speak good English yet. Even though their grandfathers lived here, they still talk Dutch. They come down-country from St. Louis a long time ago. An' here's somethin' you'll want to see." He chuckled and pulled up at the side of the road. A neatly painted sign confronted us—"Nigger Don't Let the Sun Go Down on You in This Town!"

"What's that for?" I said.

"There's only one nigger in the whole town," said Henry. "He shines shoes at the *hotel*. All the German women couldn't stand havin' 'em round 'cause they was so no-count an' careless like. So they run 'em out. An' we better run out, too, or we'll never see no footwashin' at Double Springs."

The clay road began to climb, the sun to get hot as the morning hours wore on. We passed little hamlets sleeping in strong contrasts of sunlight and shade—Clarkson, Jones, Chapel, Nesmith. Suddenly the road grew steeper and rougher. Mattie Sue gave a little scream and I looked around to see her clutching the top-supports desperately.

"Winston County road," said Henry. "Never been a good stretch o' pike in it. Folks down at Montgomery ain't through payin' 'em back for stayin' in the Union in the War Between the States."

"Do you mean they didn't secede?"

"I reckon that's what you call it. When they had the war they was some kind o' meetin' down to Montgomery an' Winston sent a man down there name o' Sheets; his folks still live round here. He tol' 'em they was only three slaves in the whole county and *they* wasn't worth fightin' over, so he reckoned he and his neighbors would stay out o' the fuss. Well, when the war started the Confederate soldiers come up in here an' shot an' hung a lot o' the men for deserters. That made the rest of 'em mad and a lot went north an' joined the army up there. Some of 'em hid up in the hills though an' kept on makin' their corn liquor same as usual. Hurst Mauldin tol' me all about it once. His grandpap was one o' those got caught by the soldiers."

"Did they all come back after the war?"

"Yes, an' brought a few more with 'em, an' for a while they had a good time—while the carpet-baggers and niggers was runnin' the state. But as soon as the Democrats got in they didn't get schools nor roads nor nothin'. Won't for a long time yet neither. County's still over two-thirds Republican."

We crossed a clear little stream that hurled itself bravely at bowlders in its path.

"Sipsey River," said Henry. "Only runnin' water in the county. We're 'most there. You'll be hearin' 'em in a minute."

"Hope most the preachin's over," said Mattie Sue. "They always have lots o' preachers an' they kin talk a long time."

"That's because they don't get their sermonts ready none," said Henry. " 'Most all on 'em can preach without havin' got posted from a book or nothin'. Reckon we'd be hearin' one of 'em now if 'twasn't fer this engine."

As he spoke we came in sight of a weathered church so like the one we had visited for the Sacred Harp Singing that its differing details escape my memory. Its tawny spire pointed lamely toward the sky. Its doorway, reached by three sagging steps, was open, the door swung inward. Narrow windows looked out on a worn-clay clearing filled with Fords and wagons hitched to mules. As we climbed out of our Ford we could hear a high-pitched voice shouting, its accents falling at regular intervals. We climbed the steps and, finding the first bench inside vacant, sat and looked about us. The preacher stood on a box rostrum. In front of him were two long low benches running the long way of the room and about four feet apart. On each of these sat a dozen people each solemnly gazing into the eyes of the worshiper across from him. Between them on the floor were six basins, one for each couple. The rest of the benches, like the one on which we sat, faced the rostrum.

"It stands to reason," shrilled the speaker, a dumpy fellow whose black coat and trousers contrasted sharply with his white shirt, white collar, white tie, "that when man fell from a state of grace there was nothin' he could do to save himself from hell. He disobeyed God an' only God could help him. It would be false and prideful to take on a feelin' that you kin rescue yourself from the wrath of the Lord. God knew what was goin' t'happen. Before this ol' world was built he knew that Jesus Christ would save as many as he could from eternal torment by sacrificin' himself on the cross. An' God knew what ones he was goin' t' save. He had 'em all picked out ahead o' time. All the rest will spend eternity bein' licked by the flames o' hell, damned to everlastin' perdition by the fall of Adam an' their own wickedness. I tell you, my brothers and sisters, there ain't a feelin' in the world that can make you so happy as to find out that you are one o' them that God picked out—an' the only way you kin find that out is by walkin' in his ways."

His voice soared in a triumphal chant. "We're a-goin' to walk with the saints who will never fall away or be lost. When that resurrection day comes God's elected will stand on his right hand and rejoice while the wicked shall groan forever in the torturing flames. Then us that believe ever' word in the Bible, us that's been buried in holy water accordin' to the only right way, us that knows the Lord's Supper and washin' the saints' feet was meant to be carried on, us Primitive Baptists, will stand an' see judgment pronounced on the dancin', card-playin', carnal-minded sinners, on them that read the unscriptural works of men on religion—abominations in the sight of God —them that belong to secret societies when they should belong jest to God's picked out holy ones, them that don't know no more than tryin' to get folks into their churches when they had ought to realize that jest those that are called by God can git into heaven."

He stopped for a moment and looked beyond the stolid group who still sat eyeing each other across the basins. Then a stubby forefinger pointed directly at us in the back row.

"Did you ever burn your hand over the top of a lamp chimney? Did you ever pick up a hot pan, not knowin' it had been on the fire? It hurts, doesn't it? Suppose you hurt that way all over. You wouldn't be able to stand it. Well, you've got to. No rest and no ending for all the time there is forever, you will be hurting like that all over—no use to scream—no water to put out the fire—no butter to put on your scars—jest nothin' but burnin' up through all eternity."

I heard a little choked gasp beside me. I turned and saw Mattie Sue sitting as if stricken by a sudden paralysis, her eyes staring intently into those of the preacher. Henry moved close to her. His face was livid and his chin was set. I could see that he was deadly angry. I caught his eye and smiled. He relaxed and gave Mattie Sue a little poke with his elbow. We three looked at each other and we all smiled as if to say, "the crisis is over and we aren't hurt a bit."

Then, rather vaguely, I heard the familiar high voice speaking again.

"Only them that is fit subjects, been baptized all over and born of the spirit, is invited to take part in this footwashin'. Jesus washed the feet of his disciples after the feast of the Passover an' he said, 'As I have done to you ye should also do to each other.' Brother John Muckle, will you begin histin' the rhyme?"

A raucous barytone lifted a plaintive questioning: "How long, O Savior, O how long shall this bright hour delay?"

Scatteringly the song gathered volume. On a sudden the motionless ones before the basins joined in and the rhythm became more marked—a strongly emphasized staccato chant:

How *long*, O *Savior*, O how *long?*

As if by some prearranged signal all twelve backs bent over at once. The people in the pews craned their necks. Each of the footwashers was unlacing the left shoe of the person he faced. Two men sat on the near ends of the benches. One was tall, angular, thin, the other short and stocky with a large protruding belly. They seemed inextricably wound up in each other and both were singing lustily. An old woman was intent on the laces of a heavy brogan worn by a wiry little man in overalls—while he earnestly drew. long black strings from the eyelets of her high shoe. No one wore stockings and soon the flesh of bare feet, strong, calloused feet, began to gleam in the basins. The swinging chant grew stronger and the movement of the washers quickened as they caressed the feet in the water with their hands. The dozen bodies seemed a convoluted whole, writhing in a slow ecstasy to the monotonous beat of the song. The preacher strode down off the rostrum, singing loudly. There was a flash of white at the far end of the benches—a towel. Slowly it traveled from one couple to the next—growing more limp, less white. Now the shoes were being replaced by their wearers. Still the chant:

How *long*, O *Savior*, O how *long?*

The preacher walked back to the rostrum. He lifted his hand and the singing stopped abruptly in the midst of a line.

"Brother Sam Sprott'll do the preachin' while our brothers and sisters here change places an' git ready for the next washin'."

The twelve on the long benches somewhat self-consciously

sought seats in the rear. Another dozen rose from the front pews and advanced to the vacated washing-benches.

A pompous, round-faced man with a big bass voice began to talk from the rostrum. Mattie Sue touched my arm and she and Henry and I tiptoed out.

As we walked toward the Ford two men climbed out of it and one of them was Knox.

"Howdy, Mist' Knox," said Henry. "How was the vote-gettin' in Lawrence County?"

"Went all right, Henry," said Knox, "thanks to Tom Nabors here. I reckon y'all know each other."

"We been hearin' 'bout each other 'most our lives anyway," said Nabors, a hearty big man with a broad smile punctuated by three gold teeth.

"Mighty pleased t'make your acquaintance," said Henry. "Meet my wife."

"Howdy," said Mattie Sue.

"You ready to come back with us, Mist' Knox?" said Henry. "An', Mist' Nabors, we'd feel mighty proud t'have you come, too. Stay as long as yuh like."

"Henry," said Knox, "Tom here's got an idea. He wants y'all and the professor to come over to his place at Mountain Home for the night an' then we can all drive in to Decatur for the first day o' court week tomorrow. They're havin' that big nigger-trial. What do you say?"

"I got plenty room," put in Nabors, "an' I sure would admire t'have yuh."

"Well, now, that's mighty clever of you, Mist' Nabors," said Henry, "but we ain't come away with no idea o' visitin' an' I don't reckon—"

"Jinny McDade was goin' t'milk the cow 'fore we got home anyway," said Mattie Sue, her eyes sparkling.

"Miz Nabors an' I got a couple o' nightshirts fer yuh. Reckon we couldn't find yuh in 'em 'thout a posse but you're welcome to 'em," said Tom Nabors, and slapped his thigh and roared with laughter. "No offense," he went on, suddenly serious, "reckon I talk too rough sometimes, specially for ladies. Mist' Knox an' I sort o' got our hearts set on your comin' though."

"We-ll," said Henry.

"We'll come," said Mattie Sue, "and we're much obliged to yuh. Perfesser, you go with Mist' Knox in his new car an' we'll follow ye 'long in the Model T."

CHAPTER IV

Sweet William Came from the Western States

TOM NABORS lived in a plank house, a comfortable home larger than Henry's. It was built on a hillside on which young pines were repairing the ravages of a cutting ten years before. Mrs. Nabors was buxom and kind. She seemed not at all disturbed at the arrival of three extra guests and we had hardly washed up with the aid of pitcher and basin on the back porch when she called us to come in.

"Set right down," said Tom Nabors. "Just go right ahead and help yourselves to what's before you. We don't have much but what we have we give unto thee."

His use of Biblical expression, typical of the Alabama north country, was amusing in its understatement of fact. "Not much" consisted of chicken and dumplings, sweet potato pie, ham from the smokehouse, corn bread in large pones, scrambled eggs, snap beans, biscuits and cane syrup, and a goblet of buttermilk at each plate.

Our meal was full of long silences as we diligently emptied our plates. After it was over Mattie Sue "helped with the dishes" and the four men sat on the wide front porch gazing down at the brown road winding through the trees. We could feel the cool breath of evening in the hill country and we were restful and full of talk.

"They ought to hung them niggers long ago," said Tom Nabors, "an' been done with it. This trial costs Morgan County plenty."

"But suppose they're innocent," I said.

There was an embarrassing silence. Then Tom said:

"We don't like niggers in this neck o' the woods. We ain't ever liked 'em. I can remember my father standin' on the mountain where you can look off down toward the Black Belt an' the flat country an' sayin': 'Them black bastards is takin' the food out'n our mouths. We oughta be down there workin' that black land but we got too much pride to work for nothin'.' They're down there sharin' the good things with the rich while good white folks in the hills have to starve."

"But you don't starve," said I, remembering the dinner.

Knox laughed. "Tom's got one o' the best stills in this section back over the hill somewhere. He won't starve as long as Decatur likes its liquor."

"Are you ever bothered by revenuers?" I said.

"Not more'n once," said Tom shortly. "There was a young feller, 'bout twenty-five, I reckon, come up here and set off with his guns int' the hills to catch him a still. He come wanderin' int' town a day later, out of his head, an' his back beat off of him with whips. There was a note pinned on his shirt said, 'If you'd sent a man we would of killed him.' "

"Don't they send out revenuers any more?"

"Sure, somebody has to draw their salary, but we got a good arrangement now. Whenever the government tells 'em to get busy or lose their jobs they just show up in Flossy or Grenada or some such small place an' let ever'body know who they are and what they're there for. They talk mighty big an' say they're hot on the trail. Then in a little while one of 'em gets a note that tells 'em where to go. Next mornin' they set out an' they come back at night with an ol' worn-out still we left for 'em out in the woods. There's more big talk about how they mos' caught a couple o' the boys workin' it—though any fool'd know it ain't been worked in months. Then the Decatur and Albany papers tell about how brave the revenuers are an' how big a still they got an' ever'body is satisfied for a long time."

"Have you got a moonshiners' organization?"

"No, I don't reckon you'd call it that. It's just us people in the hills got to stick together. We ain't done it so well since Aunt Jennie died. Ever'body was scared o' her an' used to do what she said."

"Tell him about Aunt Jennie, Tom," said Knox. "He'll put her in a book."

"She ought to be in one. I allus reckoned somebody'd come along and write about her in a newspaper or somethin'."

"I sure would like to hear about her," I said.

"When I knew her," said Tom, "she was a little dried-up ol' woman but she had talkin' blue eyes. She run this county like she was queen of it. Nobody ever candidated round here without she said so. When they had the War Between the States a lot o' people in these parts felt like they did down in Winston County, didn't want to fight fer the rich folks in the Black Belt so's they could have niggers do their work for 'em free. Folks in this county was pretty well fixed then. They was makin' liquor same as now, and the lumber companies hadn't cut over the woods an' druv away the game an' spiled the land. So Henry Brooks, Aunt Jennie's husband, said he wasn't goin' to be a soldier, he was satisfied to stay right here an' mind his own business.

"Not long after that a party of Confederates come up into the hills to force men into their army. Henry Brooks wouldn't run from 'em when they come to his house but he fought when they tried to take him away an' they shot him dead. Aunt Jennie's four boys was little shavers then but she got 'em all out o' bed an' made 'em swear on the dead body o' their pa that they'd kill the men that shot him. Well, sir, in the next forty year they got ever' one of 'em. They kep count with notches on a hickory stick. Aunt Jennie had three of 'em her-self. One was for the leader. She cut his head off an' cooked it till it was jest a skull an' made it into a wash-basin. She used it ever' day, an' jest a minute before she died she washed her hands in it for the last time. Another o' her notches was fer the man that shot her son, Henry. She sort o' set store by him, named after his pa an' all. He was six foot two an' could ride slow round a saplin' an' put a pretty belt o' lead round it. He died shootin'—with his boots on.

"After all the Confederates that killed her man was dead Aunt Jennie ruled the roost round here. Folks was righty keerful to do what she said an' they was right proud of her, too. Ever'body voted the way she said. She hated niggers, sort o' held 'em responsible, as the feller says. All the folks in these parts hates 'em fer one reason er another. Lucky we don't see 'em much. Feller round here tol' me he got to votin' age 'fore he ever seen one."

"Same way over near Sand Mountain an' in the hills round Scottsboro," said Henry. "They's good-sized lads an' gals over there ain't seen one till yit."

Mattie Sue appeared in the doorway, bearing a guitar with deep-gleaming surfaces.

"I found this," she said, "an' Miz Nabors says her husband kin pick it. I sure would like to hear some music."

Tom Nabors laughed self-consciously. "I ain't much of a hand at it, I jest pick roun' home a bit."

Mattie Sue placed the guitar in his hands and a deep mellow sound came from it as she let it go. "Knows its boss," she said.

"Don' know what to pick at," said Tom.

"Pick a ballit," said Mattie Sue, "and sing it. Pick *Barbary Allen.*"

"I don't sing so good," said Tom, "but I'll try it."

He strummed a few notes. A red arc, thin as a thread, lay on the top of the hill across the valley. Then Tom's hearty bary-tone raised the old tune:

In Scarlet town where I was born,
There was a fair maid dwelling,
Made every youth cry "Well a day,"
Her name was Barbary Allen.

All in the merry month of May,
When the green buds they were swelling,
Sweet William came from the Western States,
And courted Barbary Allen.

It was all in the month of June
When all things they were blooming
Sweet William on his death-bed lay,
For love of Barbary Allen.

He sent his servant to the town,
Where Barbary was a-dwelling,
"My master is sick and sent for you,
If your name is Barbary Allen.

"And death is painted on his face
And o'er his heart is stealing,
Then hasten away to comfort him,
O, lovely Barbary Allen."

So slowly, slowly, she got up,
And slowly she came nigh him;
And all she said when she got there,
"Young man, I think you're dying."

"Oh, yes, I'm sick, and very sick,
For death is on me dwelling,
No better, no better I never can be
If I can't get Barbary Allen."

"Oh, yes, you're sick, and very sick,
And death is on you dwelling,

No better, no better you'll never be,
For you can't get Barbary Allen.

"Oh, don't you remember in yonder town
When you were at the tavern;
You drank a health to the ladies all 'round,
But slighted Barbary Allen?"

"Oh, yes, I remember in yonder town,
In yonder town a-drinking,
I gave a health to the ladies all 'round,
But my heart to Barbary Allen."

He turned his face to the wall,
And death was on him dwelling,
"Adieu, adieu to my friends all 'round,
Be kind to Barbary Allen."

As she was on her highway home,
The birds they kept a-singing,
They sang so clear they seemed to say
"Hard-hearted Barbary Allen."

As she was walking o'er the fields,
She heard the death bell knelling,
And every stroke did seem to say,
"Hard-hearted Barbary Allen."

She looked to the east, she looked to the west,
She spied his corpse a-coming,
"Lay down, lay down the corpse of clay,
That I may look upon him."

The more she looked the more she mourned,
Till she fell to the ground a-crying,
Saying, "Take me up and carry me home,
For I am now a-dying.

"Oh, Mother, oh, Mother, go make my bed,
Go make it long and narrow,

Sweet William died for pure, pure love,
And I shall die for sorrow.

"Oh, Father, oh, Father, go dig my grave,
Go dig it long and narrow,
Sweet William died for me today,
I'll die for him tomorrow."

She was buried in the old church yard,
And he was buried a-nigh her,
On William's grave grew a red, red rose,
And on Barbary's grew a green brier.

They grew to the top of the old church wall,
Till they could grow no higher;
They lapped and they tied in a true lover's knot,
And the rose grew round the brier.

There was a long silence after the ballit. The final chord from the guitar sounded on indefinitely. The thread on the hill had grown into an inflated orange balloon that seemed to be threatening to burst.

I said: "That's a very old song. They sang it in England before there were any white folks in this country. The mountain people sing it in Tennessee and North Carolina but I never heard of it in Alabama."

"Reckon you're thinkin' o' some other ballit, perfesser," said Henry. "We don't sing it quite the same over our way but that line that says he come from the Western States can't be from England. Besides my granddad said he knew both them people when he was young."

"Maybe it *was* another ballit," I said. "Let's have more music."

"Make it a jolly one before we go to bed," said Miz Nabors, standing in the doorway. "How about 'See the ol' devil with a pick an' a shovel, A-turnin' up folks with his big toe-nail'?"

"I'd rather pick *Ol' Dan Tucker*," said Tom. "Hold yer feet to the floor":

> Big John, little John, big John Davy,
> Had a wife and three little babies,
> One in the corner and one in the cradle,
> And one in the mushpot waitin' with a ladle.
>
> Get out of the way, old Dan Tucker,
> Come too late to get your supper.
>
> My poor wife and my poor children
> Lived away in the Allegheny mountains,
> Some got drunk and some got drowned,
> Some got choked on chicken pie.
>
> Old Dan Tucker he got drunk,
> He fell in the fire and he kicked out a chunk,
> A coal of fire got in his shoe,
> And you ought to see how the cinders flew.
>
> Old Dan Tucker was a wise old man,
> He washed his face in the frying pan,
> Combed his hair with the wagon wheel,
> And died with a gum-bile on his heel.
>
> Old Dan Tucker went to town,
> He swung dem ladies 'round and 'round,
> He swing 'em to de right, and he swing 'em to de lef',
> And he swing to de one dat he love bes'.
>
> Git out of the way, old Dan Tucker,
> Come too late to get yo' supper.

"It's a shame to go in, it's such a pretty night," said Henry, "but I reckon we better if we're goin' to see that nigger tried."

"Druther see him hanged," said Tom, "I'd get up *real* early for that!"

CHAPTER V

Court Week

NO ONE quite knew how it got to be so late the next morning before we started out. Tom Nabors called us all around five o'clock. Somehow or other we wasted time, dawdling over our grits and bacon and coffee. Then Henry and I demanded to see the still and, while Mrs. Nabors and Mattie Sue made the beds and did the breakfast dishes, all the men took a cool morning walk behind the hill. There in a little hollow screened by underbrush and cottonwoods stood the graceful curved copper machine, its coils gleaming fitfully as an occasional sun's ray struck through the thick foliage. The pungent odor of mash grew stronger as the sun warmed the air. Tom said he hadn't made a run for 'most a week but he reckoned business would be pickin' up considerable, now so many Yankees had come to Decatur for the trial. On the way back we passed a rock pile and Tom lifted a thin flat stone near the top to discover a five-gallon keg from which a small spigot projected.

"Anybody have an early one?" he said. "There's a cup in that hollow stump."

The result of that was that four loquacious men arrived ultimately at the house to find Mrs. Nabors and Mattie Sue seated on the porch wearing their hats and resigned expressions.

The two cars had no sooner got to Hillsboro than we realized that our delay might prove costly. A cloud of dust hung over the main pike and we were slowed up by a long procession of automobiles all rolling toward Decatur. When we finally began to pass long rows of frame houses, each like its neighbor, traffic had almost ceased to move and we were in for a series of long stops and short advances. Nevertheless Mattie Sue's bright anticipatory spirit was not discouraged.

"They had a brass band over in Scottsboro at the first trial," she said, "and a lot of fine speech-making. I reckon it won't be as much fun as that but, my, they's a lot o' folks here already."

"I reckon Mist' Knox an' Tom Nabors figger on doin' a little vote-gettin'," said Henry with a chuckle. "I kin see 'em arguin' up there ahead of us about somethin'."

In a few minutes at Knox's signal we turned off into a side street where we parked the cars. Then we set off afoot for the courthouse. When we reached the square we knew that we were too late. A crowd of several hundred loitered about at a respectful distance from two men in army uniforms strolling back and forth, their rifles on their shoulders. We caught a glimpse of massed figures inside a window.

"Shucks!" said Mattie Sue.

"They tell me," said Tom Nabors, "the Com*mun*ists have hired a slick Jew lawyer from New York City an' you'd think it was the jury that did it the way he's goin' after 'em."

"It won't do him no good," said Henry. "It's a white woman's word against a nigger's, ain't it? Maybe she ain't all she should be but she's white an' she come from these parts an' no black bastard from down-state kin tell her she lies an' git away with it."

"Hello, professor," said a voice from the crowd, "what are you doing here? Haven't seen you since you nearly lost me my Phi Beta Kappa."

"Hello, Charlie," I said. "You got better than you deserved. How are things in Birmingham?"

"Terrible. So bad I've taken to the road to drum up the furniture trade for myself."

"Harvard Business School should have done better by you."

"You know how it is about anything you learn in college. Isn't worth a hoot in hell afterwards, if you'll pardon my saying so."

"I knew that when I taught you. Why are you at this trial?"

"I'm not. Just tryin' to sell furniture. Have *you* turned Communist or something?"

"Not exactly. I just got brought along to court week. But what do you think about this business?"

"Well, I'll tell you. I might have been for acquittin' them at the first trial. But now all this stink's been raised, we've *got* to hang 'em."

"But why?"

"That probably shocks you a bit. But listen to this. A few months ago three girls I knew, I reckon you did too, were drivin' down the mountain near the Birmingham Country Club. A nigger with a shotgun steps out of the bushes, makes 'em drive off the road into the woods and holds 'em prisoner, while he talks to 'em about how white folks oppress the niggers and about Communism. When it begins to get dark he tries to rape one of 'em and the other two jump on him. He shoots all three of 'em, two of 'em dead. The other pretends she's dead until he's gone and then drags herself to the car and drives down the mountain for help.

"Now that wouldn't have happened if it hadn't been for this God-damn Scottsboro business and I'm for seeing that it doesn't happen again. I'll admit to you I'm snob enough not to have cared much about whether these niggers were guilty or not. Those white wenches didn't mean a thing to me. But when it's a girl I know, one I've danced with and played tennis with and so on, I'll be the first to put my hand on the rope."

"Charlie," I said, "I reckon you represent liberal opinion in this state. You're an honor graduate of the state university and you've been to Harvard for a couple of years and you spent a summer abroad."

"Nobody ever accused me of bein' narrow-minded," said Charlie.

"Well," I said, "what if these boys are executed for something they didn't do?"

"It would be too bad. But I hope they're executed. It's a hell of a mess. I'm mighty sorry for 'em."

"So am I," I said.

Charlie and I parted and I sought out Knox in the crowd.

"Do you think this fellow could have got a fairer trial somewhere else?" I said.

"Probably. Maybe in Mobile or in the Black Belt counties where there are more niggers and folks know 'em and like 'em better and have some feeling of responsibility for 'em. He hasn't got a chance in this hill country where there aren't many of 'em and folks wish there were less. If they were innocent they might let 'em loose farther south. But not here. I'm sorry for them."

Tom Nabors and Henry and Mattie Sue came up to us.

"They've taken a couple o' storekeepers on the jury," said Tom. "Reckon they won't want to lose trade by votin' wrong."

"We're goin' back home," said Henry. "I got plenty to do. Perfesser, wish you'd change yer mind an' come stay with us a while longer."

"I'd like to," I said, "but I'm going back home in a day or so and I've got to get down to Birmingham first."

"We surely did enjoy havin' yuh, perfesser," said Mattie Sue, "and we want yuh to come back whenever yuh kin. Miz Nabors an' her husband are comin' over Sunday week an' I wish yuh'd jine us."

"I wish I could," I said, "and some day you'll have to teach me how to dance to fiddlin'. Knox and I have got a ride through the country to Birmingham in an hour or so."

"Well, we'll be leavin' yuh then," said Tom Nabors, "we enjoyed your visit."

"Shorely did," said Mrs. Nabors.

"Reckon we kin leave this trial to the jury all right," said Henry.

"They'll hang 'em sure," said Tom. "They can't hang too many of 'em for me."

"Reckon we don't have to worry none," said Henry.

"Must be an awful feelin' to know you've got to hang," said Mattie Sue. "I feel kind o' sorry for him."

"So do I," I said.

CHAPTER VI

Birmingham

THERE is a spot on the pike that enters Birmingham from the north where, a dozen miles away, one may catch his first glimpse of a city residence. To a man who has been traveling through wooded hills and valleys all day, passing little villages whose general stores and post offices bear the unmistakable imprint of American Southern life, the sight of a Roman temple at the summit of a mountain comes as something of a shock. Many a motorist has gazed upon that circular colonnade and driven on wondering about mirages and the tricks the sun's rays play on a man's vision. It is a far cry from the Tiber to Shades Mountain. Nevertheless, there on the topmost ridge outlined against the changing Alabama skies stands the lovely temple of Vesta, in exterior at least an exact replica of that jewel of stone that sleeps in the lowlands beside the yellow flood in distant Italy.

The fact that the temple belongs to a rich man who, having taken a fancy to its prototype while on a tour of Europe, ordered it built as his private residence only emphasizes the grotesquerie of its being where it is. This classic glory with a garage in its base is a symbol of the big town's quality, ever amazing the visitor though not always palpable to the blasé resident.

Birmingham is the *nouveau riche* of Alabama cities. With an arrogant gesture she builds her most luxurious homes on a mountain of ore yet unmined. Hardly a half-century ago she was the little crossroads town of Jones Valley. Now she numbers her population in hundreds of thousands. She has no traditions. She is the New South. On one side of her rises a mountain of iron. On another a mountain of coal. She lies in the valley between, breathing flame. The dark shafts of her smokestacks mock the beauty of the temple columns in the sky above her.

There is nothing of vanished glory about Birmingham. It is like no other Alabama town. Only the mushroom cities of the West, springing up miraculously, like Tulsa or Oklahoma City, offer fit similes. The rhythm of living is quick. The air is alive with the catch-phrases of industrialism. Rotary and Kiwanis flourish. The kings of industry are the city's idols. Even religion is keyed to a swift advertising pace. Once a great banner hung across the busiest street announcing that Birmingham had more Sunday-school students per thousand population than any other city of America. And no one saw fit to comment on the incongruity in the fact that in the same week three citizens were illegally and outrageously flogged by members of the Ku Klux Klan, doubtless all duly accredited members of Sunday schools.

Birmingham is a muddle of similar contradictions. Her rich capitalists, many of them Yankees, rule the state politically. Yet she is the one city in Alabama where the Socialist party has enough converts to wield strong influence. Frequently the processes by which her corporations or her influential citizens attain their ends are, to say the least, open to a debate on ethics. Yet no city has a braver, more idealistic public press with which to combat them. Clubs devoted to the study of literature are surprisingly numerous and probably the best-known citizen is a writer, Octavus Roy Cohen (whose pictures of negro life on 18th Street never seemed truthful observation until the last year or so when 18th Street began to imitate them). But book publishers state that few Birmingham people buy books. With characteristic enthusiasm residents spend big sums on art but always for ultra-conservative work and usually for the second-rate. Itinerant art dealers on occasional pilgrimages from New York display only academic conventional landscapes before prospective Birmingham buyers whose fortunes were obtained by unconventional and daring methods.

The valley of the furnaces is an inferno. Molten steel, pouring from seething vats, lights the night skies with a spreading red flare. Negroes, sweating, bared to the waist, are moving silhouettes. On the top of a big mold they tamp the sand in rhythmic unison—a shambling frieze. Steel cranes, cars of the juggernaut, screech above the simmering red pools of spitting, rippling metal. And in the gardens that circle the temple on the quiet mountain the irises stand straight and cool in the moon-shadows.

Such a catalogue of incongruities might be continued at length. But these few serve to show that Birmingham is not like the rest of the state. It is an industrial monster sprung up in the midst of a slow-moving pastoral. It does not belong—and yet it is one of the many proofs that Alabama is an amazing country, heterogeneous, grotesque, full of incredible contrasts. Birmingham is a new city in an old land.

BLACK BELT

CHAPTER I

Greene County Rally

A S Knox had promised on the occasion of my first evening in Tuscaloosa, I met Tennant, hero of the "shootin' at Eutaw," at the Greene County Rally. I met almost everybody else in Central Alabama on the same day, for all an Alabamian needs is an invitation to come to something festal and he comes. The invitations, published in the newspapers and by word of mouth, had been pretty general. They had included "all white persons in Greene and Tuscaloosa counties" and it was understood that anybody else who wanted to attend would be welcome.

There were nine in the two cars that bore our party and we had a gay time though the dust from the spinning wheels of countless other conveyances sometimes choked us. We stopped finally in the yard of the Banks house whose white pillars were buried at their bases in rambler roses. We were welcomed as if we had been long expected by a gracious lady whose lively blue eyes belied the whiteness of her hair. We *must* come back after a while and have a bite of supper with her, she said; she didn't get the opportunity to see us often. We expostulated weakly, politely, and consented. As we were descending the steps Tennant came up the walk.

He was tall, slim, dark and he walked stiffly if a little indolently. A slight limp betrayed his latest misadventure. There was dignity in his carriage, and pride, I thought, and something else—a courtliness that suggested the romantic Southern background. When he bowed to our hostess he inclined from the waist stiffly and she beamed upon him. The rest of our party greeted him affectionately but I noted that even with them, his best friends, he did not unbend.

When I got to know him better, much better, he told me that this was his natural manner, occasioned by extreme self-consciousness and the inability to coördinate his muscles as successfully as other men. People generally interpreted it as his heritage from his ancestors, gallant gentlemen and beautiful belles. He was the old South reincarnated, they said, and he was not loath to accept the verdict. At the state university he had been popular and his record as a beau had been brilliant, though he gave little effort to making it so. After graduating with honors he had returned to a partnership in his father's office and a wedding with Mary Louise who will soon become an important character in this narrative. He lived in a big plantation house near Livingston and he managed the place besides attending to his duties as an attorney. He and Knox were much alike in outward appearance and in mental attitudes, though Knox was the more volatile and ambitious. They were close friends.

"I've heard of you," said Tennant to me. "Suppose we walk over to the doin's together."

We had hardly reached the road when I heard a deep, sonorous baying.

"What's that?" I said.

Tennant laughed.

"That's the voice that made the state famous. 'Alabama casts twenty-four votes for Underwood.' I reckon you heard that over your radio?"

"I did," I said, "but I never knew how much of the power came from the loud-speaker. Now I guess I didn't have it in use."

"You can hear him for miles," said Tennant. "Here's your first look at a combination political rally, singin' and barbecue."

We turned into a yard separated from the road by a picket

fence. Perhaps a hundred yards from us a big, gray, rather dilapidated house sat on a little knoll. In front of it a raised platform had been built and decorated with red, white and blue bunting. On the platform was a piano, a large table supporting a single glass of water, and several important-looking gentlemen, all seated on little wooden folding chairs which they rather uncomfortably overwhelmed. A short, vigorous man, apparently in his early fifties, was haranguing a crowd of men and women who sat on plain wooden benches facing him. He opened his mouth very wide, his gray mustache moving into a curving arc as he did so—and a great deep golden sound came from it.

"I stood on the banks of the Potomac," he said and paused, looking impressively about him. "Before me spread the glorious shining expanse of a mighty river. On its further bank I could see a gleam of white in the dark shadow of a little grove. And I knew that gleam was from the white wall of the home of America's greatest soldier, statesman, patriot, that gleam which filled my heart with solemn pride and sacred homage, was from the white home of that paragon of chivalry, that noblest of gentlemen, that most revered of the sons of the Southland. I speak, ladies and gentlemen, of General Robert E. Lee." The golden voice rose in deafening crescendo. The crowd burst into wild applause, clapping their hands, shouting. A rebel yell sounded above the din. Then there was silence as the speaker raised a quieting hand.

"I am a poor man, ladies and gentlemen, y'all know how hard I had to work to get my education. Now I'm goin' to be governor of the great commonwealth of Alabama an' I want to say to you that the peepul of the state of Alabama must unite as that great soldier and statesman would have us in one great purpose. Then with the aid of God we will all go forward. Just as the little streams trickling down the sides of our everlasting mountains unite here and there, dashing on to unite again, until they form mighty rivers that roll inevitably onward to the great vastness of the sea—so shall the peepul of Alabama unite to form a resistless flood that shall bear them onward to their goal!"

He paused to mop his brow with a big white handkerchief and the crowd clapped madly, all except one man who rose slowly to his feet and stood patiently, awkwardly. As the applause died down he raised a nasal whining voice above it.

"I jest want t'ask one question. If'n you're goin' to get my vote I want to know where you stand on the liquor question —I reckon we all want t'know that one way'n another."

There was a chorus of remonstrance and approval. A score of men began shouting for permission to speak. But the little man on the platform was unperturbed. Again he raised his hand, again the silence, again the beautiful golden voice:

"When I think of all the homes the demon rum has ruined, when I think of the hearts of pure women and little children —broken by a husband's accursed habit, when I think of the lives alcohol has snuffed out in their prime—then, ladies and gentlemen, I'm *agin* it."

There was a loud spatting of hands. The audience clapped vigorously and virtuously.

"But," thundered the voice— *"but*—when I rise on a chill mornin' and pull the window down an' hug the fire and shiver an' I can't get warm nohow—an' my wife says to me, 'Ol' man, how about a bit of toddy to warm your innards?'—then, boys, i'm for it."

There was a shout. Many of the men in the audience stood up and whooped. The man who had asked the question sat down, nodding his head as if to indicate that it had been answered to his complete satifaction.

Tennant chuckled. "He's the world's champion fence-straddler. He'll tell you so himself. I like him and they might as well elect him as anyone else to fiddle while Rome burns." He turned abruptly away. "Let's go down by the barbecue."

At the foot of the knoll on which the old house stood we saw smoke rising and walked toward it. But I was destined not to reach the embers on which a whole cow sizzled in appetizing fragrance, not then to meet Antimo Williams, black raconteur, who was later to make himself a place in this book.

For a soft voice called "Tennant" and we turned to see a slim girl in a white dress standing beside the thick trunk of a water oak. Her dark, wavy hair, parted in the middle, was drawn back with severity to a knot on the nape of her neck. Her eyes were black and even in moments when she was not excited (which I later discovered were few) they were full of changing shiny light. The white dress, very simple, was adorned only by a few ruffles on its short sleeves and somehow added to the impression I had already of a little girl wearing grown-up clothes for fun.

"Hello, Mary Louise," said Tennant. "Here's the educated New York professor I've been promising you. Cancel that reading course you laid out for me now you've got somebody to be civilized with."

"That's no way to introduce two people of culture," said Mary Louise, smiling. "I'm a type," she added turning the shiny black eyes full on me. "Alabama is full of disappointed women who think they can play the piano or dance or write or paint. Most of us have had a year in New York and have been encouraged by an instructor who needed the tuition. Then we've come back down here, fallen in love and married. Out the window goes the career, but we can have the satisfaction of eating our hearts out thinking what we might have been. Now I'm a painter. I studied once under somebody you've heard of. Come to my house and I'll show you two priceless oils of his."

"If you think she's begun to talk," said Tennant, "you're mistaken. I'm going over to the Bankses' and sit in the shade hoping for a julep. You'll need one, too, if you're going to put up with my wife's monologues."

We three wandered back to the big yard after supper. Darkness had fallen swiftly. The barbecue coals were a dim red glow in the ground. People strolled restlessly about the inclosure. Suddenly the stage from which the little man had spoken in the afternoon became a square patch of light. Electric bulbs hung in a brilliant festoon above it. An orchestra in the center of the platform was tuning up. It swung into a slow foxtrot and couples began bobbing around. Soon I was discovering that Mary Louise danced expertly.

"Promise that you'll pay us a long visit after commencement in May."

"If I don't go north."

"You'll like visiting us better than going north."

"I believe I will."

Tennant laid his hand on my arm and I reluctantly gave Mary Louise over to him. As they danced off I saw a line of black faces above the white pickets of the fence that lined the yard. A great crowd of negroes stood in a close-packed mass gazing intently at the dancing. As the orchestra ended the dance with a flourish of the drum—the little man who had made the speech in the afternoon stepped to the center of the floor and turned toward the fence.

"A lot of the white folks here have heard about how good you colored boys and girls in Eutaw can sing. I told 'em I'd ask you to make some music for 'em. While the orchestra's restin' is a good time for y'all to tune up."

Hardly had the last words been spoken when a strong high tenor led off, "lining out" the song:

> Read in de Bible, understan'
> Methuselah was de oldes' man
> Lived nine hundred sixty-nine
> Died an' get to Heben in de Lawd's due time—

The singer held a long high note on the word "time" and then a deep strong refrain swelled from hundreds of throats, basses, altos, tenors in perfect accord and in such volume that the whole night seemed alive with the quivering sound:

> Methuselah was a witness
> Fuh my Lawd, fuh my Lawd.

As the last full tone ended—like a great amen on an organ —the tenor rode out high above it:

> Read in de Bible, understan'
> Samson was de stronges' man
> Went out to battle to fight one time
> Killed a thousand o' the Philistines—

The little tufted tops of the tall lolly pines beside the singers shivered as if the refrain were a gust shooting upward through them toward the low-hanging stars:

> Samson was a witness
> Fuh my Lawd, fuh my Lawd.

The white people around the dance floor were growing restive. They were chattering among themselves. A man's laugh sounded, flat and hollow on an air through which waves of melody surged in timeless beauty:

> Daniel was a Hebrew chile
> He went to de Lawd to pray a while
> God tole de angels de lions to keep
> While Daniel lay down an' went to sleep—

Something was wrong this time. On the surface of the organ's great diapason sounded a thin scratching. From somewhere came a silly beat that broke the magnificent dignified rhythm of the spiritual. For as the negroes sang,

> An' dat's another witness
> Fuh my Lawd, fuh my Lawd,

the tawdry orchestra, violin, piano, drum, had begun to play the cheapest, ugliest and most popular of all dance tunes below the Mason and Dixon Line, a college march generally known as *The Swing*.

"I'll be in Tuscaloosa for commencement," said Tennant, "and we'll start from there. We'll take a few days to do the plantation houses in the Black Belt for you and then you'll come to Livingston with me for an indefinite stay. It'd be a real favor, keep Mary Louise from remindin' me of her sacrificed career every five seconds. She won't dare show you her paintings for fear you'd know whether they're good or not."

"If you want to work, you can have the mole-hill," said Mary Louise. "I'll be afraid to use it with you around."

"What's that?"

"My log-cabin studio. I built it myself—with Antimo to do the hard work. I call it that because Tennant made a mountain out of it."

"This famous Southern hospitality of yours has got you into trouble," I said. "I'm coming."

CHAPTER II

Big House

I. THORN HILL

I HOPE I may never approach Thorn Hill without being spied upon. Years ago when I first stood in the shadow of the slope that gives the plantation its name, I felt somehow that I was being watched. Then I heard a rustle above me and saw a little black boy running madly toward the house. When I had reached the pillared veranda "Miss Betty" was coming down the curving stair in the hall to welcome me. In those days it was James who brought the news of visitors. Now it is William who lies in wait and James is a stalwart buck working in the fields and a devil with the girls.

Tennant and I had been driving all the morning—"through the country" (which in Alabama parlance means by motor) from Tuscaloosa. We had planned a few days' tour before the visit Mary Louise had planned was to begin. An hour or so after we started we had seen the red-gold of the dust turn to white. Below that white surface—black soil—the Black Belt from whose dark and fertile land rose pillared glories with names that are poems—Rosemount, Bluff Hall, Gaineswood, Oakleigh, Farmsdale, Snow Hill, Tulip Hill, Windsor, Chantilly, Athol, Longwood, Westwood, Waldwie. Some of these houses are now memories. Time has been cruel to others standing dismally in dreams of their past. But living is still more abundant in the Black Belt than elsewhere in Alabama. Candles in hurricane glasses still gleam on silver goblets and still a ham and a chicken and a roast are served with corn and okra and snap beans, cowpeas, and collard greens, and sweet potatoes, beaten biscuit and corn bread, a salad and a watermelon, for just a "pick-up potluck dinner."

James Innis Thornton is the name of "Miss Betty's" husband. James Innis Thornton was the name of the gallant Revolutionary soldier from Fall Hill Plantation in Fredericksburg, Virginia, who, riding through Alabama on the staff of the escort to General Lafayette in 1825, resolved to build a home there. He purchased the land for it when he returned to Alabama, four thousand acres of the fertile valley that lies between the forks of the Tombigbee and Warrior rivers. And he brought with him six other young men, his friends from around Fredericksburg, all with their brides; and every family built a house on a hill—so that each hill of a curving chain was crowned with a Virginia home. They made a long gay caravan traveling southward from the Old Dominion, the gentlemen riding beside their wives' carriages, behind them the mounted overseers bringing on the wagon train filled with household goods and farming tools and slaves.

These young gallants had known General Washington. Thornton, indeed, was the great man's cousin. They had seen Mount Vernon and Kenmore and the other famous early American houses and they intended to build as well. If Thorn Hill may be a criterion, they succeeded. The fluted white pillars rise from the gallery to the roof in the same tapering lovely gesture that Virginians know. A romantic balcony with wrought-iron railing hangs above the center doorway. As for the interior, one need only step into the wide old hall that runs the full depth of the house to be sure. I had a little difficulty in doing that, for William, bearing napery and silver for outdoor lunch in the deep shade of the magnolia tree, rushed outward as I was about to enter, nearly butting me to earth. But once inside I realized that I had stepped back in time a full century.

The years have mellowed but they have not changed Thorn Hill. On one side of the hallway, main axis of the house, is a reception room and behind it the dining room. On the other is a parlor and behind it a chamber that was used as a sewing room. On a rack in the hall hangs a spy glass given by General Washington to his cousin at the end of the Revolution. It has rested on this spot for a hundred years. In the reception room over the Italian marble fireplace stands a brass candlestick that belonged to Nellie Custis, and on a highboy in the dining room sit a cup and saucer once owned by Bushrod Washington, part of a set at Mount Vernon. The high-ceilinged rooms hung with long gilt-framed mirrors have not altered since the slaves of the Virginia emigrant built them from the trees on the land he had bought—heart pine, walnut, cypress, cedar and oak, every timber hand-hewn. The year 1830 saw Thorn Hill complete, house and plantation; 1933 sees it still whole. Descendants of those very slaves who came with "young master" from Virginia chop cotton for "young master" today down on Suckey's Bottom. The schoolhouse for the plantation children still stands. So does the smokehouse, hung with the former inhabitants of the hog pasture, and the gin house stuffed with cotton bales, and the carriage house and the Free Hope Church (built for the slaves and still used by the negro servants) and the slave quarter. Big Branch still runs through Persimmon Bottom down to the catfish hole and through Palmetto Slough to the swimming hole, and the plantation bell still tells choppers and fishers and swimmers when to knock off and eat.

Miss Betty and Tennant and I walked about the plantation for a while and came back when the bell rang to sit in the shade and be ministered to by William. But before lunch was ready I climbed the curving walnut stair to see "The Judge"—

Miss Betty's father—seated in his study and reading the Alabama laws. He told me of the days when his fathers bargained with Indian Chief Pushmataha in this region, and we talked until William silently materialized. Then the judge said he didn't go downstairs much now but he reckoned he would today, so we went "together down" to the feast under the magnolia. There, while we looked out over the leafy sun-caressed valley of the Tombigbee, Miss Betty told us that two boys went from this house to the War Between the States, though the best that the fifteen-year-old could do was to join the training corps at the University in Tuscaloosa. All their Virginian cousins, she said, used to come to Thorn Hill to recuperate from their wounds, and the delightful result of that was that three of the Thornton girls married sons of the Old Dominion.

After our fried chicken and beaten biscuits and iced tea—"a long drink out of silver"—we all set out for the kitchen where we found Aunt Becky, ageless and voluble, refusing to have her picture taken until she had gone to her cabin to put on her best dress, a spotted calico affair that had once adorned a white maiden younger by half a century. Then we came back to our chairs to find that William with marvelous dispatch had caused the table and all it bore to disappear. While the sun lifted a mist from the river below we read letters from a charming gentleman named Martin Van Buren to the master of Thorn Hill. And we pored over a list of the negroes who had worked on the plantation and with them the nicknames by which they were known. These held so much of interest that I copied some of them: Pie ya, Puddin'-tame, Frog, Tennie C., Monkey, Mush, Cooter, John de Baptist, Fat-man, Preacher, Jack Rabbit, Sixty, Pop Corn, Old Gold, Dootes, Tangle-eye, Bad-luck, Fly-up-de-Creek, Cracker, Jabbo, Cat-fish, Bear, Tip, Odessa, Lorenzo, Pig-lasses, Rattler, Pearly, Luck, Buffalo, Old Blue, Red Fox, Coon, Jewsharp and a hundred more.

As I finished writing, a minor tune rose out of the stillness below us—a high pitched male voice singing:

> Ain't miss my salt water tell my well went dry
> Ain't miss my goat tell she said good-by—

Miss Betty said: "I brought this old love letter of a planter's son out here for you to see. It doesn't belong to us but I borrowed it because I thought you would be interested. They wrote a different style in those days."

I unfolded the browning sheet and read:

July the 5th, 1845.

Thou only beloved and always adored by me, for so I must call you while the delightful showers of rain are falling from above this evening. I sit silently and alone unaccompanied by thy sweet presence, but blessed be the name of high heaven, I have a promise from thy sweet lips and also I trust, from the heart, which renders me happy in my imagination and which affords to me much consolation in my lonely hours when there is no one to console, or to call my attention from things upon which it is constantly running. And if I should say what they are, I must tell you that it is looking forward with fond anticipations at future prospects, at the time when I shall enjoy the sweet company of one whom I hold most lovely to my heart. Then it will be that I can look by my side and see that lovely form which I now only imagine I see,

> At midnight's lonely hour
> It is often then I see
> That love will have its power
> Both day and night with me.

Ever thine

———————

Tennant and I studied the perfect script of a lover who had learned to write from a copy-book and we speculated about him and his sweetheart.

"They were married five years later," said Miss Betty.

Perhaps there should be some exciting climax to round off

this narrative of a visit to Thorn Hill. I would rather leave us all sitting in the shade—high above the distant yellow water. For Thorn Hill knows that climaxes are never near the end. Continuance is its meaning—continuance of good things—food and shelter and beautiful belongings and love and life itself.

2. ROSEMOUNT

You must follow a winding road and cross a winding stream to come to Rosemount. You will see it at last, in a dark circle of trees, with a carved railing set like a crown upon its head. Tennant and I were fortunate to come upon it unannounced in one of its informal moments. Three black boys were mending the steps that led up under the magnificent colonnade, but they stopped work to grin and say "howdy." And just inside the widespread door a fourth, hoe in hand, did battle with a curving spitting snake while our hostess coolly directed his campaign. Over a hundred years ago Amelia Walton Glover, bride in her new Alabama home, met like emergency with the courage of a Southern pioneer. Amelia Walton Legaré, the snake dispatched, welcomed us to Rosemount.

"How's that sweet Miss Mary Louise?" she said to Tennant, "and how's Miss Fannie, you all must come over right soon. I declare, time gets by and this old house needs fixing and we don't get much chance to see old friends." She turned to me:

"I missed you last time you were in the Black Belt. We mustn't let that happen again."

"You were away—in Wedowee," I said in defense. "I came by and talked to Keith for a while."

She smiled. "Then I'll forgive you. We'd hate to have you pass by Rosemount and not stop. This time you want to know all about it for your book—I read about you in the paper—I'll help you all I can. Let's go in."

She led us through the entrance hall, spacious and high, into first one and then the other of the reception rooms which are on either side of it. In one of these a hundred years ago it was the custom for guests to await the presence of the hostess, while slaves took from them their beaver hats, their golden canes, their flowing capes, and carried them off to the coat room which adjoins the Great Hall of Rosemount. Beside a fireplace of black Italian marble from the Carrara quarries they sat until she greeted them and led the way into the spacious high-ceilinged room that saw Williamson Allen Glover, planter, at home with his family. Slaves that had cost a thousand dollars apiece built this room, its timbers hand-hewn from trees on the land. Allen Glover, South Carolina emigrant to Demopolis, gave the costly negroes to the first of his sons to marry. Beside this room's tall windows that once looked out on flower beds blooming under the care of gardeners from Ireland, a Boston governess taught the children their lessons. (Poor spinster—she died far away from her New England and lies buried in Demopolis with the epitaph above her—"A Night's Lodging on the way to New Jerusalem.") These floors have felt the scrape of the slipper of a French dancing teacher, once a soldier and a courtier in the favor of Napoleon. These paneled walls have heard the music of the German music teacher's violin.

Behind the Great Hall lies the dining room, goal of stately processions. A white marble fireplace adorns each end. A door, now always closed, once opened on a covered passage to the kitchen which stood—as in most plantation houses—at some distance from the Big House. Across the bridge two slave carriers brought savory messages in covered dishes (kept warm by containers filled with hot water under them) from the four cooks to the guests seated at the long table. Three house servants received the dishes from the carriers at the door and served them properly, moving quietly about with gleaming silver platters.

From the Great Hall the stair curves upward to the second floor—a series of chambers built around a central well of space, now a wide hall. This well, rising through the third floor (a less spacious story built above the column-supported roof-line and surrounded by an outdoor, railed-in ambulatory) provides the most interesting architectural feature of the house. Long ago, said Miss Amelia, the well was the shaft of an elevator operated by slaves who, when the ladies and gentlemen were seated on its broad expanse, wafted them by means of ropes and pulleys to the top floor where they might promenade on the outside balcony and survey the vast domain of which this home was the center.

While we sat at tea in the Great Hall, Rosemount's last "Miss Amelia" brought out parchment grants of land signed by President James Monroe in 1820, by John Quincy Adams in 1825, by Andrew Jackson in 1829. The plantation grew to be over five thousand acres, she said, and the family fortunes grew with it. The *Allen Glover,* sidewheel steamer, proudly carried its owner's cotton and tobacco down the Warrior River to the markets of Mobile. A coach and four, outriders beside it, bore visitors from Rosemount to the other Black Belt houses. There was gay dancing and the drinking of imported wines. Fox hunters rode to hounds and spent the long evenings at poker. Slaves were plentiful and happy. Milady walked in the garden with a slave to hold her parasol and another to fan the air into cooling motion about her. Life was full of pleasant formalities.

Miss Amelia rose and returned with a letter which her great-grandmother had once received and which she allowed me to copy.

Eutaw, Alabama
August 26th, 1852

Mrs. WALTON, Strawberry Hill

MY DEAR MADAM,

My valet de chambre—Jeff—who belongs to Mr. Wynn of North Carolina, but who has been hired by me for the last two years, having formed an attachment for Miss Abbey your servant and being solicitous of entering into a matrimonial alliance with his dulcinea, requests me to write a recommendation to you, bespeaking for him your favorable consideration of his application to wed Miss Abbey.

I have known Jeff for the last six years and Mrs. Sharrver, your neighbor, knows him well, to whom I refer you if you desire any additional information to that contained herein.

He is a boy of unexceptionable character—remarkable for his honesty, sobriety, morality and integrity—and indeed I may say Jeff has as much character as any slave can have.

Should you favor his suit I doubt not but that he would take great pleasure in serving you as the Mistress of his inamorata.

Hoping that you will sanction Miss Abbey's choice and allow these sable children of Africa to unite their destinies in the silken tie of Hymen.

With consideration, I am very Respectfully
Your friend and obedient servant
S. J. CHAPMAN

In the record of the slaves kept at Strawberry Hill, Miss Amelia told us, there are entries which read:

Jeff and Abbey were married in 1852.
Adoline the daughter of Jeff and Abbey was born Aug. 5, 1853.
Walton the son of Jeff and Abbey was born 9th Dec. 1854.

Prosperity and idyllic life ended with the War Between the States ("Don't you call it any other way," said Miss Amelia). Four sons of Rosemount, mounted on thoroughbreds, left the old house riding together. Behind them rode four black valets. Before the war was over each soldier, black boy by his side, was fighting in a different command.

Three white men rode back to the valley between the Tombigbee and the Warrior after Appomattox. And three black valets followed them. All were clad in uniforms stolen by the negroes from the Yankee dead, and their horses were old and lame.

Though the masters of Rosemount plunged into the problems of reconstruction at once, the three black valets took things easy for a time, a long time. Tenderly cared for by the servants on the plantation, they appeared very little at the Big House until years later one of the white veterans died. Then three white-gloved old negroes appeared at the doors of Rosemount and announced that they were the bearers, and no one denied them. And not long ago when the last of the black valets died the plantation bell tolled slow and mournful over the fields of Rosemount.

As we were leaving Tennant said, "We'll be in Demopolis tomorrow, Miss Amelia. Can we do any errands for you there?"

"No, thanks. Just tell your cousin Annalee to come over to see me for a few days whenever she can. And give our love to you-all at home."

"Sure will, Miss Amelia, and thank yuh."

"I wish you could stay longer with us. My men will be home in a little while. Sure you won't stay for dinner? We wouldn't have much but there's a turkey and a ham and some roast mutton and some vegetables."

"We really mustn't. Remember me to Keith."

"He'll be sorry he missed you. Good-by—Good-by!" The shadows of the pillars were lengthening behind us. The sedge of the fields was a deep gold from the setting sun as we rolled back along the winding road and across the winding branch. Visitors had come to Rosemount—gone.

3. GAINESWOOD AND BLUFF HALL

The architects of the plantation homes in the Alabama cane-brake were for the most part the planters themselves. History records that the Virginian gentlemen, George Washington and Thomas Jefferson, knew how to plan houses. The sons of their contemporaries, building in the deep South, had been taught in the school of their fathers. James Innis Thornton of Virginia planned Thorn Hill, Williamson Allen Glover of South Carolina, Rosemount, and Nathan Bryan Whitfield conceived the most architecturally elaborate of them all—Gaineswood. From their homes in the earlier settled states all three of these gentlemen-designers brought skilled slave-artisans capable of realizing in wood and brick the drawings their masters had made. The classical renaissance in Alabama is the more interesting artistically because each of the men who built its most beautiful examples stamped his with the quality of his individual character and background. While Rosemount and Thorn Hill have the simplicity usually associated with the houses of colonial Virginia, Gaineswood bears testimony that its author had felt the influence of his French neighbors, Napoleonic exiles living on the white cliffs above the Tombigbee. Rounded niches for statuary, mirrors sunk into the walls between fluted pillars, small rooms in which the ceiling tapers like the interior of a rounded pyramid, round-pillared "summer houses" on the grounds, formal gardens enclosed in stone railings bespeak a contact with more Latin ideas on ornament than those held by Virginian Nordics.

Since the source of that French influence was the goal of our journey now, Tennant and I did not stop long at Gaineswood. The Whitfield family no longer occupied it, but it was in loving hands, its colonnades gleaming with white paint, its flowers blooming in battalions. The columns and mirrors in the great reception room, the brilliantly lighted dining room, its windows filling the outside wall, the music room with its spiraling ceiling and light coming from windows at its top, the intricate curving of plaster frescoes molded by artisans imported from Philadelphia, the matched paneling, reconstructed for us something of the character of General Nathan Bryan Whitfield, planter and soldier. During the War Between the States Gaineswood was a haven of refuge for the wounded, a hotbed of Confederate loyalty. No wonder the deep South produced gallant fighters when there were homes like this to defend.

Demopolis lay before us. Time has made it into a typical Alabama town, happily oblivious of the great dream which gave it its name. Faithfully in the slow ordered rhythm of its people it serves them and their neighbors in the countryside. The cotton wagons come to town in the summer but no longer the six-mule teams with the bales piled ten feet high. Few residents here can tell you about plantation days or about Eaglesville or how Marengo County got its name. And fewer still are haunted by the ghosts of French dragoons galloping through the moonlit streets, or marquise and colonel dancing on the river bank to the slow music of the minuet.

There could be no ghosts in the white noon of the July day when we reached the spot where the deep South's most romantic story had its beginning. We turned aside for a little while to sit in the cool shelter of one more plantation house before we sought to reconstruct from a few timbers in the side of a negro cabin a tale of Gallic courage and romance and adventure.

Bluff Hall stands on the steep white cliff which the exiled Bonapartists once climbed with the hope of a new world in their hearts. Before, disheartened and despairing, they realized that their vision was a mirage, many had found refreshment in this home as we were finding it now. The front colonnade of Bluff Hall shelters one of the most graceful doorways in the

South. The main entrance, with its side panels of glass and its fan transom above, is echoed on the second floor by an almost identical doorway leading out upon the characteristic overhanging balcony with wrought-iron railing. The little differences between the two serve only to heighten the architectural interest—the curving tops and single panes of the lower panels contrasting with the square tops and quadruple panes of the upper. The house now faces a village street, it is no longer the center of the acres that Francis Strother Lyon, lawyer, planter, financier and statesman, collected about it. Its interior is as simply arranged as Thorn Hill—a central hallway separating the reception rooms in front, a parlor and dining room in the rear. Like some of the old New England homes it is filled with objects from the Orient, testimony to the propensities of a wandering son. Simple cordiality warmed our hearts, iced tea cooled our stomachs, in this home. The sun on the white banks outside was not inviting. But those chalk cliffs were the background of the story that had brought us across the state, and we left the cool gallery of Bluff Hall.

CHAPTER III

Plaisant Pays de France

A FEW hewn timbers in a negro cabin on the chalk bluff above the Tombigbee are left to tell a story whose roots are in empire, these and the legend that the descendants of the tale's protagonists have kept alive. I am telling it as one of them told it to me—preferring the truth that folk-say creates to the fiction of history:

Napoleon at Fontainebleau, the shadow of Elba upon him, put his arms about the gallant cavalryman hero of Saragossa, saying to his weeping officers: "I cannot take leave of each of you, but I embrace General Desnouettes for you all. Doubtless he was remembering those bitter days and nights when Lefebvre-Desnouettes sat beside him in a coach rolling southward over Russian snows, remembering, too, that he had influenced his lovely cousin, sister of the great banker Laffitte, to become Madame Desnouettes.

With the Little Corporal into his temporary retirement went another dashing soldier, Colonel Nicolas Raoul. And Raoul, commanding the advance guard of two hundred grenadiers on the triumphal march from Cannes to Paris, led his adored master into the immortality of the Hundred Days.

It was an odd fate that brought these two favorites of the Emperor's court to residence beside the junction of the Black Warrior and Tombigbee rivers in the far wilderness of Alabama. Waterloo and St. Helena left them friendless in their native land. They and their comrades must go into exile. Louis XVIII had decreed it. But where? Already many Bonapartists had been welcomed to Philadelphia. There Semon Chaudron, the poet, had found a refuge. But the city could not absorb hundreds of exiles. Perhaps, though, it might serve as a way station toward an American Provence where, wars forgotten, they might live in pastoral content among their grapes and olives. A dream of a universe where the petty hates of parties, even of nations, would die out in goodwill took possession of their minds.

Three hundred forty families, once the most influential in France, begged admission to America. It was granted and they sailed for Philadelphia. Their advance agents reported that Alabama offered best opportunity for the cultivation of fruits. So the band made the long trip down the coast to Mobile where it was happily received by the old Creole families. Then one day in 1818 a crowded boat made its way against the river current northward and stopped where the walls of the Tombigbee rise high and white above the yellow water. Here the French aristocrats disembarked to find only a few huts built of logs and clay on the site of their new adventure. They named the little settlement Eaglesville, remembering Napoleon, but soon, visioning a world of friendliness among the peoples, they rechristened it Demopolis. The county bears the proud name of Marengo, and the little towns round about in it are Linden and Arcola and Moscow, though few of their present inhabitants know why. There is no suggestion in their quiet streets of "old far-off unhappy things, and battles long ago."

Representatives obtained a definite grant of land from the United States Government. In Demopolis today descendants of the Chapron family show the charter proudly. It is signed by James Monroe, President of the United States, and William Crawford, Secretary of the Treasury. The grant is for four townships each six miles square, at a price of two dollars an acre made payable fourteen years after the date of the contract.

And the document states that the government has set this tract apart to encourage the cultivation of the vine and olive.

Then came the period of hope and enthusiastic labor. Veterans of many a victorious campaign began a new battle—against nature and the elements. Dressed in rich uniforms, they cleared wooded land, ditched it, plowed it. Their wives, delicate women still in Parisian gowns, milked the cows, carried water to the men in the fields, cooked meals over the coals in the fireplaces. From old letters and the stories of elderly people whose fathers knew the French settlers comes a fragmentary mosaic of their social life. Houses and gardens were so reminiscent of the immediate past that the settlement took on the appearance of a French hamlet. Living in some respects was abundant—there being plenty of wild game in the woods and of vegetables in their cultivated acres. The women had brought with them their silks, their laces, their books, their guitars. And often after a hard day of arduous labor the whole group gathered on the chalk cliff near Bluff Hall. Then there would be a feasting and a drinking of rich wines sent by their friends in the old world. And after that the guitars would sound and there would be dancing on the level white plateau beneath the moon while the river sparkled far down below and Indians and Yankee traders looked on the gay festival. But Fontainebleau and Versailles must have seemed very far away—as far as the days when the Bonaparte eagles screamed in triumph over Europe.

General Desnouettes, richest of the exiles and their acknowledged leader, spent over twenty-five thousand dollars in opening his estate and starting its cultivation. In the midst of his acres and near to his home he built a log cabin which he called his sanctuary. In the center of it stood a bronze statue of Napoleon. Heaped about the feet of the figure were swords and pistols Desnouettes had captured in battle. The walls of the cabin were hung with captured banners and the colors of the regiments he had commanded.

Colonel Raoul, not so fortunate in material wealth and finding agriculture entirely distasteful, soon lost his land and became a ferryman transporting passengers across the waters of French Creek, three miles from Demopolis. His wife—the former Marchioness of Sinabaldi and once lady in waiting to Queen Caroline of Italy—cooked flapjacks on the bank for the travelers' refreshment.

The colony grew daily more optimistic. With unquestioning faith these civilized, charming people sent to Bordeaux for vines and olive seeds. With religious exactness they set out stakes at distances of ten feet in one direction, twenty in the other, and trained the grape vines on them. Heedless of the lack of fertility in new ground, fearless of certain frosts, they entrusted the olive seeds to the soil.

No people would have been more unfitted for the job of bringing the forests under cultivation. Their importations frequently arrived out of season—causing the vines to wither, the seed to be sterile. Blithely they continued to sow. In 1821 three hundred eighty-three olive trees were planted on the grant. A few vines began to bear. But the grapes produced only a mediocre wine because the fruit ripened in the heat of summer. Before the vinous fermentation was complete, the acetic had begun. As for the olives, each winter the frost brought most of them to the ground.

The colony might have survived, however, had it not been for a stunning misfortune. It was discovered that the site of Demopolis was not within the grant presented them by the government. Immediately aggressive American squatters moved in on them, appropriating their lands and improvements. Sadly the French moved deeper into the forests. Despairing of clearing the land again by their own efforts and too poor to buy slaves they arranged for the importation of a number of German redemptioners to perform the heavy labor. This move proved suicidal. The Germans were worse foes than the Americans. They disregarded their obligations, stole from their masters, became only burdensome and expensive.

The want of wagons and teams and the scarcity of water in the canebrake forced the French to live in groups, leaving much of their allotted land uncultivated and unoccupied. Indians and squatters and Germans were allied against them. A few of them sold their lands to Americans and the others were the more discouraged to see fields that had lain fallow smile in abundance under the care of negro slaves. More and more the colonists gave up their struggle and the Vine and Olive Colony on the Tombigbee faded out of existence. Some of them joined their countrymen in Mobile and New Orleans. Some went back to Philadelphia. Others sought and received permission to return to their native land.

General Desnouettes, though not allowed by the Bourbon régime to rejoin his wife in Paris, received permission to reside in Belgium. Forsaking his Alabama home in 1823, he embarked for Europe in the *Albion* which struck a reef off the coast of Ireland at Old Kinsdale. The distinguished refugee was washed overboard and drowned in the sight of great crowds of people standing on the cliffs. In 1824 Colonel Raoul and his wife left their lonely cabin on French Creek. They were next heard of in Mexico where as a soldier of fortune the French officer fought with all his accustomed impetuosity for the cause of revolution. At length they were allowed to return to their beloved France and for many years Raoul held his commission in the army in which he had first won distinction.

Frenchmen and Germans and Indians and Americans, all the people who remained on the site of the colony, gradually merged into the people who now live in the typical little Southern town. Aside from the Gallic names of a few families there is nothing about the inhabitants to recall the character of their ancestors. But Demopolis, though it is not easily to be distinguished from neighboring sleepy Black Belt villages, remembers in ways of its own. Occasionally a breeze wanders, even on a hot day, into the back yards of its old homes—and a gnarled olive tree suddenly turns to tossing silver, just as the orchards do along the hillsides near Nîmes and Arles and Avignon. And on the dazzling surface of the white bluff at the edge of town stands a negro cabin into which a half dozen hewn timbers are built. They once helped to house a shrine— built by a French soldier in memory of the days when he served in the victorious armies of the Corsican.

CHAPTER IV

Front Gallery

IT was a comforting experience to turn in at a wooden gate-way on the pike near Livingston and see the home of Tennant and Mary Louise at the top of the rise. It stands where the grove of water oaks thins out and one big magnolia tree is a dark silhouette against its white columns and sides. Tennant had been telling me about Colonel Cluis, veteran of the Napoleonic Wars, who had kept a tavern at Demopolis after the French colony failed. The colonel had continued in his military profession during the War Between the States and his inn, after the struggle was over, became a kind of clubhouse for reminiscences. In fact, it had delayed so many a housewife's dinner that "visiting Colonel Cluis" became a Black Belt by-word for any inexplicable lateness of absence. The colonel, Tennant said, was Mary Louise's great-great-uncle—and this fact partially explained her. I was about to ask what he meant by that when we reached the gate, climbed the rise, and saw the slim dark girl herself standing on the steps.

"You're earlier than I reckoned," she said. "I was going to have Centennial all dressed up as an old black retainer should be. Centennial, take their bags and try to look picturesque in that dirty shirt."

"Yas'm, Miss May Lou," said Centennial, appearing from around the side of the house. "I sho' does look homely. Howdy, Mist' Tennant; howdy, perfesser." His black arms hoisted the heavy suitcases out of the car with an ease that belied the graying curls on his head.

"Centennial will show you your room," said Mary Louise,

shaking hands with me, "and don't use my Duncan Phyfe chair to climb up on your bed. There's a stool for that in the corner."

"All your kin in the state say 'Howdy,' " said Tennant, kissing her, "and we're hungry as hell and we're not interested in antiques for another century. We've had enough."

Since it has been necessary slightly to disguise Tennant and Mary Louise for reasons that following chapters reveal, a detailed description of their Big House would seem unwise. It became my home for a few months and I wandered happily among its mirrors and highboys and Colonial chairs until I was more proud of them than were their owners. I can never think of it now without a nostalgic longing to return to the ease and serenity it provided. The things that happened there during my visit are still cut deep into my memory.

It was from this haven that I made my forays into the Black Belt seeking an understanding of its people, their backgrounds, and their life today. Sometimes the Black Belt came to me. For as Mary Louise and Tennant and I sat on the front gallery night after night while summer moons waxed and waned, guests sat with us. And while they sipped minted incense from frosted glasses they grew sentimentally contemplative over the vagaries of men. Once it was "Uncle Louis" Davidson from Uniontown—cosmopolite of the Black Belt—enchanting us with sophisticated tales of Paris and Vienna and Budapest, and always coming back to his conclusion: "There are only two places in the world where one may live a happy, civilized existence— Paris and Uniontown." Once it was Colonel Breck Musgrove who regaled us with an account of the time he ran for President of the United States because he was disgusted with the candidates put up by the political parties.

It was Colonel Breck, too, who told us how Frank Derby

organized the rooster sale that built a river bridge. He said
Frank wrote to Mussolini and Queen Marie of Roumania and
Lloyd George and Coolidge and a lot of other well-known people and asked each one of them to give a rooster to be sold for
money to build the bridge. A good many of them, more than
you'd think, sent roosters. He named them after their givers
and on the day of the sale most of Alabama showed up and paid
fancy prices for them at a barbecue that hasn't been equaled
since, and the bridge was finally built from the money. The
Birmingham *Age-Herald* searched the country over for the
most beautiful proud-stepping bird. And they sent Frank Willis Barnett, orator extraordinary, spats, stick, special waistcoat
and all, down to make the presentation speech. You could
hardly tell the man from the rooster, Colonel Breck said, they
both looked so set up. Just before the sale Colonel Breck
sneaked into a drug store and then into the long shack where
the rooster crates were.

Well, when the *Age-Herald* rooster was presented his crate
was covered with red, white and blue bunting and Frank Willis
Barnett waved his arms and shouted about how the paper had
secured the proudest, healthiest, snappiest rooster in the world
to help build the bridge. Then he dramatically lifted the bunting and there the bird was—standing on one leg and leaning
against the side of the cage and looking for all the world like
a drunken bum after a two-week spree. Colonel Breck had
doped him with a bit of morphine.

Most frequent and most welcome of all our visitors was the
white-haired judge from Tuscaloosa. We were never happier
than on the long gentle evenings when we listened to his
courtly mannered speech. His voice was strong and genial and
the sound of it, as the glow from the end of his cigar made little
circles of light on his immaculate white linen suit, is a pleasant
memory. He loved to tell stories about the early planters—a

proud hot-headed lot, absolute monarchs over their vast estates. I have remembered some of them. Other friends have aided me in making a meager collection of them. They are the folk-tales of the Alabama aristocrats based, as are most communal legends, on real happenings in the long ago. Here are a few of them:

I. THE TALE OF THE GILDED MIRROR

Some years before the War Between the States a wealthy Black Belt planter sent his daughter to a private "female seminary" in New York, there to complete the education begun by her tutors. While she was at the school she met (through his sister) a pale patrician young man who was so attracted by her beauty that he sought and won her hand in marriage. The bride's father made the couple a present of one of the most coveted plantations in the canebrake and they began their married life most happily.

But the Alabama climate proved not as beneficial to the young husband's delicate health as they had hoped. Like many another Easterner, he found himself incapable of coping with Alabama life and atmosphere. Alarmed, his wife sent for a physician, a gallant young Southerner who proved so sympathetic and charming that before long the frequency of his calls was less occasioned by her interest in her husband's recovery than by her desire to see his doctor again. Suddenly a passionate love sprang up that could not be satisfied by stolen caresses in the hall, quick looks into each other's eyes across the husband's bed.

Now every afternoon old Joshua, the lady's favorite slave since her childhood, hitched the black horses to the brougham and waited for his mistress at the entrance to the Big House. The spirited team, the slave and the lovely girl became a familiar sight on the dusty roads of the Black Belt. But always in a wooded spot where a little lane soon lost itself in a green twi-light they vanished.

One day when the beat of the black team's hoofs had died out down the drive a lone rider walked his horse slowly up to the Big House, pensively gave over his reins to a slave, heavily climbed the winding stair to the master's room. There was silence for a while—then the sound of loud voices. The visitor strode out of the sick man's chamber and ran down the stair and out the door. His face was flushed and his eyes were bright. He rode off swiftly.

The next morning the invalid sent for Joshua. Then other slaves were summoned. They seized Joshua and took him down to the whipping post on the slave block beside the house. The master dressed, for the first time in months, and went slowly down. He sat in a big cushioned chair while a young buck me-thodically lashed the skin from old Joshua's bare back. When he stopped to rest the master asked Joshua in a soft voice if he were ready to tell the truth now, and Joshua said, between sobs, that there was no more to tell. Then the whipping began again and while the slave was screaming the lovely lady, on the upper balcony out of her husband's sight, was wringing her hands in an agony of terror.

Joshua kept her secret and the master, finally believing that no man could endure such torture without breaking down and telling all he knew, had him taken away and cared for. The exertion of going back up the stair proved too much for the in-valid, however, and he had gone but a few steps when he fell, his heart fluttering uncertainly. The young doctor was sum-moned. He ordered the big four-poster bed brought down and set up in the reception room just to the left of the main en-trance, for he said it would be dangerous even to carry his patient up to his chamber. This feigned solicitude proved his undoing, for, as he said farewell to his beloved in the secrecy of the hallway, the great gilded mirror above the marble mantel betrayed their guilty embrace to the sick man's eyes.

The master said nothing then. But he thought of his friend who had warned him and been sent away for his pains. A slave was dispatched to beg him to come back to the house he had left so bitterly. He came and listened to the husband's story. At its end he complained that the distressing narrative had caused his head to ache, and his reconciled friend offered him a sedative powder the doctor had prepared. A few moments after it had been taken the man sank to the floor, dead. His host, never suspecting the true cause of his demise, was so moved that he also took one of the sedative prescriptions and soon collapsed into a coma from which he never revived.

When suspicion of murder fell upon the doctor, that gentleman, always agreeable and charming, suggested that the victims of his medicine had been drinking and had taken too many of his powders. He pointed out that those left on the table by the bed contained only enough poison properly to stimulate the invalid's failing heart. There was no tangible proof that his deductions were false.

Free now to do as they pleased, the lovers waited a few months for the whisperings of foul play to die down. They waited in vain. Then in desperation they converted much of their property into money, married, and went to France where they lived happily, so far as anyone knows, for many years.

2. THE TALE OF THE WEDDING RING

A woman clothed in black sat on a rock beside the road, waiting for the stagecoach. She was young and beautiful, though her eyes were red with weeping over the death of her mother. The funeral had been held, she had said farewell to her father, she was returning to her husband and children—a three-day journey. A man stopped his team and buggy beside her, an old friend of her youth, more than friend once. The stage, he told her, had been rerouted on account of swollen streams. But he would be glad to help her catch it. She climbed into the buggy and sat beside him. Before long they came to a stream whose usually sluggish waters had been whipped by the spring rains into a raging torrent. Bravely the horses plunged through it— only their heads above water. The buggy tipped dangerously. Water splashed around its occupants. At last, wet and cold, they were on the other side. A few miles farther the man turned off the road toward the gleaming white pillars of his plantation home. He would get dry clothes there for them both. Then they would continue their journey—there was plenty of time.

No one knows exactly what happened then behind the white walls of that Big House. All the slaves were away at a baptizing. The man and the woman were alone in there. The woman never came out alive. Most people believe that the man attacked her and that she resisted so strenuously that he killed her. The only certainty is that he hid the woman's corpse. The new shed room behind the house had not yet been completed. He dragged her there and buried her in a shallow grave beneath the unfinished floor. And that very night he got word that the stage had overturned in midstream and all its occupants were drowned. He jumped on his horse and rode over to help in the search for the bodies. His companions said that he worked like a madman.

Everyone believed that the woman had been drowned with the other occupants of the stage, though her body was not recovered. And so her murderer lived on peacefully in his Big House for three years. Then came a season of bad crops, his investments were unfortunate, and he sought to sell his home. When his victim's husband bought it in order that his children might be near their mother's father, he went west. A report came, a few months later, that he had died there.

More years intervened. Then one night old black Aunt Sophie, caring for her young master who had a cold, bore a lighted lamp into the shed room to find an iron which she would warm and place at his feet. A screech owl hooted outside and, perhaps frightened by the sudden glare, dashed against the window. Down went the lamp as Aunt Sophie screamed and fled.

When the fire had been put out a big hole had been burned in the shed room floor. But the shallow grave had not yet been betrayed.

Early's raiders were responsible for the uncovering of the gruesome secret. Word flashed through the Black Belt that the Yankee cavalry were coming and the planters rushed to hide their gold and silver. One of them, remembering the hole burned in his shed room floor, crawled through it and began to dig a cache for his treasures. He unearthed a skeleton and on one ghastly, bony finger he saw a wedding ring—his wife's!

3. THE TALE OF THE WHITE DOVE

When the mistress of the Big House lay dying, so the house slaves said, she raised herself on her elbow and vowed that she would come back to her home: she would come back as a white dove to her husband and to the garden where they had been happy together.

No white dove came to the garden for months nor for years. But on the day the master carried a bride inside the pillared portal the slaves heard a low grieving and in the garden, hardly distinguishable against the white blossoms on the snowball bush, they saw the white dove. Every afternoon after that, at exactly the same time, the bird appeared, uttering heartbroken moans. The slaves were frightened, they said their first mistress had kept her word, the whole community became excited.

People began peering over the garden wall to see the dove. The bride became tearful, the master exasperated.

Finally one afternoon, gun in hand, the master strode from his house in a towering rage. As he approached the snowball bush the dove rose in the air, fluttered toward him. He raised his rifle and fired. A woman's scream sounded over the garden, and the dove flew away never to return, a crimson hole staining the whiteness of its breast. That night as he lay in his bed the master died. No one has ever known the cause of his death.

4. THE TALE OF THE STUD NIGGER

Many a planter claims that his acres were once the stamping ground of that black stallion, Jim the stud nigger. According to gallery gossip, Jim was chiefly responsible for the ratio of three negroes to one white in the Black Belt. All the big slave-owners, so the legend goes, kept a big black buck at stud to produce more slaves—just as they kept a blooded bull to increase their herds. But Jim was the best of the lot. He need serve a black wench but once; nine months later, maybe less, as sure as death and taxes there'd be another pickaninny to grow up into a strong field hand, a trusted house servant or a chattel to be sold down the river.

So Jim became famous. His master was so pleased with him that he didn't make him work at all, just kept him around to exercise his one talent. Other planters used to rent him from time to time to help replenish their depleted stock.

There are many stories about Jim. A book could be written from them, though it would be quite Rabelaisian. One of the most characteristic (which has the doubtful advantage of being sworn to as gospel truth by hundreds of God-fearing Alabamians) has to do with his trip to a plantation near New Orleans. The owner of the Louisiana estate had heard of Jim's value as a multiplier of property and, being in Alabama on business, approached the gifted black man's master with the proposal that he rent him. Jim's owner, a kindly man, said he had no objections so long as the slave would not be unhappy so far away from home. "If Jim wants to go," he said, "take him and welcome."

"How fur is it, boss," said Jim, "to down aroun' New Orleans?"

" 'Bout five hundred miles, Jim."

"An' how fur is it back?"

"Just about the same."

"An' how many gals you got down there on your plantation?"

" 'Bout two hundred."

"Well, boss," said Jim, "I'll go. But it seems a mighty fur piece for just a few days' work."

These tales came to me. Others were more difficult to obtain. I went after them. Through the long lazy days straggling in sunny procession down the summer I was searching for stories and people who live them. Sometimes my importunities won me Tennant's company—oftener the lovely presence of Mary Louise. All the remaining chapters in this Third Part of my narrative are the fruits of our expeditions into the little towns and wide fields near us. And after we had gathered the legends of the past, had come to know the people of the present, the Black Belt became in my mind a unit, a country apart from the rest of the state—perhaps under an especial enchantment—exerting a softly insistent influence on all those who have ever trod its dark soil.

CHAPTER V

The Tombigbee Outlaws

I. RAILROAD BILL

MORRIS SLATER, turpentine nigger out of the pine woods of Escambia County, went to town one day with his rifle under his arm. A policeman came up to him and said:

"Nigger, hand over that gun."

"It's my gun," said Morris Slater, "I needs to have it."

"Hand it over quick 'fore I clap you in the jail house."

"You let me be," said Morris, and the policeman grabbed him. The negro swung around, lifted his rifle and pulled the trigger. The policeman fell down, and his assailant ran. There was a freight train pulling out down by the railroad station. Morris Slater jumped on it and got away. That trip was his new baptism. It was Railroad Bill who got off the train in the deep woods.

Railroad Bill is a god of negro mythology. A rifle was the symbol of his godhead. A freight car was his chariot. The white gods pursued him—but he escaped. The freight train provided him food, booty to be sold for money, and a means of flight.

As a long line of rattlers rolled through Wawbeek on a summer night in 1893 a black shadow drifted against it, vanished. The next morning at Bay Minette a brakeman discovered the seal of a car broken, its contents gone. Back along the track Railroad Bill was collecting what he had thrown out. Canned food was cheap along the L. & N. for a while. Bill was underselling the lumber company stores. Negroes dared not refuse to buy from him, not that they wanted to. White men sought

122

him out to purchase his loot. The sheriff got up a posse and set out after him. They were close behind him when he changed himself into a sheep and stood in a field watching the man hunt pass. At least that is what the negroes who remember him well will swear to. Bill was a conjure man, they say, and he could change himself into any kind of animal he wanted to be.

Sometimes his pursuers got too close for Railroad Bill to change himself. Then he would have to shoot them. He did not like to shoot people but he would not be arrested. The list of his killings grew to a half dozen, a dozen. Every new sheriff in the south Alabama counties in order to be elected had to swear he would get Railroad Bill or die trying. They knew he would never be far from the railroad and they set traps to catch him. One night he robbed a car on a train that carried a special posse out after him. And after every crime he disappeared into the woods where, scattered here and there, lay the cabins of black men who worshiped and loved and feared him.

Sheriff E. S. McMillan was a brave man and when he went into office he said he would keep his word to get Railroad Bill. When Bill heard about it he wrote to the sheriff: "I love you and do not want to kill you so do not come after me." Nevertheless, on July 3, 1895, the sheriff set out. The tragic result is best told in the words of the *Standard Gauge,* Escambia County newspaper, for July 4:

At twelve o'clock last night, E. S. McMillan died from effects of a shot fired by the notorious outlaw, Railroad Bill. Sheriff McMillan has been endeavoring to capture "Railroad," who has been beating about between Bluff Springs, Bay Minette and Flomaton. Parties were keeping him supplied with ammunition and knowledge of the movements of the officers. Sheriff McMillan knew it would be a difficult capture but, hearing that "Railroad" was in Molino, he, Dr. O. Brannon and son, Charles, went down to hunt him. They located him near Bluff Springs by a tip of another "nigger." When they started to the house, someone called "Who's there?" and then fired, hitting no one. Sheriff McMillan came from behind a tree and raised his gun, when another shot hit him through the heart. The other men fired but McMillan needed their attention. They asked him if he was hurt and he replied, "Yes, I'm killed." He was taken to John Mc-David's house and there asked the men to pray for him, as he would be dead shortly. Superintendent McKinney sent a special car with doctors and friends but this came too late. The body was brought to Brewton. Sheriff McMillan was the fifth son of Malcolm McMillan.

In the woods cabins around Nymph and Volina and Astoreth and Piney Grove and Elwy and Keego, the black boys were tuning their banjos:

> Railroad Bill mighty bad man
> Shot all lights out brakeman's hand
> Was lookin' fer Railroad Bill.
>
> Railroad Bill mighty big spo't
> Shot all buttons off sheriff's coat
> Was lookin' fer Railroad Bill.
>
> Railroad Bill was worst old coon
> Killed McMillan by the light of the moon
> Was lookin' fer Railroad Bill.

A few more months now for the black god but the white gods were closing in. Once a lean brown short-haired dog appeared from nowhere to yelp with the Mississippi bloodhounds on the trail. But as soon as he joined them, the beasts with the big ears and red eyes lost the scent. Then the brown dog disappeared. Once a white hunter fired at a little red fox as it raced through the woods and he heard a wild laugh, like a nigger's, when he missed and it disappeared.

On an early spring day in March, 1896, Railroad Bill who had been hiding in the budding woods near Atmore, set out from a negro shack for Tidmore's store. Behind him screened by the flowering dogwood and the blossoming honeysuckle lurked Leonard McGowin. Before him squatting behind the counter in the store, his rifle beside him—waited R. C. John. As the black man searched the counter John fired. The outlaw reeled. (No time to change into a fox now, black god. They got you.) He took a step toward the door and fell. Leonard McGowin entered at that moment and fired. The charge almost blew the negro's head off.

Speeding from Brewton an hour later—an engine and coach brought Sheriff McMillan, brother of Railroad Bill's victim, to Atmore. On arriving he and his party hurried to Tidmore's store. Somebody said:

"Reckon you wouldn't walk so fast if you knew Railroad was still living." The reporter of the *Standard Gauge* described the scene in the store:

All was quiet about the premises and the night was dark. Lying near the center of the store was the body of the negro in a pool of blood. He presented a terrible appearance, his face having been badly torn with a load of shot, said to have been fired after he was down. He had on dirty, greasy looking clothes, shoes worn through the toes, a much used leather belt around his waist and his Winchester on his left side down his pants leg.

Leonard McGowin and R. C. John shared the reward of $1250 for Railroad Bill, "dead or alive," and McGowin received also a lifelong pass on the L. & N. The body of the famous outlaw was exhibited at Brewton and later at Montgomery, and even at Pensacola in Florida. Every sheriff in South Alabama was happy at the funeral.

But there are people in the little shacks far back in the woods who do not believe that Railroad Bill is dead. "Not *him*," they say, and laugh and tell of the time he changed himself into a sheep to watch the posse go by.

2. THE OUTLAW SHERIFF OF SUMTER COUNTY

Steve Renfroe rode a milk-white horse into Livingston. The Black Belt town felt his presence, tall and blue-eyed and handsome, when he swung into Main Street, the horse dancing along beside the bored well and the courthouse in the square. Straight to the undertaker's he rode, and bought a coffin for his dead wife.

Some said he came from Virginia; others that they knew his people up in North Alabama, near Anniston. Folks from the south of the county reported he had bought a big cotton plantation down there.

Steve Renfroe had a way with women. They liked him because he was beautiful and reckless and courtly. He soon had another wife from one of the finest families in the Belt. Men liked him because he liked them—and hated the Yankees.

Sumter had been having a hard time before Steve came. The Republicans and the niggers had been raising hell. Black congressmen were sitting in the state house at Montgomery. Carpetbaggers were sitting in judgment at the Livingston courthouse. The Ku Klux had tried to help matters but only made them worse, for after they had ridden a few times a detail of Yankee soldiers had been sent to Livingston—to prevent further "outrages." Then things began to happen. Steve took a hand.

Over in Greene County conditions were just as bad. Yankee soldiers were in Eutaw, too. But one night when all the Harwoods and the McQueens and the Jemisons and the rest were having a friendly game with the Yanks down at the courthouse, a Republican judge disappeared. A trembling negro told the soldiers on the next day of seeing a little group of ghosts gallop up to the judge's house. He said a tall ghost on a white horse rode ahead.

A week or so later, while Steve and a few friends and the Livingston Yankee soldiers were putting aside all hard feelings, the bodyguard of a certain Livingston magistrate was shot down. The magistrate left town the next day at three o'clock, bound for Boston.

Then there was that business about Mr. Byrd. He's still alive and his sons are grown men but I think none of them knows how near he came to death about a half century ago. He was going to make a Republican speech in Eutaw and the Livingston Ku Klux fixed it up to kill him while he was making it. The hall had a center aisle and the Klan arranged to have one of their men at the end of each row on the aisle. The man who sat in the front row was to shoot Mr. Byrd and toss the gun to the man behind him. It would then be passed from hand to hand to the back of the hall and thrown in the fountain outside. But just as the appointed killer was taking aim, another objector to Republicanism could stand heresies no longer and let go at the speaker with a quart whiskey bottle. It knocked Mr. Byrd off the platform and out. And it saved his life.

But secret methods seemed roundabout to a man who was never very good at deception. The next time a carpetbagger overstepped himself Steve Renfroe met up with him on Main Street and ordered him to get to hell out of town on the next train or take the consequences. The man went. The soldiers and the scalawags and the carpetbaggers decided that this was too much. So they had Steve arrested on the charge of being a Ku Klux raider. They did their best to fake some evidence but Steve was acquitted—the most popular man in town. When the election for sheriff came around he rode into office as jauntily as ever he rode down Main Street.

God help the carpetbaggers and the scalawags then! Sumter County was saved and the damn Yanks were licked and Steve Renfroe did it. Men warmed to the sight of the white horse and its rider. They went out of their way to receive a wave of the hand from their champion who was a prince of good fellows. And hearts fluttered, a little panic-stricken, when he swept his hat from that curly head, and a smile came to that firm mouth and crept into those blue eyes. Children loved him. Negroes worshiped him.

But like many another pretender to power Steve Renfroe proved a better champion of rights than an administrator of them. The good-fellowship of politicians, the admiration of his fellow townsmen and a few bad cotton crops were contributing causes. On one sad day in Livingston the civil authorities were forced to arrest Sheriff Renfroe for embezzlement of county funds and to confine him in the same jail to which he had committed many an offender.

Imprisonment was not for Steve's free spirit, though. One night he broke down the jail door and set all the prisoners free (save one negro who chose to stay and be hanged). Then followed a day of anxiety in the town. Steve's indictment papers were in the circuit clerk's office and that officer feared for their safety. Being a brave man, he watched over them all day and all the following night. When the little town square grew light again, however, he thought all danger past and walked home. Standing at his own doorway he turned to see the flames from his office licking up into the gray morning sky.

No man had more loyal friends than Steve Renfroe. Despite the case against him, the men of Livingston raised a large sum of money and gave it to him. Take this, they said, go somewhere else and get a new start. He took the money, but he came back, hiding near Livingston. Then his friends said, come back and stand your trial, we will sign your bond and defend you. And so he rode around the square again, as straight and tall and arrogant as ever. A few days before his trial he was rearrested and put in jail. His friends had discovered his plan to run away. The next morning the jailer found the bars of Renfroe's window all but sawed through. Then they bound him and took him north—all the way to Tuscaloosa where there was a stronger jail. And another dawn saw a great hole burned in the eighteen-inch floor of the Tuscaloosa jail and Steve Renfroe, the outlaw Sheriff of Sumter County, free again.

More money from friends, more promises. Then James Little's best mule and Nathan Weisenburg's beautiful saddle disappeared at the same time. They and Steve were found together in Slidell, Louisiana, a few days later.

"Well, Frank," said Steve to an interviewer from the Livingston *Journal* as the two sat together in the (improved) county jail, "when I left here the first time I tried to do right. I struck some good jobs but just as I'd get to doing well, along would come some man and say: 'That's Steve Renfroe. He used to be sheriff of Sumter County,' and that would almost kill me and I would go to drinking. I haven't been any account since I left here just because of that."

While he was in jail this time Steve sent the following letter to the editor of the Livingston *Journal*. It tells its own story:

It would be better for me perhaps to say nothing, for I feel that I cannot gain, nor do I expect to get any sympathy from the citizens of this county, but inasmuch as the *Journal* has of late made pretty free use of my name, I have concluded to drop you a line in regard to the note written by me to one J. C. Giles. I did write the note and the following is a copy:

DEAR JAKE:
Please go to Meridian and get me four ounces of nitric-muriatic acid and a bunch of pure yarn thread. Dip the string in the acid and pull it across a piece of iron and see if it will cut it. Get the acid put up in two ounce bottles so I can get them through these bars. Come at night, at the back of the jail, and fasten them to the end of a fishing pole about eight feet long and poke them to me. I am in the second

story a little to the right of the window. You can't miss it; since it is the only window in the back of the jail. You can come in sometime in the day light to speak to me. Then you can take in the whole thing. If the acid will not do the work, try and find out what will cut these bars. It will be no trouble to get out of this place. Try and get everything ready before the August term of court. You can get the acid at any drug store, and it is not very costly.

Truly your friend,

STEVE

I am informed that he objected to the note being published because he did not wish the public to know that he had received such a friendly note from me. This is strange for he has always, when I was at large, professed the greatest friendship for me. When I have been in the neighborhood he has endeavored to impress upon the community the fact that he knew where I was, and could see me whenever he liked. Professing such friendship, I had the right to believe that he would not betray me, at least. I find, however, that I was mistaken and that he is a traitor. I would not have censured him if he had burned the note up, and said nothing about it, but I suppose he thought he could safely betray me, now as I am in jail with no hope of escape. Does anyone believe he would have done it if I had been at large? Why did he not tell the sheriff where I was when I was in the county, not in jail?

I am accused of some bad things, but none so mean as being a traitor.

Yours truly,

S. S. RENFROE

Indictments charged embezzlement, grand larceny, burglary, assault with intent to murder, and a number of lesser offenses. The prisoner pleaded guilty to embezzlement and burglary and was sentenced to the penitentiary for five years. Livingston felt a relief it had not enjoyed in a long time. But the men were a little shamefaced. After all, Steve was their friend and they had not forgotten carpetbag days. They did not like it much when they heard that he had been set at hard work in the mines of the Pratt Coal and Iron Company. Neither, apparently, did Steve, for in less than sixty days the

Pratt Coal and Iron Company was spreading the alarm for an escaped convict. A posse tried hard to find Steve. They worked with bloodhounds, but their prey escaped them by walking backward for miles down a small creek to his favorite resort and, from then on, to his headquarters—the "Flat Woods." This was a belt of uninhabited and mostly sterile timber lands about ninety miles in length and from five to fifteen in width. Here he lived desperately, making quick forays into the surrounding country to rob plantation homes, even daring to plunder houses in the small towns. At last he came to be known, even to his despairing friends, as the "outlaw."

Negroes living about the Flat Woods worshiped and feared Steve. They served him faithfully and they kept watch against the officers of the law. He had them cut him a special road through the woods to Mississippi, and whenever a posse was on his trail, he made for that and galloped madly to the state line and safety.

By this time he made no discrimination between former friend and foe. None were secure from pillage or violence. The little, widely separated communities of the Black Belt were thrown into a panic at the report that Renfroe had been seen near by. Almost every day a new and more reckless crime was laid to him.

Still he could not stay away from Livingston. The scene of his former triumphs always drew him back. Never, even, did he give up the idea of returning there to live as he had once lived, proud among his friends.

On the day before Steve Renfroe's final capture a negro slunk across the fields behind the Pickens plantation home. He came to the back door with a message for Mr. Pickens. The master of the house received him and was informed that "someone" wished to see him behind the house and across the railroad track. Mr. Pickens said: "It's Steve." Despite the entreaties of his wife and daughter (who are my authority for this anecdote) he went with the negro—answering their protestations simply: "He will not hurt me. He is my friend."

When Mr. Pickens came back from that interview he told little of what had transpired. His wife gathered that Steve wanted to know what would happen if he gave himself up— hoping that his friends would again rally to his defense. Perhaps, too, he told Mr. Pickens, what several of his contemporaries have alleged he told others—that if his old Ku Klux friends would not raise a large sum of money for him he would furnish the Federal Government with a list of their names and evidence of their affiliation. There is still much dispute on this point in Livingston. Many insist he never descended to this form of blackmail. But there are others who are quite sure.

What Mr. Pickens told Steve is not known, but it must have been discouraging, for on the same night a mule belonging to the outlaw's brother-in-law disappeared. So did the silverware of a kindly lady with whom he had boarded and who had befriended him many times in former years.

Some days later three Mississippians who had read the story of the crime saw a man riding a mule like the one described therein. Surrounding the man, they called on him to surrender. He drew a pistol and one of his captors fired. A load of small shot in the back and side considerably facilitated his arrest.

Then began the long journey to the nearest town, Enterprise, sixty miles south. It was only when they arrived there and Steve was recognized that the three men learned how important a capture they had made. They brought him back once more to the Livingston jail. And once more his old friends came to see him there. But the jaunty air, the spirit in the blue eyes were gone.

About eight-thirty on the second night after his capture a silent group of twenty men appeared before the jail. Two of them entered and seized the jailer's keys. Then they got Renfroe and moved off. As soon as they had gone the jailer gave the alarm and a posse started in pursuit. They did not go far. At the old "Tan Yard" about a mile south of town they found the body of Renfroe, hanged to a chinaberry tree.

There are people in Livingston who know who the members of that group of twenty were. Although the executioners were bitterly condemned by many of their own friends, it is still impolitic to ask about them. But a little has seeped out about that journey of a mile and its tragic end. Renfroe rode as he had always ridden, fearless. When they came to the tree and he saw their purpose, he struggled, called them cowards and challenged any one of them to single combat. No one accepted. One of the men said: "We're doing this for your own good, Steve, and the good of the community."

He was quiet while they put the rope about his neck. He looked about him at the stern faces of these men who had for so long been his friends. Perhaps he was thinking of the days when he wore a silver star and the milk-white horse danced down Main Street, for he said at last: "Will no one say a word for me?"

There was a grim silence. Again Steve said: "Won't someone say a prayer for me?"

Then the leader of the company, his boon companion in another time, said in one and the same breath:

"God rest your soul—string him up, boys!"

The chinaberry tree still stands. And the story of Steve Renfroe is so well remembered that to this day whenever Livingston children play about it they stop for a moment while the bravest of them says in a quavering voice: "Renfroe, Renfroe, what did you do?"

And the chinaberry tree says: "Nothing."

3. RUBE BURROW: ALABAMA ROBIN HOOD

Rube Burrow could lift a seven-hundred-pound sack and walk off with it, no sign of buckling in his six feet of straight man. One day he went hunting with only his pistol. With twenty shots he killed nineteen quail—and broke the wing of the twentieth. He was the outlaw king of Alabama—some say he was a bolder train robber than Jesse James—and he never robbed a poor man. All the songs about him and the old paper-covered dime novels will tell you that.

And over west in Lamar County (old-timers still call it Rube Burrow's County) the first story they always tell about the fearless bandit is of the time when, pursued by deputies, he stopped at the home of a widow-woman and asked for a meal. While she prepared it, Rube saw tears on her cheeks and asked her why she was sad. She said her landlord was that very day foreclosing the mortgage on her little home.

"How much will clear the mortgage?" said Rube.

"Seven hundred dollars."

"Here's the money," said Rube; "what time will he come?"

"Around two."

"Be sure to get a receipt," said Rube.

That afternoon as the landlord walked smiling back toward town—seven hundred dollars in his pocket, he suddenly looked into the muzzles of two pistols.

"Hand it over," said Rube.

At eighteen Rube Burrow was finding the forests and farms of Lamar County pretty tame. That was in 1872. So he was off to be a cowboy in Texas. Four years later his brother Jim joined him and for ten years after that it was a wise rancher who could recognize his own cows after the Burrow boys had done a fancy job of superimposing their own brand.

After a decade of it, cattle rustling seemed neither exciting nor lucrative enough. And so in 1886 the passengers and crew of a train that had just pulled out of Bellevue, Texas, looked down the muzzles of rifles in the hands of four determined men and gave up what valuables they had—which were few enough. A scared soldier surrendered a brace of pistols, however, that were to become famous throughout all the Southeastern states. Two months later a train, boarded at Gordon, gave up $2500 from the express and a thousand from the registered mail. And an express car, looted at Benbrook in September of the same year, added another $2450 to the swelling hoard of the bandits.

Then the brothers went back to their Alabama home in Lamar County for a visit. They had money and they spent it. There was swaggering and boasting—and the people of Lamar, many of them kinfolks, looked upon them fondly.

Their visit at an end, their funds low, the Burrow boys invaded Arkansas and there at Genoa they took $200 from Express Train No. 2 of the Arkansas & Texas Railway. The Southern Express Company, proud of its record of seventeen years without a robbery, set detectives to work to apprehend those responsible for its humiliation and the brothers were at last given the notoriety they had so richly deserved. Handbills announcing rewards for their capture and giving complete descriptions were distributed throughout the Southeast. Hastily the Burrow boys fled to Lamar County where they might be secreted by relatives and friends. But even the fastnesses of home country proved unsafe, and one wet night they boarded a southbound Louisville & Nashville train below Birmingham.

At Montgomery station three policemen disguised as railroad men waited in the rain. When the train had pulled in they entered the car where the Burrow brothers sat and loudly announced that the downpour had washed out the tracks ahead. Rube asked the officers if they knew of a boarding house where two lumbermen might spend the night. One of the conspirators replied that he and his companions were going uptown and would guide them to a place where they could put up. The party was on the narrow covered stair leading to the police station before either of the robbers suspected their danger. Then Rube turned about in the darkness, knocking men right and left, and fought his way to the street. There, his pistols drawn, he fought desperately to save his brother, but Jim, unarmed, was not strong enough to beat off his captors, and the people of Montgomery were aroused. Neil Bray, a printer, joined the officers with his shotgun leveled, only to fall severely wounded. Under cover of a spray of lead from his pistols Rube fled to safety.

Back to Lamar County he went, plotting his brother's rescue and writing to Joe Jackson, comrade of his Texas days, to come to his aid. Joe came. Hunted like animals but always protected by loyal friends, the two outlaws succeeded in boarding the train on which Jim was said to be a prisoner on his way to Texarkana for trial. But Jim was too ill for travel. Typhoid fever killed him in prison, and Rube turned again bitterly to his trade. A passenger on an Illinois Central train which was robbed at Duck Hill, Mississippi, showed fight and Rube put a bullet through his brain. Six months he hid out in Lamar County for that, while the public raged and detectives scoured the South. Then things got so hot for Rube that he sent to a mail-order house for false whiskers and a wig, signing himself, appropriately enough, W. W. Cain. But when the parcel arrived at Jewell, Alabama, some of the hair was sticking out of it, and Moses Graves, the postmaster, refused to give it to Rube's messenger. Rube strode down to the post office in a mighty rage, shot Graves through the heart and took the parcel away with him.

Detectives were camping now in the wilds of Lamar. Nevertheless, Rube's mother brought him word that his first cousin, Rube Smith, wished to join him. At midnight in Fellowship Cemetery the cousin and Joe Jackson met to make their pact. Its first fruit was the robbing of a crack M. & O. train which railroad men and press alike had claimed impregnable even to attack by Burrow. As he jumped from the train near Bucatunna, Mississippi, with a loot of over $3000, Rube said: "Tell the boss to put steps on his express cars. It's too much trouble to rob them."

Lamar County now benefited by an influx of book agents, lightning-rod salesmen, tinware peddlers, even hoboes. But its residents bought little and talked less. They knew a detective when they saw one—no matter what he said he was—and they were loyal. But the situation was desperate. One day in early fall of 1889 Rube's father said:

"There's a detective under every bush in this county. You boys had better leave."

So Rube Burrow and Joe Jackson walked to Columbus, Mississippi, bought a yoke of oxen and a covered wagon, and set out for Florida. Perhaps because of the strangeness and slowness of their method of travel no one suspected the two men in the pioneering conveyance, who said they were on their way to a logging camp to the southward. When detectives picked up the trail in Pickens County they were forty-five days behind and Rube Burrow was in the swamps of Santa Rosa County, Florida.

But Joe Jackson had doubled back. The detectives still camping in Lamar County reported him hiding there again. Orders were given to watch him but not to make the arrest. Then Joe got on a train one night at Millport, Mississippi, southbound. Three officers were waiting for him in the car he entered. Unarmed he surrendered, saying that he was on his way to visit an uncle in Louisiana. He denied he was going south to join

Rube. His confessions were easily obtained but, like his idol-
ized leader, he never stood trial. On the day his case was called
he jumped from a jail window in Jackson, Mississippi, to death
on the stone pavement far below.

Rube was a lone outlaw now. All his band were dead or in
prison. The net spread by the railroads and the law was closing in on him. Capture was inevitable. Yet in the very heart of
danger he went on his terrorizing way. As an L. & N. passenger
train waited a few moments at Flomaton, Alabama, to allow a
connection from Pensacola, Rube took a coal pick from the
tender. As the train pulled out he ran alongside in full view
of the station and yards, and climbed aboard the engine. Wit-
nesses thought him an employee. Hiding between the tender
and the express car until the train was moving rapidly, Rube
suddenly climbed into the engine, his pistols covering fireman
and engineer.

"Pull ahead and stop with the express car just over the
Escambia River bridge," he said.

As the train stopped Rube fired several shots into the air,
as if signaling to his confederates. Then he forced the crew to
open the express car with the coal pick and took what currency
he could find, only $250.

Money in his pockets and the law on his trail had always
meant but one thing to Rube Burrow—headlong flight for
home—for the protection of the woods and canebrake of Lamar
County—for the security afforded by loyal friends and admir-
ing family. He set out northward but he was never to see
Jewell and Molloy and Blowhorn and Fernbank and all his
old haunts again.

He strode into a negro cabin in Clarke County about noon
of an early October day in 1890. Frank Marshall and Jesse
Hilton were there, and he offered the latter money to go to
J. D. Carter's store at Myrtleville near by and get him canned

foods enough to last for the rest of his trip. Carter's suspicions were aroused by the large order. He questioned Jesse about his white visitor—then offered him and Frank Marshall fifty dollars apiece if they would capture the desperado. Jesse went back to the cabin, and while he prepared Rube's dinner he succeeded in telling Frank of his plan. A rain had begun to fall and Jesse offered to wrap up Rube's rifle to keep it from rusting. Once it was well wrapped and set at a safe distance Jesse lunged at the outlaw from behind and Frank Marshall leaped to his assistance. A terrific struggle took place but the two powerful blacks finally succeeded in overcoming their dangerous guest. While Frank was binding Rube with rope, Jesse held him so tightly that he shouted:

"God damn you, don't hug me to death."

"Boss," said Jesse, "I jus' *got* to hold you now. I *can't* turn you aloose."

"I'll give you a hundred dollars if you'll let me go," said Rube.

"I couldn't use it then," said Jesse, " 'cause you'd kill me first."

Now the white storekeeper appeared, bound Rube to the saddle of his horse and, riding behind his captive, set out for Linden and the nearest jail. Beside them rode John McDuffie, a friend of Carter's, and behind them walked Frank and Jesse, Frank carrying the outlaw's "croker sack" which held his few belongings.

At the Linden jail Rube was confined in the "bull pen," his feet chained to a ring in the floor, his hands shackled. The news of his capture spread and the townspeople came to the jail to peer through the bars at the notorious bandit and joke him over his plight. Rube laughed with them. His droll humor was infectious, everybody had a good time, and the night wore on. By midnight only McDuffie and the two negroes remained to guard the prisoner. Carter had gone to a friend's house to sleep.

"I'm hungry as hell," said Rube.

"No place is open this time o' night," said McDuffie, "or I'd get you a snack."

"There's a piece o' cake in that croker bag there," said Rube. "If you'd just hand it to me and loose my hands I could eat that."

McDuffie unlocked the handcuffs while Frank Marshall handed over the burlap sack.

"Have a New York *Times?*" said Rube. "I always read that instead of these hick newspapers down here. And here's some cake for you niggers, too."

"And now," said Rube, drawing the famous brace of pistols from the sack, "McDuffie, come in here and unlock my feet, and one of you boys come in here and lock him to this floor ring. Lock yourself to it, too, or I'll blow your God-damn heads off."

Silently they complied.

"Take me to Carter," said Rube to Jesse Hilton. "I'm goin' to kill him and get back that sixteen-chamber rifle. And if you two make a sound I'm comin' back and kill you both."

Through the dark gray of approaching dawn Jesse walked, lantern in hand, two pistols at his back.

"Don' know where he *kin* be, boss," he said. "Reckon it might be this house."

A rap at the door—a sleepy voice answering Jesse's questioning "Mist' J. D. Carter stayin' with you-all tonight? They wants him at the jail house."

Three times the wily negro took the outlaw to the wrong house while the eastern sky was growing red.

"They wouldn't pay me no mind," Jesse complained later. "By that time the town should of been illuminated with men."

Then Rube Burrows said: "Boy, if this ain't the right house this time I'm goin' to kill you," and Jesse knew he meant it.

The strange procession stopped at Glass's Store and Carter answered from the rooms above.

"Mist' McDuffie wants you right away," said Jesse.

"I'm comin'," said Carter.

As he left the door a few minutes later, his revolver in his pocket, Rube Burrow stepped from behind a tree.

"Rube Burrow is a free man, God damn you," he said, "and he's killin' you."

Two shots were so close together that they sounded as one. Both men reeled and then began firing wildly. There was a silence for a moment, then three more shots. When townspeople found them Rube Burrow lay dead beside the horse-rack in the street. Carter lay unconscious on the store steps, wounded so severely that, though he lived for some years, he never recovered.

In Fellowship Cemetery, just a few miles from Vernon, is the headstone of Rube Burrow. Folks around there will tell you the body lies under the very spot where Rube and his cousin and Joe Jackson made solemn pact before they robbed the express at Bucatunna.

"He robbed the rich and gave to the poor," they say, "and he could outjump and outshoot any man in this neck of the woods."

CHAPTER VI

God in the Canebrake

I. BEN DELIMUS

BEN DELIMUS is a dying legend now. Only a few old-timers in Alabama, fellows who know a good story, speak of him. My friend, the late Colonel Breck Musgrove, who was a page boy in the carpetbag days at Montgomery and knew Ben well, told me about him not so long ago. And one February night in Montevallo, about a year before he died, T. W. Palmer, President of Alabama Women's College, told me just about the same tale. Here it is:

The youngest soldier with Croxton's raiding Yankees on their quick tour of Alabama was a little dark-haired black-eyed drummer. His name was Ben Delimus and he was a French Jew, born in Paris and brought over to New York when he was very young. He was about sixteen when he rode through Alabama, his drum strapped to his saddle. But he was old for his years and his little black eyes saw many things. Among them was the dark soil beneath his horse's hoofs—promise of fertility. And in Lowndes County he looked on wide reaches of the level black land punctuated only by negro shacks and widely separated plantation homes. Then and there he resolved that when the war was over he would come back to this place.

Ben did not have much to pack into his carpetbag when he set out on his return journey. His discharge papers, probably, and his army wardrobe. He could hardly expect to buy land and wait for crops to grow on it. There is no record, however, that such considerations, even momentarily, deterred him. He went straight down to Lowndes County. Then he looked about for some means of acquiring wealth, and his genius immediately asserted itself.

The newly freed negroes were in a highly emotional state. Emancipation, no matter how their former masters might look at it, was no doubtful blessing to them. Father Abraham and General Grant had become deities no less powerful and generous than the Christian God, and somehow all three were fused in their simple minds. It was natural, then, that when Ben Delimus rode about the county announcing himself as Massa Lincoln's closest friend, and the right-hand man of the great Yankee war-god, they listened. Ben said he bore a message from Father Abraham to his black children. The great man in Washington was worried over their souls. A negro baptized in slavery, he said, could never hope to escape the torments of hell-fire. Such a ceremony performed when the convert was owned by a wicked slaveholder could not be expected to take effect. In fact, Ben reported Mr. Lincoln as saying, all baptisms that had taken place before the Emancipation Proclamation were null and void, and all negroes so baptized were inevitably bound for eternal torment. But there was a ray of hope. Mr. Lincoln's good friend, the bearer of this message, would be willing to save all thus exposed from the danger of the devil's grip by rebaptizing them at a dollar a head.

Mr. Lincoln's good friend did a land office business. Negroes poured out of the Big Swamp to be immersed in the muddy stream near Haneville where Ben saved them for the Lord. They came from Bogahoma and Collirene and Big Union Church, even from Soapstone over in Dallas County. Payment was strictly in advance, to avoid the calamity of receiving Confederate money, and the dollars rolled in. A great religious revival swept the county, and for weeks there were singings and visions. Then business began to let up. There was no one left to save.

But Ben had prepared for this. Immediately he delivered the second part of the Emancipator's message. It was that, for reasons similar to those stated before, all weddings that had been solemnized before his proclamation were also ineffective and participants in them were living in a state of sin. His good friend and duly appointed representative, however, would save them from the horrible consequences of such wickedness by re-wedding them at the absurdly reasonable rate of a dollar a couple. Again the roads were dotted with mules and wagons on their way to the deliverer. Giggling couples paid their dollars, received his blessing, and drove away on second honeymoons. Unexpectedly for Ben a number of negroes used his announcement as authority for immediate divorce. Failures to remarry cut into his receipts, but the wedding ceremonies, while not as numerous as the baptisms, brought in a tidy sum.

The fertility of Ben's inventive faculty now became more strongly evident. He was no man of a single idea to be run at last into the ground. He left the county for a week or so. When he returned he brought a carload of bottles containing a dark liquid—the first of the long line of hair straighteners for kinky heads. Ben brought with him two letters, one of which stated that the writer had observed the workings of this wonderful boon to the negro race on the curls of many of his colored friends and its straightening powers in each case had proved infallible. This letter was signed Abraham Lincoln.

The other epistle was more laudatory than the first but stated conservatively in conclusion that should one bottle fail of its purpose, the writer had no doubt that two would be sufficient. The name subscribed was Ulysses S. Grant. Ben Delimus had somewhat unethically anticipated modern endorsement advertising by more than half a century.

The sale of the unkinking mixture at a dollar a bottle was fabulous. Ben was growing rich. Now that he was a man of popularity and influence and means, the will to power descended upon him. He felt sure that he could command much of the newly acquired negro suffrage in the county, and the successes of other carpetbaggers in the state pricked his ambition. He announced himself as a candidate for the Alabama Legislature. But other white men, envious or disapproving, had been watching Ben, and to his surprise he found a sudden and bitter opposition to his nomination. He called on his negro friends for aid and they responded manfully. Still the issue was in doubt when the day of the convention dawned. It would be a close fight. Fate seemed against Ben from the start. As he and one of his trusted henchmen were driving to the convention, they found a bridge down, destroyed by enemies to delay them. When they arrived the meeting was under way, the opposing forces had elected the chairman and were in full control, and the tribe of Ben was weakening. The chairman would not recognize their leader when he rose to speak.

"I call upon this convention to witness," thundered the little man, "that it has committed sacrilege, that unlike any past convention it has sinned against God."

There was a silence. Even Ben's enemies were a little awed by that charge.

"No convention has ever begun in Alabama," shouted Ben, "without a prayer to the Almighty for guidance. In his name I now offer that prayer."

There was no shutting him off. The chairman, well aware that all the negroes might turn against him if he ruled out a prayer, was helpless.

"O Lord," began Ben, "although the chairman of this convention obtained his position by lies and deceit, bless him and make him see the light. Although he and his friends are full of false promises, although they would rob the black man and swindle the white, make them realize the truth before it is too late." On and on he went in a masterpiece of prayerful vituperation.

At last one of his enemies could stand it no longer. Rising, he leveled an accusing finger at Ben and roared out:

"Who is this who dares to accuse us? There stands one of the men who crucified our Lord."

There was a great gasp from the convention. Ben saw the black faces of his negro supporters turning away. In another moment his cause would be lost.

"It is not true," he said steadily and with rising force. "Your Lord was crucified almost two thousand years ago. I am not that old. You can see that. And furthermore, gentlemen," his voice rose in a great peal of sound, "furthermore, *if I had been there, I would have put a stop to that business.*"

Ben was elected. He went to Montgomery and he sat in the carpetbag legislature. He bought a nice house in Montgomery and married. He had made his money, had had his share of public favor—and he took life quietly and serenely from then on. Few of his neighbors knew about his strange past. He lived quite to himself, was happy with his wife and family. He died hardly a decade ago.

2. THE SIMS WAR

Bob Sims was a better man than most until he was fifty years old. He had been a brave soldier in the War Between the States and after he was demobilized he became an earnest God-fearing family man. He was a better quoter from the Bible than anybody in Choctaw County except the preacher.

What strange quirk of circumstance changed Bob into the man he was when he was hanged, no one will ever know. Some think it was liquor. At any rate, when he was fifty he and his four brothers had built themselves a big house over by Womack Hill—just south of Butler, the county seat. That house was of strange construction. It was stronger than any house around—with extra thick walls and doors. In a cluster about it were other dwellings, easy-built shacks in which lived those of the Simses who couldn't find room in the big house, and the six Savage brothers, wild youngsters who had taken a liking to Bob. And in the hollow behind the big house stood a copper still bigger than any in South Alabama.

The possession of a still was no novelty in Choctaw County. But it was a subject not discussed. So when travelers saw at the crossroads which led away from the main pike towards Womack Hill a sign which read, "Three Miles to Bob Sims' Still," they shook their heads and wondered.

The Baptist church to which Bob belonged numbered among its members several who were not averse to making their own whiskey or even parting with a bit of it for cash. But a church could not countenance an open defiance of constituted authority. The board of elders met and sorrowfully excommunicated Bob Sims. The mantle has ever been laid on the shoulders of the prophet in mysterious wise—and few of those well-meaning churchmen could have surmised the story that was to lead to six dangling corpses at a crossroads.

Bob was a religious man and so he built a church of his own near the cluster of houses that circled his home. Perhaps the next step in the tragedy was his realization that he might dictate the creed of the people who worshiped here. Holding power like that is dangerous to anybody. In Alabama during the late nineteenth century, as elsewhere throughout America, a man need only announce himself a prophet to have disciples. And so the sect of the Simsites was born. They adopted the beliefs God had imparted to Bob Sims who had been able to clear away the mists that separate man from his Maker and

thereby to understand the divine meaning with heretofore unknown clarity. And they published a proselyting journal aptly
entitled *The Veil Is Rent* in which these beliefs were attrac-
tively set forth.

Judged by standards of today, the Simsites were partly com-
munistic, partly anarchistic. They believed in no central federal government, in communal enterprise, in the open practice
of their creed, in Christ as God and in Bob Sims as his prophet.

The thirsty heeded the sign at the crossroads, for Sims'
liquor was cheap. A few converts joined the Simsites—some
even moving out to their settlement to be with them. There
were rich crops in the fields, horses to ride, abundance of food,
wives and sons and daughters to be gay with. The church
people over at Butler began to growl, but the county authorities dared not interfere.

Then one October morning in 1891 two grim silent men
walked through the cluster of houses and into the thick-walled
house. They found Bob Sims there and marched him out at
the points of their revolvers, down the hill, and to their wagon
which was hitched to a swift team. Before supper they were in
Bladon Springs awaiting the Tombigbee River boat to take
them to Mobile where Bob was to stand trial. The Simsites in
their happy security had not reckoned with the United States
government or its marshals.

While Bob Sims sat shackled beside two hired guards in the
ornate lobby of the hotel at Bladon Springs, "Saratoga of the
South," three horsemen were galloping down the road from
the north. The Simsite women had spread the news of their
prophet's capture and two of his brothers, Neal and James, and
his son, Baily, were riding to expiate the sin of their careless-
ness. Most of the guests of the hotel including the government
marshals were at dinner in the high-walled, mirrored dining
room, and the citizens of the town were in their homes when

the three climbed the steps of the veranda and strode through the wide entrance. There was a roar of gunfire and four men leaped out of that entrance, one handcuffed, and the others carrying smoking revolvers, looking behind them as they ran. In the lobby two guards slumped in grotesque death on the red velvet of the big chairs.

The Sims band had run but a few yards up the street toward their horses when one of the marshals darted from the hotel, dropped on one knee, and fired. James Sims threw up his hands and fell headlong into the dust. Bob and Neal were almost to the horses now. But doors were opening in the town. From a window came the sharp spat of a rifle. Both marshals were in the street firing steadily. The two brothers were mounting. Behind them, between them and the gunfire, stood the slim figure of Baily Sims guarding his father's escape. A man rushed from a doorway, shotgun in hand. Baily lifted his rifle. The man fell, squirming on the sidewalk. There was a sound of galloping hoofs and Baily turned and ran for his horse. At that moment a man stepped from the hotel into the roadway, raised his rifle and took slow aim. Baily almost reached the side of his horse before he fell, slid a foot or so, and was still.

Bob and Neal Sims rode back to the big house, strengthened its defenses, and waited. But no one dared come again, not even the marshals. The people of Butler were openly hostile but nobody in Gilbertown or nearer was brave enough to speak out against the Simsites, nobody, that is, except John Mc-Mellon.

McMellon kept a general store about ten miles from the Sims stronghold and he had a moral sense inherited from his Scotch ancestors. He called upon all decent people to unite and drive from the county the scourge of honor and right living that had infested it. Bob Sims heard of the storekeeper's attacks and grew restless. A prophet of God and ruler of a domain over which even the United States had no power could brook no such insolence.

"As far back as I can remember," he said, "I never have liked a McMellon and the world would be a better place if they were all out of it."

On the afternoon of December 23, 1891, the Sims brothers and the Savage brothers, and a negro, Harry Hinton, surrounded McMellon's home. Inside there was much before-Christmas gayety. The school-teacher was spending the holidays with the McMellons, Ed Kennedy and his family had come to visit, and the whole crowd were joyfully awaiting the arrival from Butler of a wagonload of toys. This the Simses had already seized and confiscated. Dinner was about to be served when the first fusillade apprised the merrymakers of their fate. In the kitchen, which stood apart from the rest of the house and was connected to it by a bridge, the school-teacher and two of the children saw flames shooting up through the floor and realized that they must be burned to death or run across to the main house. As they ran a volley riddled them and their bodies lay charring in the flames of the bridge for hours.

Desperately the McMellons and the Kennedys fought to put out the fire and for a while they succeeded, though at terrific cost, for anyone who ventured outside was immediately butchered by the high-power rifles of the besiegers. As night settled the besieged families discovered that by hiding behind the shrubbery in the garden they could escape to the shelter of the woods, and one by one they made the perilous journey, Mrs. McMellon, Ammon McMellon, Ed Kennedy, John Mc-Mellon (wounded three times and carrying in his arms his little wounded baby). Then the Simses closed the gates in the picket fence surrounding the house, stationed themselves to command all exits and set the flames to eating their way once again. There were no other escapes. Nine corpses lay in the embers when the gutted house fell.

Just before dawn of the day before Christmas the Sims band rifled the McMellon store and then set out for home and the security of the big house. But the prophet had overestimated his power. No God of the Simsites and no high-powered rifles could long protect him now. Before he and his band had reached their goal an army of a thousand men was setting out in pursuit from McMellon's store—men from Gilbertown and Butler and Toxy and Tullis, Souwilpa and Okatuppa and Water Valley and Paragon, Ararat and Bogueloosa and Coffeeville and Silas and Turkey Creek, all under the command of Thomas Bonner who had fought by the side of Bob Sims in the old war days.

As the vanguard rode up the road toward the Sims house— the long-range rifles barked from within and the besiegers knew that it would be foolhardy to advance. The army drew up in a great circle around the Sims fort and waited. Scouts reported that the whole group were together in the big house —the shacks below it were empty. The rifles of the army could not carry as far as the Simses' and so they waited for the shelter of darkness. In the gray of the twilight Thomas Bonner crept unnoticed up to the Sims kitchen, poured coal oil on it, and set it afire. As the first curl of smoke appeared Bob Sims ran from the house, rifle in hand. His shot just missed Bonner dodging among the trees.

"Eh, Bob, you lack to get me," yelled Bonner, running back to his command.

Sims got a bucket of water and extinguished the flames, then filled the bucket again and returned to the house unconcernedly.

The night vigil set in. All through the hours of darkness great fires flamed toward the sky lighting the house and its surroundings lest anyone escape unnoticed. On Christmas morning a party of besiegers left for Bladon Springs to drag back an old Confederate cannon while horsemen scoured the county for powder with which to load it.

At noon came the message that the cannon was only eight miles away and would be available by two o'clock.

A man bearing a white flag approached the house. He was beckoned to come on and he stood at the door and talked to Bob Sims. He said that the besiegers did not wish to harm the women and children but that they would be obliged to fire cannonballs into the house unless its occupants surrendered. Bob asked the messenger to return in a half-hour for his decision. Behind the prophet the messenger could see the main room of the house. The furniture had been placed against the walls to aid in stopping bullets, and the children sat on the floor in the middle of the room.

Before the half-hour was over Bob sent his own messenger to say that he and his men would surrender if they would be taken under guard to the Butler jail, and if the women and children would not be harmed. These terms were agreed to, though the Sims women had been manfully using rifles in the defense, and a guard of fifty was deputized to escort the prisoners to jail. Then the Simses and the Savages walked out of the house, Bob's wife by his side. Neal Sims, though, had disappeared and was not to be found.

The cavalcade got under way riding toward Butler and had ridden perhaps two miles when their erstwhile comrades galloped upon them, fifteen hundred of them. The fifty guards made scant resistance—indeed, they had been expecting to be overtaken. Then the whole vast swarm swung about and retraced its steps to the big oak tree that grew at the crossroads in front of the James Sims house—still standing on what is now known as Prophet Hill. Never did Christmas tree bear more grisly ornaments! One by one the crowd strung up the Savages and the Simses until only old Bob Sims, prophet leader of the Simsites, was left. He climbed up onto the seat of the old-fashioned road-cart that was being used as a gallows and placed the noose about his own neck. Then he stood straight and defiant, his white beard blowing a trifle in the December wind.

"Old Lady," he said to his weeping wife who sat by a front wheel of the cart, "get my dinner ready for me on the third day from today. At that hour I shall arise and walk upon this earth again."

He turned to the men beside him.

"I am not afraid of death. Don't tie my hands and I'll not catch at the rope."

But they tied his hands and as they did so he called out:

"I can lick any man here in fair fight. Will anyone try it with me?"

Then he began to dance a jig on the wagon seat. The sorry business of preparation quite done, he stood alone.

"Have you anything to say?"

"Only that you're a sickly bunch of cowards. Look," he held his roped hands out behind him, "I have the steadiest hand of any here. And I can whistle the loudest tune." A shrill piping came from his lips—the notes of *Home Sweet Home*. It stopped suddenly.

The last time I was in Butler I stopped by an attorney's office to have a chat and to confirm some of the facts in my history of the Sims War.

"Yes," said the lawyer, "that's about the way it was, and I ought to know, for I was a sizable lad then, old enough to know when my father was up to something."

"Now *my* father," said his partner, "never missed a hanging from the time he came back from the War Between the States until he died in nineteen-fourteen."

"That accounts for two out of the two thousand," I said.

"You misunderstand us," said my friend. "We don't know who any of those two thousand were. Still my father was an active man interested in most of the things that went on around here."

"I don't misunderstand you at all," I said, "but there's a question unsolved in that story. What became of Neal Sims, the brother that was missing when they surrendered?"

"They say he's livin' over in Texas under another name right now—as decent and law-abidin' a citizen as you'd want to see. The sheriff here just a few years ago wanted to organize a band of night-riders and go over there on the q.t. and hang him. Some of us wouldn't let him—said we'd had enough hangin's in this county—especially after they took Mr. Will Sims, who was my school-teacher, out o' the jail and hanged him when he hadn't even taken part in the McMellon business. That was a week or so after Bob was hanged. It was a bad job and I hate to tell you about such unpleasant things happening in Choctaw County when most of the time it's as uneventful and pleasant a place to live in as you could ask for."

"You're right," said his partner emphatically. "Of course there was the time when that boy killed himself over his best girl. His father never believed it, always said her old man shot him from the doorway and then fixed him to look like he shot himself. The two of 'em met downtown one day and the boy's father nearly killed the other with an umbrella—cut him up so he was in the hospital for weeks."

"That was just before one of our farm boys here shot his father for openin' the gates and lettin' his horses graze over his new pasture. Some say he was justified, though, because the old man had a gun and threatened to shoot him for bein' a disobedient son—though he was a good thirty years old at the time and a deacon in the—"

"But we ain't had nothin' recent," interrupted the partner, "except last week that little moonshine business one of our town lads got mixed up in. He was a sort of good-lookin' boy an' he started runnin' liquor just to get money to carry his girl to parties, they say. Anyway some of the white lightnin' crowd around Desotoville and Climax got the idea he'd sold 'em out somehow. He didn't come home for a couple of days and his folks finally found his body out in the woods near here. They had wired him upright between two big tree trunks and set a fire under him—burned him to a crisp."

"Well, aside from one or two things like that once in a while this is a decent, home-loving county," said my friend, "and I'd hate to have you get a wrong impression of it. If you could only come down here and live among us for a little while you'd realize that we are a peace-loving, serene people."

"I don't doubt it," I said hastily, "and I'm obliged for the invitation, but I'll have to be going now. I've got a special reason for wanting to be back in Livingston before sundown."

3. THE PROPHETESS OF EUTAW

Nancy Vaughn said that her story would be written into a book, the Lord had told her so. Now that it appears in print the least of her prophecies finds fulfillment.

The first time I saw her Aunt Nancy was seventy-five years old, but she was slim and straight—standing in her cabin door in her starched white prophet-robes. She clasped my hand firmly and she looked into my eyes and spoke with the assurance and simplicity of all true prophets. The Lord, she said, had told her I was coming.

The Lord had begun speaking to Nancy Vaughn more than sixty years before our meeting. Her mother, who had belonged to Colonel Irving in Greensboro, had not believed the story that little Nancy heard a voice when there were no people around. So Nancy went on hearing the voice and not telling anybody about it for many years. Indeed, she was a grown woman before she knew it was the Lord's voice and understood what it was saying. Then she heard it distinctly:

"Dress yourself in a white robe," said the Lord, "I'll tell you how to make it; and go tell the Pope I say his time is nigh."

"I'll go, Lord," said Nancy, "but I was born in slave times and all I been doin' since the war is a little washin' for the white folks here in Eutaw, and I ain't got no money."

"You go and see Sister Jane about that," said the Lord.

So Nancy made herself a white robe according to what the Lord told her and she walked over to see Sister Jane.

"Sis Jane," said Nancy, "the Lord tol' me to dress this way and go tell the Pope his time is nigh. I tol' him I ain't got no money and he say, 'You go see Sister Jane about that.'"

"Well," said Sister Jane, "if the Lord say so, must *be* so. This is my house and land and maybe we can get enough money from it somehow."

Sister Jane got six hundred dollars for a mortgage on her place and she made herself a white robe and she and Aunt Nancy went to Rome. They took a steamboat from Mobile and then a train.

"We got a 'terpreter when we got to the city of Rome," Nancy said, "and he took us to the Pope. 'Course the Pope didn't speak nothin' but Latin an' all we could speak was English, so the 'terpreter had to tell him what I said. First we kneeled down and then the Pope come in an' I riz up an' I said, 'Pope, you ain't been rulin' right an' your time is nigh.'

"The 'terpreter tol' him what I said and then the Pope said somethin' in Latin, I never did know what it was. Then we

went away from there an' took a steamboat an' went to Jerusalem an' Japan an' come home. An' by the time we got back
to Eutaw the Pope was dead. An' the trip cost the Lord just
seven hundred an' eighty-eight dollars."

Neither Aunt Nancy nor Sister Jane ever elaborated on the
details of their trip so far as I know. This is the story of their
journey as they have told it to me again and again and as they
have told it to many others. The facts of it have been authen-
ticated.

When Aunt Nancy and Sister Jane came back to the Black
Belt, Sister Jane went on with her washing and ironing and
planting. She never got her land back. It was sold when the
mortgage came due. But Aunt Nancy heard the Lord's voice
plainly again. He spoke to her deep down in her heart and
told her to go to Birmingham and tell the folks there that they
were wicked and a great trouble was coming to destroy them.

A big crowd gathered in 18th Street while the black woman
in the white robe was prophesying destruction. Aunt Nancy
spoke calmly and certainly, and fear came upon her hearers.
Then a policeman forced his way through the people and arrested her.

"They put me in jail, honey. Throngin' the streets was the
charge. I tol' 'em one woman couldn't throng the streets but
they put me in jail anyhow. An' I tol' 'em, if'n you don't let
me out of this here a big wind'll come, bigger'n the tornado
that blew the year the stars fell, an' it'll blow the city of Birmingham down. Then in a little while a black cloud come up.
It looked like a storm, an' a man come with some keys an' said
he wasn't goin' to take no chances an' he let me out."

After the Birmingham prophecy Nancy Vaughn wandered
the dusty road of the Black Belt, barefoot, white-robed. She
stopped at roadside cabins to foretell dire events. She preached

against the wicked in the streets of the towns—and the jail doors of Demopolis and Greensboro and Uniontown opened to receive her. When she needed food or clothes she entered white folks' stores and told their owners, "The Lord say to give me this." Usually, since her needs were modest, the suggestion was enough. People laughed at her and made fun of her prophecies but they were afraid of her, too. Once a storekeeper replied: "Then tell the Lord to send me a dollar for it," but her dignity and her concern over what she considered a sacrilege broke down his resistance.

I saw Aunt Nancy for the last time at the end of a hot Alabama summer day. Her weathered cabin was a golden brown in the mellow light. The white robe stood out against it in sharp relief.

"I tell you, chile, somethin' terrible goin' happen. I don't jest know what 'tis, but hit's goin' to be somethin' awful. So take care of yourself an' behave yourself an' the Lord bless yuh, honey."

She opened her door, standing before the dark interior of the cabin. Her robe was a silver glimmer in the blackness within when I left her.

Now the news has come that Aunt Nancy Vaughn is dead. White folks write me that they miss her on the Black Belt roads, miss her calm sure voice, her oddly worded prophecies. Her death, they tell me, was as strange as her life. It is something from which to make a religious legend. Had she been a white woman of another age she might already be destined for sainthood. The white robe, symbol of her devoted life, became a terrible winding sheet. It caught against her stove one night and Nancy Vaughn left the world she had admonished in a pillar of flame.

CHAPTER VII

White Man's Nigger: I

ANTIMO WILLIAMS is about seventy years old. All his life he has been pleasing white men. By this time he knows how so well that he can take any liberties he wants to with them and they just laugh at him. Antimo is very black. His deep-set shrewd eyes are quick with understanding though they gleam from a heavy face whose flat nose and thick lips give it a brutal quality. His neck is thick and powerful and his long arms swing forward from the sides of his barrel chest like a gorilla's. Legends have grown up about his strength in the old days when he was young. He says he could carry a full-grown cow across his shoulders without difficulty, and there are those who will swear they have seen him do it.

I had heard a hundred tales of Antimo before I ever saw him. Not a white gentleman ever waited on a deer-stand in the Dollarhide Swamps but boasts his intimacy with Antimo. He has seen more men blooded with the crimson dye from their first buck than any man alive. Many a rider, trotting back to camp in the evening with the air turning cold and a slow rain falling, hollas "Antimo!" and is cheered by the distant deep-voiced bay, "Yes, *Sir*, boss, Ise a-comin'." Then, while Antimo unsaddles the horses and feeds them and rubs them down, there is a drying out beside the fire Antimo has built, a warming of the soul with the toddy Antimo has mixed, a feasting of the stomach with the steaks and biscuits Antimo has cooked.

It has become a kind of tradition in the Black Belt that no public celebration is complete without Antimo. He hasn't missed a big barbecue in years. And not a white man goes to one who doesn't sooner or later get down where the red coals are glowing in the ground and the smell of the whole cow roasting on them is a gourmet's ecstasy, to pass a word with the shambling black man who bosses the job.

After the speech-making and the singing are over and the whole crowd is stuffed with good beef and maybe a little edged with corn liquor there is always a circle of white men around the soft embers to hear Antimo's stories. Some of the listeners may have heard them a score of times at huntings on the Dollarhide or pigstickings in Eutaw but, like every real artist, Antimo improves with each performance. A classic may not be heard too often.

Usually the story-telling starts off with an anecdote told by one of the white gentlemen. It is always the same one, probably because it is the only experience which Antimo modestly refrains from telling himself:

"I reckon y'all remember the time Antimo went up a tree and brought down five coons, all alive. I was down on the Dollarhide on one of Mr. Alison's hunts and Joe Searcy came in from his stand one night and said he had seen an old coon and four young ones playing around a big oak tree. He couldn't shoot 'em because it's against the law to shoot anything from a deer-stand except buck, gobbler or wildcat.

"Antimo heard him tellin' about it and he says: 'Let's go get him and catch the young 'uns and anybody that wants can have one and I can get a dollar apiece in Eutaw for the leftovers.'

"So we went to the tree and Antimo climbed it and there sure enough was the coon den. He peeps inside and he hollers down to us: 'They sho' is still in here, but how's I gwine git them coons down alive?'

"Joe hollers back: 'Tie 'em'; and Antimo takes off his suspenders and tears 'em up into strings. Then he breaks off a limb and begins pokin' around in the den but no Mr. Coon comes out. So he quits that and climbs a little higher to a big fork in the tree. He gets out his knife, scrapes off some bark, lights it with a match, and starts a fire with it in the krotch. After it's been burnin' a while he reaches up with his bare hands, grabs a live coal and drops it in the coon den. Same time it landed out comes a coon and mighty mad. Antimo grabs him, stuffs his coat in the mouth of the hollow to keep the other coons in, and ties him up. The coon hollers and bites and scratches, but Antimo won't let go till he's tied him. Then he drops him to the ground, takes his coat out the hole and drops another piece of fire in. Five times he does it and then he comes slidin' down the tree, all scratched and bitten from his face to his waist, his shirt torn off, and more of his trousers gone than was decent."

There is a murmur of laughter and admiration. The men around the fire all know how a cornered coon can fight.

"Wouldn't touch one of 'em with a ten-foot pole," says somebody. "Antimo, tell us about the time you fit Mr. Clay Dunlap's cow. Tyin' up coons must'a' seemed easy alongside of that."

"Nigger come down the road one night," says Antimo, grinning. "He say Mist' Clay Dunlap done give up on that fightin' cow o' his. Ever since she hooked that black boy an' chased Mist' Clay over the pasture fence he ain't had no use fer that cow. So now he say anybody kin tie that cow kin have her.

"Next mawnin' Mist' Clay was a-settin' on his front gallery an' he sees me corroboratin' 'round with a rope an' he say, 'Antimo, what you doin' here so early?'

"I say: 'Mist' Dunlap, I hears that you say anybody what kin tie that fightin' cow o' yours kin have her.'

"Mist' Dunlap say: 'That's so, Antimo. That cow's hooked a lot o' people an' chased me out'n my own pasture an' it's got so I'm jest tired o' that cow. Anybody kin tie her kin have her.'

"An' I say: 'Mist' Dunlap, you mean that?' an' he say: 'Sho''
an' I say, 'That's my cow.' I opened the pasture gate and I
said: 'Mist' Dunlap, where is that fightin' cow?' He pinted way
back in the pasture an' I walked over there an' I walked by
that cow an' that cow didn't stop eatin' grass. Then I come on
back a little closer an' that cow didn't stop eatin' again, an' I
'lowed Mist' Dunlap ain't pinted out the right cow. But about
that time I heerd somethin' an' I looked around an' that cow
had got het up and yonder she come abulgin'. But that was
what I wanted that cow to do, so I jest turned around and took
my stand as still as a stump. Jest when she was goin' t' stick
her horns in me I steps aside and jest when I steps aside I puts
out my right hand and grab her nose an' my left hand an' grab
her horns an' I just flings that cow head over heels. When
she hits the ground I turn her head back an' set right down
on that cow an' she can't do nothin' but bellow. An' then I ties
her feets together an' then I ties her head to her side an' I was
just 'bout ready to pick that cow up an' fotch her out o' the
pasture when I looks up an' there is Mist' Dunlap an' he say:
'Nigger, git right off o' my cow.'

"I say: 'Mist' Dunlap, is you gwine back on yo' word?' an'
Mist' Dunlap he say: 'Nigger, you get out o' my pasture, you
ain't gwine have my cow!' Then he turns and walks back up
to his sto' an' I unties that cow and follows him an' I say: 'Mist'
Dunlap' (an' I takes off my hat), 'is you gwine treat a po' nigger that-a-way?'

"An' he say: 'Nigger, can't you take a joke?' an' he goes
back in the sto' an' I thought sho' he's gwin fotch me a dollar
an' he comes out an' gives me a nickel's worth o' chewin'
tobacco. I puts that chewin' tobacco in my pocket an' I say:
'Much oblige, Mist' Dunlap. Next time you has a fightin' cow
I hopes to God she hooks yuh!' "

There is a roar of laughter from the white men. Mr. Clay Dunlap and his thrifty practices are known to them all. The black fire-tenders look a little frightened at that last remark. The whites of their eyes shine in the light and they glance quickly and covertly at each other. But Antimo is grinning. He knows what he can say to the white gentlemen. He understands them and they think they understand him and all is well between them.

"What's that word you used a while back, Antimo?" says a white man slyly. "You said you were 'corroborating 'round,' what does that word mean?"

Antimo smiles. "Boss, it's this way. I ain't got no education and so I uses words for what they sounds like 'stead o' what they mean. I'm all time havin' to listen to white folks and when the big court in Eutaw meets I goes there and listens to the big lawyers an' they do a lot o' talkin' about corroboratin' an' I 'lows that's the best word I ever *did* hear."

Antimo knows that they will laugh and he is satisfied to have his words sound like what he means.

"Antimo," says the white-haired judge, "tell 'em 'bout that time you treed a hant."

Alabama's most famous raconteur is in full swing now. His teeth glisten in the firelight. His black face creases in wrinkles, his eyeballs are gleamingly black spots against their milk-white backgrounds.

"Esaw Bell come down to my house jest before sundown an' he say: 'Let's go coonhuntin'.' I 'lowed to him it's Sat'day night an' we can't hunt after twelve an' I likes to hunt all night if the varmints is running. He say with his dogs we can cotch all we want by twelve o'clock an' not hunt Sunday. So I tells that yellow boy o' mine, my grandson, git on my mule an' go tell Henry Webb to come jine us. Henry's the best tree-climber an' coon-shaker in these parts. I reckon they ain't a coon he can't shake down onct he puts his mind to it. He come down right after supper an' we started out. None o' my dogs could run coons much, but Esaw had a couple o' good coon dogs an' I had that bugle dog o' mine an' he sho' was a fighter. His ma was Mist' Barnwell's big shepherd dog an' his pa was one o' them bugle hounds. He took after his ma, though, an' wouldn't run like a huntin' dog but when it come to fightin' coons he'd kill any of 'em.

"So after hit was good an' dark we started out an' when we got in them big swamps we got down off our mules. We come to a creek an' jest then them dogs of Esaw's struck a track an' sho' did have a good race an' they treed him about the mouth of the creek. Henry Webb, he climbed plumb to the top o' the tree an' he shook an' shook an' the coon fell out. My bugle dog grabbed him an' the other dogs piled in an' we killed that coon right now.

" 'Bout a mile up the creek we hit another track an' that coon run us 'round the edge of a pond an' it took a long time to tree him an' then Henry shook him out. He was a big coon and put up a big fight but finally my bugle dog an' the rest stretched him out.

"When we had him in the bag I looked up at the seven stars and I said to Esaw it's 'bout twelve o'clock an' we can't hunt on Sunday 'cause it's bad luck an' Esaw said that's right. So we started back home. But when we got over there by Sid's New Ground them dogs struck another track an' I told Esaw to blow his horn and Esaw blew his horn but them dogs was so hot in behind that coon they didn't pay no attention, jest kept runnin' that coon right towards the river till they treed it. We went over there an' the dogs was clean down on the river bank on a big drift that the river left behind after it was up. They was scratchin' an' barkin' an' my bugle dog had scratched near out o' sight an' was barkin' like he seen him. I fetched me a stick an' I held my bugle dog back an' I started feelin' 'round an' the coon began growlin' louder'n any coon I ever heard. Sounded like a thunderstorm was under there. I give him a jab with the stick an' the next thing I see the coon run out from the other side and run up a cottonwood tree right beside the water.

"I told Henry and Esaw to get the dogs there an' I'd step down to the water an' shake the tree. Lord bless you, at the first fling o' that tree that coon done jumped right in the river. But he didn't start swimmin'. He jest stood there a-treadin' water like a man an' when my bugle dog got to him that coon jest grabbed him right behind the ears an' pushed that dog under water an' jumped right on his head. I couldn't see nothing of that bugle dog but his tail. I reckon he would of drowned but Henry Webb's dog got there 'bout then and that coon grabbed him behind the ears an' pushed him under water an' jumped on him jest like he done the bugle dog. Every dog that come after him he done that-a-way an' the dog would come up coughin' and swim ashore an' start barkin' along the bank. So I say: 'If'n that coon don't come out o' there I'se gwin after him.' He heerd me say that an' he come swimmin' right up to the bank an' crawls up on it an' begins fightin' all them dogs. My lands, they fit and they fit all 'round there an' every onct in a while that coon would bite one of them dogs right on their nose an' the dog would run off hollerin'. So I fixes to stomp him to death, an' I runs an' I jumps right on him but that coon jumps sideways an' I lands right on my bugle dog. There I was stompin' jest like I'd stomped a thousand coons but I couldn't git on that one.

"So I grabbed a big stick an' I made for that coon an' he took a big jump an' landed 'most halfway 'cross the river and went swimmin' to the other side growlin' to himself like rollin' thunder all the way. When he got there he climbed up on the sand bar an' shook himself and give a big growl an' went pacin' up into the bushes.

"Then I looked 'cross the river an' I says to Esaw: 'Ain't that that broke-off oak tree where the nigger got kotched that got drownded up at Lock Six? An' ain't that that sand bar where them white folks buried that nigger?'

"An' Esaw said: 'Sho' is!'

"An' I said: *'That's that nigger's hant!'*

"An' I looked 'round and I saw Henry Webb just leavin' that bank. Then me an' Esaw got over that bank 'most as fast as Henry Webb an' I said to Esaw: 'Untie them mules but don't take no long time 'bout it.' An' Esaw untied Henry's mule an' ours an' we sho' made 'em run an' when we got back out there in Sid's New Ground we come up with Henry Webb an' we asked him what was the matter. He said his mule had got away and he was tryin' to catch him. I say to Henry: 'No use lyin', nigger. You know you been runnin' from that hant an' you never untied that mule because Esaw did.'

"And then I look up there again and I see the seven stars and it was a long way past twelve o'clock and I says: 'That's what we git fer huntin' on Sunday.' We sho' did git home quick an' if that warn't a hant we fitted that night I don' know what it was 'cause that thing whipped six dogs an' three niggers an' I never seen a coon before could get away from my bugle dog an' I know I ain't never let a coon away in my life. Besides I knowed it was a hant, 'cause every time I jumped on him he warn't there."

The tale of the treed hant is usually the evening's last. The white folks will be going now and soon Antimo will fetch a pail of water from the branch and pour it on the hissing embers. Then he will untie his patient mule, whistle for his bugle dog and the trio will set out on the journey homeward. It may be fifteen or twenty miles to the little dark low-spreading cabin on the edge of the swamp, but the seven stars are over him, his mule under him, his dog beside him.

I paid Antimo a special visit not long ago. Guided by negro children along the way I drove over a plank road, across two cotton patches, through a flowing branch and finally arrived at the cabin just after sunset. Antimo's woman, a strange, gnarled little creature, came out to meet me.

"He ain't home yit," she said. "He went to a barbecue over by Boligee yesterday. Reckon somebody took him home with him." Three children clung to her skirts, the oldest hardly five.

"Those Antimo's children?" I asked.

"Yes, sir, boss," she said proudly.

A sudden whirring noise beside the gallery made me jump, and with a sickening sense that I had moved too late.

The little black woman laughed.

"It's all right, boss. They's in a cage."

On a bench beside me was a box of wire netting. In it three rattlesnakes writhed about, hardly distinguishable in the gathering dusk.

"What are they for?" I said a little tremulously.

"Dr. Brooks over at the university told Antimo he'd give him three dollars apiece for 'em. Reckon he works some conjure with 'em."

"But how does he catch them? With a net or a forked stick or a noose?"

"No, sir, boss. He just picks 'em up by the back o' the neck. He say we gwine to be rich 'cause he knows where there's a lot of 'em near here."

"I'll be going back to Livingston," I said. "I'm sorry I missed Antimo. Tell him to come see me when he can."

"I'll tell him," she said, and as she spoke we saw him coming striding along beside his mule, the bugle dog, tail waving, in advance.

"Howdy, boss," he said. "I heerd you was here an' I hustled along. Thought you might like to take these here snakes back to Dr. Brooks with you when you go."

"Antimo," I said hastily and severely. "I'm going to be in Livingston a long time and I'm not going back to the university."

His eyes twinkled.

"I reckon I kin git 'em up there," he said.

"I just came by to tell you I was going to put you and some of your stories in a book," I said.

He did not seem surprised. He reflected a moment.

"White folks sho' do like 'em. They sho' do laugh at 'em." His heavy face twisted into an infectious smile. Then he laughed.

Listening to his husky, melodious bellow and looking into his little bright eyes, I suddenly knew I was listening to a happy man. He lives as he wants to live. His white friends provide him with all of his meager material needs and desires. Few people, moreover, become legends in their own day. Yet I know and Antimo knows that if he were to die tomorrow he would be remembered a long time. Already fantastic tales are spreading over the canebrake about his prodigious strength, his ability to hold fire in his bare hands and not be burned, his uncanny marksmanship with his old shotgun, his supernatural power over rattlesnakes, his familiarity with spirits, his immunity from the white man's rules. Antimo has made his impression on Black Belt life. After the lawyers and the judges are forgotten the tales and the teller will be recalled.

CHAPTER VIII

Miss Polly

"I'M hatin' this special trip of yours," said Tennant. "Somehow I feel like I'm lettin' somebody down—some of my own people."

"You promised," I said inexorably, "and you know I don't want to let anybody down—not even you."

"I reckon I'm in for it." The Ford slewed about in the heavy dust as we saw a wooden arrow with the faint legend "Sumterville."

For a few miles we rode in silence and then stopped. We were in front of a plantation house, its tall fluted pillars gray and rotting with age. The road had dared to come within a few yards of it, disdainful of its vanished acres. I felt that there was something puzzling and ugly about the house. Then I saw that the great middle entrance had been boarded up with unpainted weathered lumber. On either side of it were plain oblong openings, and gray unpaneled doors were swung to over them like the shut eyelids of a corpse. Close by the roadside stood a wire fence, breast high, and there was no gate in it. About ten yards from each wall the wire mesh ran its unbroken length along the sides and vanished in the rear, shutting the house off completely as far as we could see.

"Good mornin', Miss Polly," said Tennant loudly. Then I saw her, sitting in a rocking chair beside the door. Her gray hair and her gray dress blended her into the aging white of the wall behind her and made her almost as invisible as a bird of protective coloring in a thicket. She was rocking back and forth and did not answer.

"Good mornin', Miss Polly," shouted Tennant.

Suddenly she straightened her back which had seemed to follow the curve of the rocker.

"We have so few distinguished guests," she said in a clear voice, "living as we do at some distance from Mobile, that I am doubly happy to welcome you to our home."

"We just came by to see the haunted house, Miss Polly," said Tennant. "We can only stop a minute."

"I trust that you will be with us a week or so," she said as if she had not heard. Though her face was turned toward us, she seemed not to see us. "My daughter who is more active than I will be glad to show you to your rooms."

She clapped her hands and called sharply: "Emma Jane! Emma Jane!"

In a moment one of the twin gray doors opened and a little girl stepped out. She wore a neat red and white gingham dress. A red hair ribbon tied in a large bow sat on her little head. Suddenly I saw that her black hair was short and curled over her head in little ringlets, and her face was a yellowish brown.

"Emma Jane," said Miss Polly, "welcome these gentlemen to our home and make them comfortable. They will be with us for some time, we hope."

"We came to see the haunted house," said Tennant, a little brusquely.

"You'll have to climb the fence. They ain't no gate," said the little girl sullenly.

We climbed and descended to the yard. As we approached the steps Miss Polly lifted a slim withered hand though no light came into her troubled eyes. Tennant went swiftly to her and took it.

"It's nice to see you, Miss Polly," he said. "This gentleman has come from a long way off."

She moved her hand from his to mine but she did not speak.

The little girl had opened the door at the right of the boarded-up main entrance.

"You can only see this side," she said shrilly as if we were arguing with her. "My mammy's in the other side and my pap won't let nobody but him and me in there."

"I thought—" I said in surprise, but Tennant shook his head at me and I stopped short.

We entered a high dark chamber, apparently once used as a reception room. There was a white marble fireplace at one end and facing it at the other was a long mirror in an elaborately carved wooden frame that had once been gilded. Something had hit the mirror in its center so hard that a circle about a foot in diameter showed the bare wall on the other side. The rest of it was cracked into long splinters leading away from this point of impact. A leather trunk, old and sagging, stood in a corner. It was the only furniture. The three windows were covered by outer blinds but one of these had partially fallen from its hinges, admitting a little light.

We moved through a graceful arched doorway into the room behind. It had probably been the dining room but now in one corner stood a white iron cot on which there was a welter of rumpled sheets and blankets.

"This is all you can see," said our guide. "It ain't safe to go upstairs no more." She pointed to a pillared gallery on which double doors of glass had once opened. Most of the panes were gone and they had been patched with boards.

"That's where the ghost used to come." Her eyes grew wide. "I ain't never near here at night, believe *me*."

Tennant tried the door and found it open.

"Run along and play a while," he said. "We'll just sit down on this porch and rest a bit."

She left us reluctantly, suspiciously.

"I thought that old woman said this girl was her daughter," I said.

Tennant sat down on the gallery floor and leaned his back against a pillar.

"It's a long story," he said; "you might as well sit down, too.

"Miss Polly hasn't been around as long as you'd think," he went on. "My father and mother say she used to be a pretty little old girl down in Mobile when they were children and used to go down there to visit Aunt Valerie. The steamboats were still runnin' then. Must have been their last year or so. The *Hattie B. Moore* was the best of 'em and when she came down the river churnin' up the yellow water she was a pretty sight and folks at Mobile used to go over to the dock to see her land. Well, one time there was a smart young fellow aboard her from up around Tuscaloosa—his parents were Yankees and poor folks and nobody knew much about 'em. He was standing on the forward deck watching the niggers on land throw ropes to the crew and pull the boat up to the dock when he saw the prettiest girl he'd ever seen. She was carrying a ruffled parasol and wearing a flowered dress and she was mighty excited at seeing all the shiny brass on the boat and the strange people and hearing all the noise. They used to tell about it right after they got married and everybody thought it was the kind of romance you read about.

"Miss Polly was an orphan and she had quite a little income from the money her father left her—so his bein' poor didn't make any difference. But her bein' rich did. He had ideas about bein' landed gentry and havin' a big house and all, and the first thing anybody knew she'd bought this place up here, eight hundred acres, and built this house. But even that wasn't enough for him. He made her buy him some horses and he began racin' 'em at the meets in Mobile. He lost every nickel she'd give him on that. So when she wouldn't shell out any more he said if he was goin' to manage this place she'd have to deed it over to him. She got up some spunk then and said she wouldn't do it. When he found out she meant it he up and left her.

"Miss Polly stayed right on here pretendin' nothin' had happened but she had to sell some of the land and the place didn't yield much of a living. She had one letter from him, from some place in Texas. Said he wouldn't come back until she changed her mind. But she didn't write back.

"After about two years the ghost came. She'd be sittin' at her dinner after dark in that room behind us and all of a sudden a white shape would appear on this porch, swayin' back and forth and moanin'. At first she tried to pretend it was just imagination but her niggers didn't wait to light out and they wouldn't come back. The thing scared her so she hired a white woman to come and stay with her, but the first night the woman jumped up and ran screamin' down the road all the way to town and wouldn't come back.

"She begged some of the men in town to take pity on her and come and help her. Finally some of 'em did go out a couple of nights but nothin' happened. As sure as there was a man in the house—no ghost. And then the long-lost husband showed up. He said he wasn't afraid of ghosts and he sure would like to come back to her but he wouldn't do it unless she'd deed the place over to him. She held out for a while but at last she gave up and he moved in.

"The first thing he did was to have the main hall of the house boarded up so nobody could get into it or across it—and he had those two front doors cut like you saw them there. Then he moved some mulatto whore he'd brought with him from New Orleans into the other side of the house. She's been living there ever since. That's her girl brought us in here."

"But why," I said, "why did Miss Polly call that negro child her daughter?"

"Crazy," said Tennant. "She's been pretending for a long time now that things are all right. She can pretend just one thing more."

"Let's get out of here," I said. "I don't like this at all. And I don't like ghost stories. It's getting towards evening and I don't want to see anything white and swaying for a long time."

"You won't," Tennant said. "And what's more you don't suppose I brought you out of our way this far to tell you a ghost story?"

"Well?" I said.

"A few years ago a lot of the men from Sumterville had a possum hunt. They found one in a tree about a half-mile from here and they couldn't shake him down. So old Antimo, the nigger, climbed up the tree and dropped him. Well, when he was climbin' down he saw the tree had a hollow spot in it near the first crotch and he saw a piece of white cloth in it. He stuck his hand down there and pulled it out and brought it down with him. It was quite a big piece cut up and sewed a bit and at first the men thought it might be a Ku Klux robe that somebody from Tuscaloosa County or around there had hid. But down in one corner was a tag sewed on it with the name of somebody that owned it or the store that sold it or some such information. They couldn't make out anything but three letters at the end. The rest had been washed out so you couldn't read it. But the letters were T-e-x and there was a period after 'em. Now, let's go or Mary Louise will be sore about the fried chicken bein' cold."

As we passed the old gray woman on the front gallery, Tennant said:

"Good night, Miss Polly."

"We have enjoyed your visit," she said in her high clear

voice. "It has been very pleasant to have you with us for a few days. I regret that my husband is not here at the moment to wish you Godspeed." Her eyes were empty and dull.

"Isn't there such a thing as public opinion in this section?" I said as we started off. "I should think his white neighbors would resent his living with the mulatto in the same house his wife lives in."

"Well, I reckon they couldn't do that," said Tennant, "but they sure would raise hell if it were the other way round."

CHAPTER IX

Brer Rabbit Multiplies

"CENTENNIAL," I said, "I've walked all the way down here from the Big House on the hottest night 'of the summer to ask you a question."

Centennial threw back his old head and shut his eyes and let laughter pour out.

"Go on, boss, ain't nothin' I know you don't."

"Listen to me. Did you ever hear of a white man named Mr. Joel Harris?"

"He any kin to Mist' Norfleet Harris down Greensboro Avenue?"

"I reckon. He wrote a book about an old uncle, white-headed old fellow, called Uncle Remus."

"Remus?—I ain't never heerd o' any nigger by that name but I reckon I'd know Mist' Harris. All them Harrises look jest like as two peas."

"Well, Mr. Harris put down on paper all the stories Uncle Remus told the children about Brer Rabbit and Brer Fox and Brer Bear and—"

"I bet that old man didn't know half the stories I know 'bout them critters."

"That's what I came down to find out. I want you to tell me one Uncle Remus didn't know."

Centennial laughed again. "What'd I be tellin' a grown man sich-like for? They's for young 'uns—"

"I know, but I want to hear one of 'em."

"Waal, I dunno." He scratched his head. "Jest don't feel

right tellin' baby-stories like that to a man. Wait a minute. Celinda—*Celinda!*"

There was a stir inside the house.

"Yes, grampa."

"You send me a couple o' them young 'uns o' your'n out here—sort o' in-between size—an' hurry up!"

A soft admonishing voice—then two little figures in the doorway.

"Set down here on the step," said Centennial, "an' I'm goin' to tell you 'bout de knee-high man." White teeth in round black faces. "This is de story 'bout de knee-high man:

"De knee-high man lived by de swamp. He wuz alwez a-wantin' to be big 'stead of little. He sez to hisself: 'I is gwinter ax de biggest thing in dis neighborhood how I kin git sizable.' So he goes to see Mr. Horse. He ax him: 'Mr. Horse, I come to git you to tell me how to git big like you is.'

Mr. Horse, he say: 'You eat a whole lot of corn and den you run round and round and round, till you ben about twenty miles and atter a while you big as me.'

So de knee-high man, he done all Mr. Horse tole him. An' de corn make his stomach hurt, and runnin' make his legs hurt and de trying make his mind hurt. And he gits littler and littler. Den de knee-high man he set in his house and study how come Mr. Horse ain't help him none. And he say to hisself: 'I is gwinter go see Brer Bull.'

So he go to see Brer Bull and he say: 'Brer Bull, I come to ax you to tell me how to git big like you is.'

And Brer Bull, he say: 'You eat a whole lot o' grass and den you bellow and bellow and fust thing you know you gits big like I is.'

And de knee-high man he done all Brer Bull tole him. And de grass make his stomach hurt, and de bellowing make his neck hurt and de thinking make his mind hurt. And he git littler and littler. Den de knee-high man he set in his house and he stidy how come Brer Bull ain't done him no good. Atter wile, he hear ole Mr. Hoot Owl way in de swamp preachin' dat de bad peoples is sure gwinter have de bad luck.

Den de knee-high man he say to hisself: 'I gwinter ax Mr. Hoot Owl how I kin git to be sizable,' and he go to see Mr. Hoot Owl.

And Mr. Hoot Owl say: 'What for you want to be big?' and de knee-high man say: 'I wants to be big so when I gits a fight, I ken whup.'

And Mr. Hoot Owl say: 'Anybody ever try to kick a scrap wid you?'

De knee-high man he say naw. And Mr. Hoot Owl say: 'Well den, you ain't got no cause to fight, and you ain't got no cause to be mo' sizable 'an you is.'

De knee-high man says: 'But I wants to be big so I kin see a fur ways.' Mr. Hoot Owl, he say: 'Can't you climb a tree and see a fur ways when you is clim' to de top?'

De knee-high man, he say: 'Yes.' Den Mr. Hoot Owl say: 'You ain't got no cause to be bigger in de body, but you sho' is got cause to be bigger in de BRAIN.' "

"That's a good story, Centennial," I said, "and it's got a good lesson."

"Some on 'em don't always have sech a good 'un. Sometimes de wicked git the best of it. Yes, sir, that slick Brer Rabbit wins out onct ever' so often."

"Tell about that one. Tell about that one," came a duet from the steps.

"Well, chillun, this is the story about Brer Rabbit and Sis Cow:

"Brer Rabbit see Sis Cow an' she have a bag plumb full of milk, an' it's a hot day an' he ain't had nothin' to drink fur a long time. He know 'tain't no use askin' her fur milk 'cause las' year she done 'fused him onct, and when his ole 'oman was sick, too.

Brer Rabbit begun thinkin' mighty hard. Sis Cow is grazin' under a persimmon tree, an' de persimmons is turned yellow, but they ain't ripe enough yit to fall down.

So Brer Rabbit, he say: 'Good mornin', Sis Cow.'

'Good mornin', Brer Rabbit.'

'How is you feelin' dis mornin', Sis Cow?'

'Poly, thank God, Brer Rabbit, I'se jest sorter haltin' 'twix a balk and a breakdown, Brer Rabbit.'

Brer Rabbit express his sympathy and then he say: 'Sis Cow, would you do me the favor to hit this here persimmon tree with yore head an' shake down a few of dem persimmons?'

Sis Cow say 'Sure' an' she hits the tree, but no persimmons come down. They ain't ripe enough yit.

So den Sis Cow git mad an' she go to the top of de hill an' she hists her tail over her back and here she come a bilin'. She hit dat tree *so* hard dat her horns go right into the wood so fur she can't pull 'em out.

'Brer Rabbit,' says Sis Cow, 'I implores you to help me git a-loose.' But Brer Rabbit say: 'No, Sis Cow. I can't git you a-loose. I'm a mighty weakly man, Sis Cow. But I kin 'suage your bag, Sis Cow, and I'm goin' to do it fur you.'

Then Brer Rabbit he go home for his ole 'oman and de chillun an' dey come back to de persimmon tree an' milk Sis Cow and have a big feastin'."

"Tell us one more, tell us one more." Dark eyes roll about on shiny white surfaces—they plead as eagerly as the words.

"You chillun ought to be in bed—but I ain't goin' give yuh advice widout tellin' what comes to folks dat do. So here's why Brer Rabbit wears a 'round-'bout:

"Brer Rabbit wa'n't al'a's de prankin' tricky fellow he is now; not him, he was rankin' wid de biggoty onct. He didn't wear no short tail 'round-'bout dem days. Not him, he was buttoned up befo' and swingin' round de behime same as any long-tail broadcloth nigger preacher is now. He was a good un to rise and foller den. He special lay down de law to his family and his folks.

One night Miss Rabbit she done stepped crost Quarters to beg Miss Goat fer a pail er fresh milk. Mist' Rabbit he had all his chillun settin' in a row befo' him tellin' 'em how dey bes' do to live long and get wise besides.

He stan' wid his back to de fire, he done made 'em chillun cut a big back log and put in de light 'ood chunks a-top dat back log. He wa'n't no worker even den. He stan' frontin' dem little rabbits tellin' 'em dey gotter live to thrive. He say: 'Chillun, al'a's you do dis, think twict befo' yuh speak onct. Lil' rabbits all settin' wid de gooseflesh risin' on 'em foh lack er de heat dey pa keep off 'em standin' befo' 'em.

He say: 'Dar was Sis Mole; she speak fust 'fo' she think, an' she say she too proud to walk on de groun', she was put under de groun'.' He say: 'Dar was Mist' Mockin' Bird, he speak onct 'fo' he think twict, and he up and sing de birds' notes—he keepin' up de interest on dem notes twell yit.' He say: 'Dar was Mist' Robin say he choose a red breast, 'fo' he know what choice was de best.'

All dem lil' rabbits set des as solumn thinkin' twict, 'bout what dey pa say. Miss Rabbit she come er runnin' home crost de Quarters, she say: 'I see smoke! I smell fire!' she burst into de do'. Old Brer Rabbit he yit standin' 'fo' de fire. Brer Rabbit coat tail was burnt off clean 'round de crock, er rim er fire, still creepin' up an' 'round. Miss Rabbit she say: 'Chillun, didn' yuh smell smoke? Chillun, why didn't yuh spoke?'

Lil' rabbits say: 'Us thinkin' 'case Dad tells us to think twict 'fo' us spoke onct.'

Brer Rabbit been wearin' a 'round-'bout ever sence. Chillun, it's might' bad when yo' own advice turn agin you.' "

"Tell us 'bout Brer Fox an' the Goobers, Brer Fox an' the Goobers, Brer Fox an' the Goobers," the children chanted in unison.

"Promise y'all go right spang to bed if I tells you dat un?"

"Yes, grampa, we'll go to bed."

"Well, here 'tis den."

"Brer Rabbit seen Brer B'ar one day a-settin' out to dig goobers wid de donkey draggin' de dump cart. Brer Rabbit say me an' Miss Rabbit an' all them little rabbits sho' is hungry fo goobers. So he go home an' fin' him a red string an' tie it 'roun' his neck an' he run an' lay down in de road where Brer B'ar would be com'n by wid de cart carryin' his sack filled up wid goobers.

By'n by Brer B'ar come along an' de donkey shy so he 'most upset de cart. Brer B'ar git out an' he say: 'If'n it ain't Brer Rabbit as dead as a doornail wid his throat cut. Make good rabbit stew foh me an' Miss B'ar. So he pick up Brer Rabbit an' fling him in de cart an' go on. Soon's his back is turned Brer Rabbit fling out de bag o' goobers an' jump out heself an' run home. On de way he meet Brer Fox an' Brer Fox say: 'Where you git dat bag o' goobers?' an' Brer Rabbit tell him.

Soon's Brer B'ar come in sight er his house, way behime dem dark pines, he holler to his ole 'oman:

'Hello dar. Come heah, Miss B'ar:
Goobers heah; rabbits dar!'

Miss B'ar she run out de cabin. She run 'roun' de dump cart.
She look in. Des a lil' rattlin' load o' goobers in de bottom er
de cart.

She say: 'Goobers gone, rabbit gone, bag gone!'

Brer B'ar tu'n 'roun' an' look, he scratch his head, he say:
'Dat 'ar rabbit done left me bar.'

Nex' day he hitch up de donkey to de dump cart an' start
to de patch to haul up mo' goobers. His ole 'oman, she tell him:
'Watch out, don' drap noddin' on de big road wid dis nex' load.'

Dis time Brer Fox he 'low he'll git his winter's pervisions by
speculatin' wid Brer B'ar's load, labor and land.

Brer Fox git a red string, he do. He tie hit 'roun' his neck.
He go to de big road. Same place what Brer Rabbit done lay
down, Brer Fox he done lay down. He keep des' as still.
D'reckly heah come Brer B'ar wid 'noder heapin' load o' goobers.

De donkey he shy agin at de same place. Brer B'ar he git off
de cart, he look at Brer Fox, he say: 'What dis mean? Un-hum!
Maybe perhaps de same thief what stole my goobers yestiddy.
You got de same like red 'roun' your th'oat. Maybe perhaps
you dead too. He feel Brer Fox, he say: 'You good weight too,
I take you to my ole 'oman, maybe you'll make er good stew.'

Wid dat Brer Fox think he sho' goin' git good chance to git
his fill er goobers.

Brer B'ar he lif' Brer Fox by de behime legs, he say:

'Maybe you be dead, er maybe no,
But I will make you dead fer sho'!'

and wid dat he swing Brer Fox 'roun' and 'roun' and lam his
head 'ginst de wheel er de cart.

Dat lick like to kilt Brer Fox. Hit all he can do to jerk his behime legs loose from Brer B'ar and run home t'rough de dark pines. He had de swole head some seasons frum dat lick. Chillun, de same cunnin' trick ain't apt to work twict."

"An if'n yuh know what dat means you'll git to bed right quick an' not try trickin' yo' great-gran'pappy no mo'."

CHAPTER X

Lynching

THE shadows of the magnolia leaves were black and still on the withered grass. From the high darkness of the reception room in the Big House I looked out past the white flutings of a column into a world of dark shapes and amber light. The drought had lasted so long now that the air was filled with dust that mellowed the sunlight. I heard Tennant's Ford; heard it make the peculiar chugging noise it always makes when it turns off the pike and starts the climb through the cornfield to the house.

Soon it rolled under the magnolia and stopped. Tennant got out—a little slowly, it seemed to me. When he came into the hall he called to Mary Louise, and in a moment I heard her coming down the stair.

"There's trouble over at the store." His voice sounded tired.

"What is it, Tennant?"

"There's a family of niggers live over by Tishabee—four brothers besides the women—name's Wilkinson."

"I've heard of them."

"Well, one of them bought an old phonograph from Tom Shelton Saturday, paid ten dollars for it. When he got it home it wouldn't run and he and his brothers fetched it back this morning and asked for the money. Tom just laughed at them. The niggers had been drinkin' and the first thing anybody knew Henry Wilkinson—that's the eldest—picked up a Coca-Cola bottle and hit Tom over the head with it. Byrd Johnson was standin' there and saw it, and he pulled out his gun to

NATIONAL BOARD YMCA EMPLOYEE BENEFIT PLANS
(formerly headquartered at the YMCA of Metropolitan Chicago)

NOW AFFILIATED WITH THE YMCA OF THE USA

EFFECTIVE JANUARY 1, 1985

our mailing address is:

National Board YMCA Employee Benefits Plans
c/o YMCA of the USA
101 North Wacker Drive
Chicago, Illinois 60606

George A. Georgandas, Director	(312) 269-0560
Janice Protzmann, Associate Director	(312) 269-0561
Connie Karduck, Assistant Director	(312) 269-0562
Chris Willis, Administrative Assistant	(312) 269-0563

shoot Henry when one of the younger boys shot him through the stomach. They say Byrd is dead now."

"What did they do?"

"That bunch of checker-players was in the back room and they came pilin' out just as the niggers started to run. They caught the youngest one—and strung him up to a tree. He's hangin' over the road out there now. They think the rest of 'em are in a cabin up the road a piece. They've got it surrounded—say they're goin' to burn it."

"It's makin' me sick."

"I wouldn't have told you except I was afraid somebody else would say something. And we don't want to let *him* know."

I knew a thumb had jerked in my direction and I rose and tiptoed back into my room. I lay on the high white surface of the four-post bed feeling the soft monotony of the heat.

Another car drove up and stopped—almost under my window. After a moment I heard steps in the hall and then a high, tense voice.

"Mist' Tennant, you reckon we kin use your telephone? We want to git them dogs over from Mississippi."

"Why, I thought you didn't need 'em, Fred."

"We did, too, when we burn up that cabin, but they wa'n't no signs o' the black apes in the ashes. So I better be phonin' for them dogs. Reckon they won't git here 'fore six or so."

I heard Mary Louise's voice, unnatural and thin:

"But, Mr. Smith, I'm afraid it's out of order. I couldn't get central all day."

"I better make a try at it, anyway, please, ma'am. Can't waste any more time."

"It's just to the right of the stairs," said Tennant.

Steps in the hall again, and then Tennant's voice—almost a whisper:

"You shouldn't have said that."

"I couldn't help it," said Mary Louise desperately. "It's horrible for them to get the dogs by usin' our phone."

"Sh-sh—listen. We'd better get our niggers in from the lower forty."

"Shall I ring the bell?"

"And let everybody know? Send William and have him say we've got something for them to do near the house."

There was a long pause. I could hear Fred Smith's voice dimly as he talked to a man who lives in Mississippi and keeps bloodhounds. After a while he stopped and then came the starting roar of the car outside my window.

"Much obliged, folks," called Fred Smith. The house was silent.

I lay still and tried to sleep—but my mind wandered ceaselessly over the hot dusty road, through the wide cornfields. Finally I rose, bathed, dressed, and went out to sit under the magnolia and wait for supper time. The air was motionless.

There was a rustling in the cornfield behind the house. Tall tops near the edge were swaying violently. Then a small black boy came out and ran toward the house.

"William," I called.

He stopped and turned a hopeless face toward me.

"Come here, William," I said. Slowly he came.

"I know what happened this morning," I said. "Mr. Tennant and Miss Mary Louise don't want me to, but I do. Have you heard any more? I'll give you a quarter to tell me if you'll not tell anybody I asked."

"They killed my aunt," said William breathlessly. "My Uncle Lafe, he's deaf, and he was drivin' Aunt Susan into town. White folks say 'stop 'at car' but Uncle Lafe he don't hear. White folks shoot through the back of the car an' kill

Aunt Susan. Uncle Lafe took on awful, but they tol' him he mighty lucky to git out alive heself. I got to go tell my mammy." He turned and ran into the house forgetting his promised reward.

I sat looking down toward the road. The sky was beginning to redden with sunset. A low rhythmic moaning came from the house. I had not noticed its beginning. It seemed to me to have been going on a long time.

Tennant's Ford was climbing the rise again.

"Well," said Tennant, "I certainly am ashamed we've left you alone most of the day. I reckon it's been pretty hot, though, to do anything much."

"I had a long nap this afternoon," I said. "How are things with you?"

"Pretty good. Haven't got as many watermelons as I thought I had. Some black rascal's been gettin' up early these mornin's." He laughed. "Let's go in an' have some dinner."

Mary Louise sat at the foot of the long table—the big silver coffeepot beside her.

"You'll have to excuse the service tonight. Lucy's not feeling well and Aunt Mattie is helping out."

Aunt Mattie, ageless and slow, teetered about the table, muttering.

"You haven't begun to tell us about your life in New York," said Mary Louise. "It must be awfully exciting."

While I was in the midst of a description of new skyscrapers and newer subways the kitchen door opened. A black man entered and stood just inside. I wavered—stopped.

"What is it, Dolph?" said Tennant sharply.

" 'Scuse me, Mist' Tennant, but them dogs run over our land down by the branch right by Preacher Ben's place, an' Preacher Ben, he out in front an' the men with the dogs shoot him."

"On my land?" said Tennant and his face grew white.

"How could they?" Mary Louise burst into tears. "That sweet old man!"

"He been preachin' fer forty year," said the black man.

Tennant turned to me. "There's been a little trouble at the stores today. Some niggers got a little out of hand."

"Tell me about it," I said.

He looked at me uneasily. "Why, I reckon there ain't much to tell. Just a little trouble—the niggers that started it took to the cornfields and the sheriff got the dogs to help catch 'em. I'll be out in a minute, Dolph."

The black man went out.

"I'm sorry," said Mary Louise, drying her eyes, "I reckon I must be tired. Do go on about New York. It's fascinatin'."

After dinner Mary Louise and I sat on the porch behind the towering pillars and watched the moon creep up from down below the road. Aunt Mattie brought juleps and we sipped at them in silence. The air was cool now and a little breeze filled it with rustlings. Out in the corn that spread its tossing leaves over almost half of the county we knew that men were striding behind the tugging, whining dogs. Tennant came out in a short while, took his glass from the tray and sat down heavily. We had almost finished our drinks when Mary Louise spoke:

"Do you reckon the governor—?"

"He was elected by the Klan," said Tennant grimly.

Then no one said anything for a long time. The moon was just above the tops of the tall pines down by the road. Its light made the shadows of the pillars on the porch floor into deep black oblique stripes.

"If you'll excuse us," said Tennant, "I reckon we'll go to bed. It's been a right hot day." They left me and I sat a long time in the weird beauty of the Black Belt night before I returned to the friendly softness of my bed.

Aunt Mattie waked me in the morning—bearing down on me rather uncertainly, loaded tray held high.

"Miss May Lou say she don' think they'll hol' meetin' at Bethel Hill this mornin'—but they will."

"I want to go," I said obstinately. "You tell Miss Mary Lou if she'll lend me the Ford I'll just run over there by myself."

Aunt Mattie walked off, muttering.

In about an hour Mary Louise appeared.

"I'll just put on my hat and drive you over there," she said, "but I'm sure they won't be having services. They're too frightened."

"Why don't you let me go alone?" I said.

"Oh, no, I'd really enjoy it." Her voice had the same thin ring that it had when she told the sheriff the telephone was out of order.

"Well, then, let's go," I said.

We drove down the pike a few miles, then turned off on a narrow climbing rocky road. After about two miles we could see the weather-browned little bell-tower of Bethel Hill church.

As we drove into the scant yard we saw a few negroes gathered under a sycamore tree beside the steps. We stopped, and immediately a straight black man with a grizzled mustache left the group and approached us.

"Good mornin', preacher," said Mary Louise.

"Mornin', Miss May Lou. Mornin', sir."

"Mornin', preacher," said I.

"You're a little late in startin', ain't you?" said Mary Louise.

"Yes'm. It's takin' 'em a long time to arrive here this mornin'. Couple of our deacons started walkin' 'long the road an' somebody shot at 'em. They won't let any of us folks on the road on account of all the trouble yistiddy. They's a-comin' though."

His arm swept in an arc that covered the valley. We looked down and saw the cornfields dotted with people. In the cleared spaces we could see them plainly—men and women moving upward toward us.

"That was an awful thing that happened yesterday," said Mary Louise.

"Yes'm," said the preacher. "It sure was awful. We was mighty sorry to lose Preacher Ben. He was a good man an' he preached 'round here for forty year. His wife says he died prayin' for them that shot him."

"We're all terribly sorry," said Mary Louise, a little tremulous.

"Reckon we might as well begin," said the preacher. "We are honored to have you-all's company."

We walked across the yard and entered the little church. The pews were board benches. At the far end in the center was a platform on which were a bare table and two chairs. The preacher mounted the platform.

"We are honored today by havin' the company of distinguished white friends, an' I'm goin' to ask them to name the first hymn we sing. What'll it be, Miss May Lou?"

"*Somebody's Knockin'*," said Mary Louise. "I love to hear y'all sing that."

The simple melody rose, gathering volume. More people were entering the church. It was almost full.

> Knocks like Jesus
> Answer Jesus
> Somebody's knockin' at your do'.

Now the benches were full and men were sitting in the windows. Their voices grew louder.

O sinner, why don' yo' answer
Somebody's knockin' at yo' do'.

When the song ended the preacher announced the "first collection."

"That's for us," whispered Mary Louise; "he's afraid we'll leave before the end of the sermon."

After he had blessed the offering the preacher began to speak, slowly. His text, he said, was from Isaiah, the thirty-fourth chapter and the second verse:

"For Jehovah hath indignation against all nations and wrath against all their host."

He said it was a mighty bad thing for men to get mad. And it was a bad thing to make men mad. Usually it was the fault of both people when they got mad at each other. But when the Lord got mad at a man it couldn't be anybody's fault but that man's. The Lord was always right. He didn't get mad often but when he did, awful things happened.

The preacher was warming up now—striding nervously from side to side of the platform.

"Anythin' the Lord do is right," he shouted.

"Have mercy, Lord," came back at him in a hysterical feminine shriek from the front bench. He broke into a chant—beginning on a high note—ending in a low breathless husky minor:

"The Lord can throw a thunderbolt
An' burn your cabin down
An' he'd be right.

The Lord can raise a hurricane
An' blow your chimney stones away
An' he'd be right.

> The Lord can raise a mighty flood
> An' drown your mules an' children, too
> An' he'd be right.
>
> *Ain't he a terrible God?"*

Cries came from all over the little chapel:
"Oh, yes, Lord."
"Jesus, have mercy."
"You're right, brother."
Behind us a big black woman began to shake convulsively. Two men rose and held her.

"Let me alone," she screamed, "I'se bound to shout. I see the light—I can see Jesus." Above the rising babel—the preacher again:

> "The Lord can make the sun so hot
> Burn up all your beans an' corn
> An' he'd be right.
>
> The Lord can make boll-weevil come
> Eat up all your field of cotton
> An' he'd be right.
>
> *Ain't he a terrible God?"*

Mary Louise lifted her bowed head and leaned toward me. "Please let's go. I can't stand it. These poor people!"

When we got to the Ford a tall black boy was sitting on the running board.

"Jes' waited to see nobody touched your Ford, Miss May Lou," he said.

"Thank you, Rafe," said Mary Louise.

We turned back towards home. The noise inside the little church was very loud now. But above it all rode the preacher's voice—asking his proud question.

CONJURE COUNTRY

CHAPTER I

Two-Toe Tom

I CAME to Opp a little before sunset. Less than ten miles to go, now, Tennant had told me. The broad gravel pike southward was lined by furrowed fields, newly plowed. In some of them the mules still plodded up and down ahead of harrows held to the reddish earth by straw-hatted black boys. At distances of a mile or more weather-browned shacks, set back from the road, were partially hidden by flowering bushes.

A white woman sitting high in an old-fashioned buggy drawn by a drooping mule pulled back on her reins as I stopped to ask my way.

"Gilmore? Is he a-farmin' for somebody over in the Black Belt?"

"Yes, that's the one."

"You crosses the river and takes the Moores Bridge road fer about seven mile. There's a old sorghum mill close by and you'll see the mash in the road. You turns to yo' lef' there and takes the Rue road and you goes about a couple more mile I reckon. On the top of the hill there's a crossroad, and settin' to the lef' is a graveyard and New Prospect Church, and right down in de bottom, back uv the church is the Painted House, leastwise hit used to be painted, so hit still goes by that name. Well, thar's whar the Widow Cox lives with her woods colt chile, po' thing, but hit ain't none of the chile's fault, nor her ma's neither fer that matter, fer she 'lowed old man Johns was gonna marry her, an' anyhow she's peculiar to the rest of us. Well, he done right by her at that, when he give her the five-acre patch en that thar piece of new ground, and then he lef' her the Painted House an' a mule or two."

"Yes," I said, eager to get on; "now which way do I turn when I get to the crossroads?"

"Lord, man, you don't go to the crossroad, you turns due west about a quarter 'fore you gits thar."

Somewhat discouraged, I started out on the Moores Bridge road, and by asking everyone I passed, the way to the Painted House, or New Prospect Church, the two places I didn't want to go to, I finally used up my ten miles, and feeling that I must be somewhere in the right neighborhood, I stopped an old black man plowing in the field and asked if he could direct me to Gilmore's.

"Sho' ken," he said. "Take all lef'-han' turns, and the secon' house you come to after you leaves me, is the fus one you stops at."

"Isn't there a sign at the crossroads?"

"Not a thing in the worl'."

"Is it far?"

" 'Tain't no piece a-tall."

I had begun to think I had overrun my goal when I saw "Gilmore" printed on a roadside mail box. I turned in the winding drive toward a little low brown house with a single pine standing beside it. A white man in blue overalls rose from the steps as I stopped my car.

"Howdy, perfesser. I'm Gilmore. Mist' Tennant wrote me you'd be here this evenin'. Sorry he an' Miss Mary Louise couldn't come, too."

"They send you their best and want to know how you're getting on."

Gilmore's face, long and angular, suddenly stiffened.

"If'n these niggers 'round here'd work—I might have some cotton for us later on. Had a mule standin' up all yestiddy 'cause a nigger run out on me to take his Sat'd'y off. If Sunday's enough fer me I reckon it'll do fer him. But come on in. There's soap an' water on the back porch an' Sairy's gittin' our supper ready."

Sairy proved to be a sallow blonde girl whose bare feet slapped the kitchen floor in swift rhythms as she set our food before us. Beyond a muttered recognition when Gilmore introduced me to her, she said nothing, but she listened to our conversation and her face showed pride in her husband's facile answer to my questioning. Our pork chops and sweet potatoes and collards soon disappeared and Gilmore and I went out on the gallery to sit. In the west a dull red glow radiated from a bank of lowering clouds. Thunder heads moved toward us slowly. I was glad my journey was over.

"Looks like the drought'll end soon," said Gilmore. "That's good news for us farmers—and for the alligators too. A few more weeks and some of 'em would be pretty well dried out."

"I came down here to find out about alligators. Do you have trouble with them often?"

"Well, they ain't exactly pleasant neighbors."

"Tell me some of your experiences with them."

"I don't have so much trouble—all my livestock is mules and I got 'em well stabled—but old man Haines down the road a piece has had plenty—I could tell you about him."

"Go ahead."

"Pap Haines lives down between Opp and Florala on the old winding road that they don't keep up any more since the straight clay pike was built. In Model T days people had to drive right careful when the old road went through pond hollows and swamps, and sometimes they had to stop and switch off their lights to let a blinded alligator get out of the way. If he was a baby 'gator he might find himself next day taking it easy in a backyard pond in some town. But if he was big and red-eyed folks mighty well let him take his time. Any alligator will go after anything, take it in water. But a red-eye will go after a man on land and he will more than go after a woman if he catches her off by herself. The farm boys and the lumberjack boys can tell of time after time when an alligator has raped a woman before he ate her. They say old Two-Toe Tom has had more than one.

When Pap Haines bought his forty from the lumber company twenty years ago, folks told him he better not keep any stock on account of old Two-Toe. Two-Toe is a red-eyed 'gator and about fourteen feet long and he can knock a mule into the water with just one flip of his tail. When a farmer sees that track with just two toes on the left fore foot (the rest was cut off by a steel trap long ago), that means he has shore got to pen up his calves and pigs and he can't be too careless with his mules and grown cows either. Got to well-water them for a while instead of letting them wander around just any pond because you can't never tell which one he is in. But well-watering doesn't look out for calves and pigs enough. Any good-sized 'gator will come right up to the lot or cow-pen at night. And Two-Toe Tom is an eating fool. If the farmer's got a dog old Two-Toe just says dog-meat is dessert for a 'gator.

But Pap Haines said he'd run his chances on the forty. Said he would keep some light-wood splinters handy for a light and some big hard-tearing pine knots. A pine knot is better than a gun. Ordinary shots shell off an alligator's back like water. But a good hard lick on the back of the head or the neck with a pine knot will tear in and keel him over—then you can kill him on his tender belly. Of course Pap didn't reckon he could do any good with a steel trap. Ever since Two-Toe left the rest of his foot in one he has known more about steel trap layout than the men who set them. But a good dose of dynamite under that red-eye in some pond would make him feel pretty sick.

Pap Haines says he had right bad luck just at first. He has to go back 'way before his son was married to recollect when Two-Toe Tom threw him back for a cow. The 'gator caught her drinking at a pond and he came two nights later and got the calf out of the cow-pen. Then Two-Toe kind of fell out with this neck of the woods. He didn't bother around for ten years or more. Pap's wife died and his son got married and his wife borned four children, about two years apart. The state began building the clay pike, so they began sleeping four man-boarders in one shed room and Pap had to sleep in the room with his son and his wife and all the children because they used the other shed room to eat in. Boarders made good company, living back country, and their rent helped out when times were bad.

Then after laying-by time Pap Haines and his son lost another mule. They had been keeping all the stock in the lot by the window at night. In the daytime they turned out the mules but they tried to watch them and not let them get off too far. There was no work to do one morning, and the son decided he would like to go over with the old man and take dinner to the boarders and kind of see how they were coming along with the new road. The old lady and the kids wanted to go, too, so they hitched one of the mules to the old buggy and didn't bother about catching up the other mule.

When they got back along towards night they found the mule half eaten down by a pond. A little further along in the mud was that Two-Toe left forefoot track.

One of the boarders said he was acquainted with a man down close to Brewton that could get any 'gator he set out to. He used a blind and a high-powered rifle, and he had a sharp-shooter pin that he got back in the army. The boarder set out in a Model T the next morning and was back with the man by noon. They had stopped at the courthouse in Andalusia and found out that that old ten-year-ago hundred dollar reward for Two-Toe Tom was still in force. Pap Haines said to the man:

'We'll give you twenty-five more and board you even if it takes a week or two.'

'It jest takes patience,' the man said; 'the trouble about a blind, folks generally git too close. A 'gator can smell a man before he gets his head high enough out o' water for the man to see him. I don't like to brag but I most generally git a bad 'gator, give me time enough.'

He followed some tracks for a ways and then he said:

'Jedgin' by these tracks he's in one of these three ponds.'

Then he climbed high up in a thick-limbed tree with his rifle and his dinner, three hundred yards or more from any one of the ponds. He said the 'gator couldn't see through the limbs that far and he would just naturally come out to the sun in a day or two. It might be a week the man reckoned but he would spot that devil's head somewhere, and one look would be enough.

'It jest takes patience,' he said.

So the man was patient in the tree for nigh onto a week, every day, until they heard about Two-Toe Tom's track seven or eight miles down the country where he had killed two calves.

The man went down there but Two-Toe Tom must have had a good nose, or good eyes, one, for he hasn't yet got clipped off with a rifle.

Pap Haines never had any more trouble with that 'gator till last March. He had begun to reckon somebody had got him and then one of his mules didn't come up in the morning. Any mule will get contrary sometimes and not come up, so the old man went down in the brush to look for him, not bothering much, not until he saw that track. It came from a pond up yonder in a clump of water oaks and crab grass and followed along a sluggish branch too shallow for fish, much less a 'gator, and went down the hollow.

'Uh-uh,' Pap Haines said. 'Hell's up now.'

Sure enough, over in the bushes where the spring rains had overflowed the pond he saw the mule lying with his side torn open and a part of the top shoulder and the top ham eaten away. Some of the bushes were bent and torn showing there had been a struggle. And there in the mud was that track. Two-Toe Tom was still alive and he was on the move again.

Pap Haines and his son didn't wait for breakfast. They got some pine knots and they mortally lit out after those tracks. They didn't have any trouble following them past two ponds and on to another one. And there were no tracks leading out anywhere. It was a good piece to another pond in any direction. No two ways about it, Two-Toe Tom was in that pond all right. The son got to where he could see all 'round the pond and told the old man to hitch the other mule to the buggy and light out to town for some dynamite, some fuses and some caps.

'Make it plenty of dynamite,' he said, 'and get back quick, and tell my wife to send me some breakfast.'

While Pap Haines was gone his son waited for the old redeye to come out. He was going to let him get some distance and then cut him off from coming back to the pond and whale into him with pine knots.

But Pap got back with the stuff and nothing had happened. They filled about fifteen syrup buckets with dynamite, packed the sticks tight in dirt and cottonseed and cut off some fuses. They lighted three at a time and threw the buckets in the pond. The water shot way up in the air and roots and trees came up from the bottom. Nothing could have been left alive in that pond. Just the same everybody, and there were eight of them by now, went stepping around pretty careful.

After they threw the last bucket Pap Haines said:

'We got him now. He'll be a floatin' belly up in this pond by mornin'.'

They had all started back toward the house when they heard a big splashing down by the first pool Pap had tracked the 'gator through. Then somebody began screaming. Everybody ran as fast as he could and the screams kept up but it was a good ways down there. Pap Haines is over sixty but he got there first, just in time to see two red eyes sinking under the water. Beside the pond was what was left of his twelve-year-old granddaughter. She had heard the blasting and was coming down to see what it was about.

They spent the rest of the day shooting into the water and they set off some more dynamite but nothing happened. Two weeks later a farmer down by Stedman ten miles away lost a couple of shoats and found the two-toed track.

Pap Haines lives alone now. His son and family have moved up north around Tuskegee. They want him to come there for he can hardly scrape a living by himself but he says he has never been above Montgomery and he can't get 'round to it. Besides, he says he plans to kill that red-eyed hell-demon before he dies. He acts a little queer about it and some folks laugh at him.

They tell him Two-Toe Tom has got tunnels all around from one pond to another and lots of secret ways to get in and out of swamps.

'I know that,' he says, 'but he won't fool me no more.'

They tell him Two-Toe Tom has been heard from down Florida way and he won't be back. He says,

'He might be down there, but he'll be back. And I'll be waitin'.' He keeps one old mule and lets him run loose for bait."

"That reminds me of the stories they used to tell in the old days about battles with dragons," I said. "There was one about a fearful beast named Grendel who was killed by Beowulf."

"Sounds foreign to me," said Gilmore. He called out "Sairy!" and his wife came obediently to the door.

"Fix the perfesser's bed across the dog-trot in the shed 'cause that boy of ours is likely to wake up an' holler plenty early."

"I heard about the baby," I said, "and I've been wondering where he was."

"Willie George put him to sleep a while back and we ain't heard a peep from him since. Beats me how an eight-year-old nigger can do more with him than his own mother. Willie George is a hum-dinger though. I reckon Sairy and I are plum silly over Willie George—most as silly as we are over Baby Jim." Gilmore laughed self-consciously.

CHAPTER II

A Good Man to Work For

WHEN I heard Gilmore stirring around the next morning I got up and dressed though the sun had not yet risen. When I stepped out on the dog-trot my host was standing in the half-light whittling leafy twigs from an oak branch about and inch thick and four feet long.

"Breakfast'll be ready after a little," he said. "Sairy is takin' care of Baby Jim right now."

Two shadowy figures appeared at the steps. "Nathan," said Gilmore, "you go out an' start hitchin' the mules. Henry, you go git the water pail in the kitchen."

Nathan started off briskly. But Henry's eyes for some reason I did not know grew big with terror and he spoke in a trembling voice.

"Don't make me go in the kitchen, boss. Jest let me 'splain to you how it was."

"Go get that pail," said Gilmore and there was a hard edge to his voice.

As the negro entered the kitchen Gilmore stepped quickly in after him pushing him roughly in the middle of the back. The oak stick trailed in his left hand. As the kitchen door shut I heard a click and knew that Gilmore had locked it.

"Put your hands up."

"But, boss, if you'd let me talk to yuh."

"Put your hands up."

There was a muffled thud—wood against cloth—the stick against the negro's shirt—and a yell of pain.

"Keep 'em up, I tell you."

Thud, thud, thud—stunning blows that bruise flesh and make it sting unbearably. Thud, thud, the blows were rhythmic—punctuating the frightened wails of the negro.

I felt sick. And I wondered where I was. Whipping negro servants died out after *Uncle Tom's Cabin* and the War Between the States, I assured myself. This was only a nightmare. Then the door opened and in a moment Henry came out carrying the water pail in his right hand. His left held his cap with which he made futile dabs at his streaming eyes.

"If you'd only let me talk to yuh, boss, yuh wouldn't had to whoop me."

"You've had all day Sat'd'y and Sunday to talk to me. No nigger that works for me is takin' Sat'd'y off in plowin' time. Git along with yuh."

Grits and bacon held little attraction for me. I was really ill from what I had seen and heard. Gilmore said nothing about it and Sairy seemed to take it as a matter of course. After breakfast I went with Gilmore out to the field. Two mules were already at work and the black boys were plodding along behind the earth that turned from green to reddish brown. As Gilmore made ready to join the slow procession Henry passed us. To my surprise he was singing. I followed along, behind, listening:

> Bo-weavil, bo-weavil, don't sing dem blues no more
> Bo-weavil here, bo-weavil everywhere you go.
> I gonna sing this song to ease Bo-weavil's troubled mind,
> Come 'long, Bo-weavil
> Let's have a great long time.
>
> Bo-weavil, bo-weavil,
> Please leave me 'lone,
> Don' eat up my cotton and
> Gnaw on my new ground corn.

Went to the merchant's to get my lard,
Merchant said, times too hard
Bo-weavil, bo-weavil please leave me 'lone,
Done eat up my cotton and
Gnaw on my new ground corn.

"Henry," I said, interrupting him, "I was sorry to hear you getting whipped this morning."

Henry laughed. "I reckon I had it comin' to me. But I jest *had* to have last Sat'd'y off. They was a meetin' o' my lodge an' the grand officers from Montgomery come down. Little whoopin' don't hurt much. An' Mist' Gilmore's a good man to wuk foh. He don't mean nothin' by it."

I went back to the houses. The sun was hot and I lay down in the shade of the pine tree and went to sleep. By and by I was dimly conscious of a droning hum. Half awake, I looked toward the steps. A little black boy was bending over a dilapidated baby carriage and singing softly while he jiggled it. I was gradually aware of the words and the fact that he was making up his lullaby as he went along. This was Willie George's song:

Someday Baby Jim gwine git grown
Someday I'm gwine git grown
Me and Baby Jim gwine farm.
Baby Jim gwine say
"Ol' nigger go down in that fur bottom
An' haul up my corn."
I'm goin' say
"Don' feel like it
An' ain' gwine do it."
Baby Jim gwine pick up a big stick
An' lam me 'cross my haid,
Den I gwine say
"Yes, sir, white man, I orter been gone."
Den I'm gwine fly out'n hitch up the mules
An' go singin' down to the fur bottom to git the corn.

Then Sat'day come along
An' Baby Jim come out to the field
And hole out some money, an' say
"Here, ole nigger, take this money
An' go git you somethin'."
I'm goin' up town Sat'day e'ening
With the money an' buy me bottle licker.
I'm gwine git drunk; den save Baby Jim
Some o' the whiskey an' come home.
Den we both git drunk together.
An' if they puts me in jail
Fo' I gits home to Baby Jim
He's gwine come round Monday mornin'
An' git me outen de jail.
Don't reckon shorely they'd lock up Baby Jim too.

CHAPTER III

Processional

DOWN in the township of Nokomis, Alabama, in Escambia County, they tell a queer story. Many years ago, they say, two brothers named Ezekiel and Uriah Smith lived in Nokomis. Their father was a rich man, and when he died Ezekiel took his share of what was left to him and left town. But Uriah stayed. He took some of his money and built himself a fine house at the top of the hill above the spring. Uriah used to say that the water from the spring was the best water anywhere in the country.

After a while Uriah married a girl from Nokomis and she lived with him in the house at the top of the hill. He hadn't been married very long before he got to drinking. People say there "wasn't hardly a time when ole Man Smith wasn't daid to the worl'." He used to have to try pretty hard to get up the hill.

One Saturday night "ole man Smith" came home drunk as usual. The water bucket on the porch was empty and he picked it up and started back down to the spring. When he was almost there he stumbled and fell. His head caught in a forked branch of the sycamore that grows just above the spring. When he was found next morning he was dead and his face was completely black.

It is strange that an accident that happened so long ago should have had an influence on what I saw on a spring morning in Alabama many years later. Black Nathan had told me: "The colored folks is studyin' to have a parade to make the

208

crops grow. They have it every year. Hit's goin' to be down by the spring." And so I was down by the spring to watch.

I saw them walking down the hill from the direction of the old house (now in decay and "hanted," I am told). They wore their Sunday best—black suits and white shirts and collars for the men, black skirts and white shirt-waists for the women—adding to the silhouette effect as I looked up at the long line of them in sharp outline against the red clay of the barren slope and the light blue of the sky beyond it. They were singing a spiritual, one I have rarely heard, *Break Them Chains*, and they were swaying slowly in time to its minor cadences. As they walked nearer I saw that their leader—a lanky negro, very black—carried a handful of brightly colored feathers—chicken and turkey feathers. When he came to the sycamore tree he lifted his long arms and tied the feathers in the fatal fork where "ole man Smith" had strangled. He tied them so that they hung down brushing the top of his head. The heads of the negroes following him kept them swinging. Some of these followers carried forked sticks tied together to make crosses. Others clasped bits of broken colored glass—here a shattered green teapot, there a jagged gleaming golden bottle. One proudly bore a little light blue glass tower such as telephone linemen use in stringing wires.

The tall man in front led the procession in a series of wide concentric circles about the spring. When the last figure had passed under the swaying feathers, the tune faded into silence. Each negro bent down and planted his cross or his colored glass upright in the earth. As soon as this had been done a group of them solemnly approached the tree. They took from their pockets old glass snuff boxes brilliantly variegated. (I looked closely at them later and discovered that they were filled with bright pebbles.) The negroes tied them to the branches of the sycamore and returned to their places in the circles. Then without any apparent signal they all joined hands. At once a mournful minor dirge arose, growing stronger with each word:

> Long time ago
> There used to be
> A man whose name
> Was Ur-i-eee.

There was a short silence, then from all those negro throats came a low moaning wail. Its volume increased—died away—a shuddering cry that had its roots far back in the past in a distant tropical land. After each stanza of the dirge, this cry was repeated and each time, though I came to expect it, it frightened me. This was the rest of their song:

> He lived on top
> Of the big hill
> Till the night before
> That he got killed.

> His woman waited
> At the door
> Till late that night
> But he came no more.

> His woman waited
> At the door
> But he went way down
> And come no more.

> He got a bucket
> From the stand
> And down the hill
> He almost ran.

> And down the hill
> He almost ran
> And, yes, oh, Lawd,
> He was a man.

> We found him there
> In this forked tree
> And, oh, his face
> Was black to see.

> And, oh, his face
> Was black to see
> And, oh, my Lord,
> We will be free.

> And now he's gone
> So far away
> But he'll be back
> For judgment day.

The last wail did not end as had the others—it continued in a low rhythmic moaning as the leader swayed back up the hill—making the feathers swing again as they touched his close-curled head. The rest walked after him, moaning, moving as if in a slow ritual dance. The last one reached the top of the hill and vanished over its edge. I heard them wailing for another minute. Then the silence of a hot Alabama noon settled down. I wondered by what strange circumstance "ole man Smith's" accidental death many years ago had caused this rite of fertility. Black Nathan had told me: "He was a bad man an' he treated his niggers bad." Perhaps the blight of his cruel spirit lingered on the land. But now its power was broken. In irregular circles about the spring stood the crosses and the glistening colored-glass fragments. There would be good crops for another season.

CHAPTER IV

White Man's Nigger: II

ASK any Chambers County nigger about Wade Finley and he will keep his mouth shut unless he knows and trusts you. If you can get him to talk, he will tell you that Wade Finley is a bad nigger. Ask any white man and he will tell you Wade is the best nigger in the county—a real white man's nigger—the highest compliment he can bestow on him.

Wade was raised by a white family, the Huckabys. He studied to please and he worked hard even when he was little more than a pickaninny. The Huckabys swear by him and there isn't anything he wouldn't do for them. When old man Huckaby died a year ago Wade came up to the house and stayed night and day, waiting on the old boss-man, sleeping in the same room with him, not letting anybody else serve him.

It is a long time since Wade Finley killed his first nigger, and no one seems to know just what it was about. He said it was in self-defense, and old man Huckaby and a lot of his friends testified that Wade was a good hard-working boy, so the judge let him go. Chambers County niggers were afraid of him after that and he had and still has a great power over them. Wade can hit a small sapling a hundred yards away and he never takes much aim. It is talked around that when a nigger gets too fresh to white folks in Chambers County, some day he is likely to be found dead with a bullet hole through him and nobody around to blame for it. Wade has been tried for killing niggers two or three times, sometimes when he was said to have done it for white folks, but he has always got out all right except once and that was when he was fool enough to kill a nigger up in Randolph County.

He was with a crowd of white men on a man hunt and the brother of the nigger they were hunting was along. This brother was a pretty good boy and well thought of, although the hunted man was a bad character. But on some short talk Wade pulled out his gun and shot him. Wade was pretty surprised when the white folks up there turned on him and he was lucky to get away into the woods. He stayed there two days and then he started south to Chambers County. He got a ride with a white man from Lafayette in his buggy and just before they came to the Tallapoosa River he got out, thinking a posse might be looking for him on the bridge. He walked down to the water, put his gun and his clothes on his head, and swam across. He was lying in the bushes near the bridge when the buggy reached it and he heard the men looking for him stop and search it. He slipped on up the road and got into the buggy again but he was a little too soon. A posse of white men came around the next bend and caught him.

The man in the buggy went on down to Chambers County and told what had happened and the white folks down there made up a party in a hurry and drove up to Randolph to help Wade out. It was lucky for him they did, for the men in the posse were hot about it and they had a rope around Wade's neck and were just about to hang him when his friends showed up. They told the posse they didn't want anything to happen to Wade because he was a good nigger and mighty handy to have around among the other niggers. Finally the two sides compromised and let him stand trial and he got sent to the penitentiary for two years.

Wade had it pretty easy at the penitentiary almost from the first. There was a big bullying nigger there who used to take every other nigger's tobacco from him right after it was issued. He took Wade's one week and Wade went to the warden and complained. The warden told him that was his own lookout and it was up to him to keep his tobacco. The next week the big nigger came to take Wade's tobacco and Wade lifted a pick and ran him through with it.

The warden gave Wade fifty licks for the murder. But the big nigger had been in the gang for killing a white man and when that man's family heard about it they were so happy they gave Wade a fine suit of clothes and every week he stayed on in the gang they sent him a box of good food. They came to see him regularly and when he got out a little while ago they wanted him to come and live with them and work for them.

But Wade decided he didn't want to work. So he has taken a cabin back in Chambers County and turned to doctoring, mostly root doctoring for venereal diseases. He is beginning to conjure a little. Niggers come to him because they are afraid of him and because they think he has supernatural powers. The other day a nigger asked him to conjure his wife back from a big buck she had run off with. Wade gave him a conjure ball and sent him home. Then he went to see the woman and told her she better go back, and she was so scared of him that she went. Her husband gave Wade a big hog and so he has had plenty of meat in these hard times. Wade laughs about it to the white folks and says all niggers are damn fools.

CHAPTER V

Conjure Woman

IDA CARTER was seven years old when, on the first night of May, she burned seven candles all night long. For seven successive May nights she did the same thing, though her mother and sister, too frightened to stop her by force, tried to dissuade her. Every May for seven years she repeated her ritual and by then she was a conjure woman and her name was Seven Sisters.

Seven Sisters lives in Hogansville. Her clean white house is trimmed in green, and its porch is shaded by a honeysuckle vine. In the neat yard are seven white posts set in an irregular pattern. She was standing among them when I first saw her. A negro couple stood before her, the girl holding a few weeks' old baby in her arms. Seven Sisters is a big woman and she seemed to tower over her companions. As I stopped beside the road she lifted a long thick right arm and pointed at the man.

"You been crawlin' some other woman while Cena was pregnant," she said in a loud clear voice, "and you and that other woman have worked a trick on Cena so she can't get well."

"You're a damned lie," said the man gruffly. "I never done nothin' like that to Cena."

"Then the other woman did it by herself," said Seven Sisters triumphantly. "You listen to me. They's a little clump o' weeds out in front o' your cabin, ain't they?"

The man grunted, inarticulate in astonishment at this revelation.

"Yas'm, they sho' is," said the girl with the baby.

"Well, y'all go right back an' look there for a little ball that woman mixed up or got a conjure woman to mix up. You find it quick as you kin and tear it up an' Cena'll git well. If'n you don' find it you come back here to me an' I'll fix up somethin' to untrick her."

Disconsolately the little trio climbed into a mule-wagon and started for home—to search the weed patch.

"Git along," said Seven Sisters, "I got white folks visitors."

"Seven Sisters," I said, "I've come sixty miles to see you—"

"You ain't come nowheres. Folks come from foreign states to see me."

"I got troubles," I said, "and the white folks up around Birmingham say you can help me."

"You got money?"

"A little."

"It costs a dollar to me and a quarter to the city council at Hogansville."

"I reckon it'd be worth more'n a dollar to me."

"Well, what's the troubles? Women, I reckon."

"One of 'em."

"You can't git away from her. You sick of her but she can always bring you back."

"That's right, auntie. How does she do that?"

"Well," said Seven Sisters, "they's a lot of ways. Easiest way is to git a piece o' thread out'n your pants or a dirty string from your drawers. Then she can trick you with 'em an' you can't git away."

"Reckon it was some other way," I said.

"She might git some fishbait worms an' boil 'em and strain the water, and then put in a spoonful of lard an' boil some more. Then if she can jes wet the bottom o' your drawers with the water—or your stomach—they ain't nothin' you can do— she's got yuh, you won't never fool with any woman but her.

"Or she might take your right sock and bury it so deep rain kin never reach it, an' then piss over it all along through the June (middle) of the days an' when the sock rots she got you.

"Or stick nine pins in the left sock and bury it under the doorstep right under the eaves o' the house with all the pins pointin' to the edge of the roof. That's mighty powerful, too."

"But, Seven Sisters, what'll I do? Sometimes I tell her I'm through and then she says: 'I can always get you back like I did the first time.' And she can."

"You jes' want to bust loose or you want to kill her?"

"What do I have to do to kill her?"

"Best way so nobody catch on is take a big auger an' go out in the woods an' bore a hole in a tree an' git some o' her dung and put it in the hole an' fit a peg in the hole. Then for nine mornings you drive that peg more tighter. On the ninth morning when you done got the peg as tight as it will go, that woman can't go out a bit [becomes constipated]. She'll begin to git weak about the second morning an' about the sixth she'll have to go to bed, and on the ninth she'll be done stopped up tight."

"There ought to be a quicker way than that, auntie."

"You can do it quicker. Jes' take nine hairs out o' the tip of a black cat's tail, nine hairs from a hog's snout, nine tail hairs from a horse and nine hairs from a black cow (don' make no difference what part) and mix 'em all up with gunpowder into a ball. Then you say 'East, West, South, North,' and you call out her name three times and throw the conjure ball in the air. It'll sail like a kite an' blow up an' when the blue smoke comes out of it, she'll drop dead—no matter if she's in Montgomery."

"Seven Sisters, how did you learn all this? Everybody says you can help out on any kind o' trouble—howcome you get to do that?"

"It's a spirit in me that tells—a spirit from the Lord Jesus Christ. Used to be old voodoo woman lived next my mammy's cabin. She tol' me how to trick. She say her mammy in Africa teached her. But she was a bad ol' woman—a voodoo conjure woman. I tricks in the name o' the Lord."

"I reckon all the old voodoo people are gone now," I said; "they don't have meetings like they used to."

"Well, there's Ella James down by Lafayette, they say she a voodoo and they's an old woman lives 'bout a mile up the pike I've heard tell about. But I reckon they don't have no meetin's."

"Seven Sisters, you've sure helped me a lot about this woman. Reckon I can get rid of her now. There's a lot of ways you could help me—with women and gambling and all that. I wonder if you'd tell me all the things you know and I'll write 'em down and keep the paper by me when I get in a jam."

"That'd cost yuh a lot o' money. I reckon I couldn't do that for less'n fo' dollars and a half."

"You can start right in. I'll get out my pencil and paper."

SEVEN SISTERS' MANUAL OF VOODOO CONJURING

To Keep Your Wife From Flirting Around

Take a persimmon sprout about six inches long and bury it under the doorstep while her flirting spell is on.

To Get a Girl to Sleep With You

Steal something dirty from being next her skin—a string from her drawers, moisture from under her right arm, best of all a menstruation cloth—stick nine pins in it and bury it under the eaves of the house.

Take hair from her head, make it into a ball, sew it up, and wear it under your right arm.

Take moisture from under your right arm and mix with Hoyett's Cologne. Sprinkle the mixture on a handkerchief and then touch her hands and arms with it. Then you can have anything you want.

To Drive Your Rival Out of the County

Take a limb from a poplar tree that has been struck by lightning and tie a dogwood sprout to it with a raw thread (thread from a feed sack) and measure your rival's track with the sticks, measuring the same track nine times. (Just place one end of the sticks in the heel track and the other in the toe.) Then bury the sticks where he will walk over them, and in nine days after he walks over them he will be in another county.

To Keep Your Girl Coming to You Regular

Spill one drop of turpentine on the doorsill of the room you want her to come in and that will time her coming and make her keep on coming.

To Give Your Rival Bad Luck

Take a snake shed (discarded skin), mix it with pepper and bury it where he will have to walk over it and it will bring him the kind of bad luck you want him to have.

The Uses of May Water and John the Conqueror Root

May Water is the first water caught off the roof from the first rain in May. (Seven Sisters sells it for a dollar a gallon.) Mixed with John the Conqueror Root, it makes you successful in business, lucky at gambling. Drinking it will make a gambling hand. (Seven Sisters made a gambling hand for a man one night. She charged him five dollars and he made six hundred dollars in thirty minutes and came by and gave her ten dollars more.) Drinking May Water will bring you health and good luck.

Mix John the Conqueror Root with a lodestone and it will draw dimes right off a store counter, unless they are fastened down.

Warning: Never let John the Conqueror Root come in contact with snuff or tobacco; that will kill its effect.

To Keep Your Land and Have Good Crops

Take four persimmon limbs about nine inches long, cut from right next to the trunk of the tree and bury one at each corner of your land and you can never lose the land and you will always have good crops.

To Revenge Yourself on an Enemy

Catch a snake, cut off its head and hang up the body by the tail on a long-leaf pine sapling (it must be long-leaf). Take the first drop of blood dripping from the snake and mix it in whiskey or something to kill the taste and smell and offer the drink to your enemy. If he drinks it snakes will grow under his skin and he will die. At the moment of his death all the snakes will crawl from his body unless, of course, you get somebody to kill the spell.

Or substitute for the blood of the snake that of a spider hung by the legs from a long-leaf pine sapling and spiders will grow under his skin.

In like manner lizards or ants may be made to grow under the skin, killing the victim and forsaking him in a swarm at death. (One woman who "sat up with" the corpse of a woman who "died from a perishing" vowed to me that the breath had no sooner left her body than thousands of ants came out of her nose. She had stolen another woman's husband and the jealous wife had had her "fixed up.")

Plant nine needles in something and slip it under the house right under the head of the bed. They will cause nine pains to the person sleeping directly above them and kill him. (Seven Sisters was called just too late one time recently. Death was already on the woman when she got there but she told the relatives to look under the house and they found the needles.)

To Know When You Have Been Tricked

Wear a dime, on which either the number 3 or the number 7 appears twice, on a string around your belly or your ankle. When it turns black you will know somebody is trying to work a trick on you and you can go to a conjure woman and get it untricked.

Take two pods of pepper and one tablespoon of salt and put them in your right shoe, take one pod of pepper and one tablespoon of sulphur and one of salt and put them in your left shoe. Then whenever you walk over any conjure balls, bad luck plants, buried needles, powders, etc., your feet will burn and warn you. If the conjuration is very bad, sometimes the sole will burn right off your shoe. But you will know somebody is after you and go and get untricked.

To Cure Warts

Tie as many knots in a cotton string as there are warts and then suspend this string under the eaves of the house so that the water dropping off the roof will run down this string and wash the warts away.

Cut a slit in the wart and pass through it a string dipped in kerosene oil and lighted.

If it is a large wart, it should be penetrated with a small brass pin, which should be thrown away or "hid from yourself," and after three days the wart will disappear.

Rub seven grains of corn on the warts and then feed the corn to the chickens.

Pick the wart with a brass pin, let one drop of blood fall on a stone, cover the drop with another stone, and then bury them secretly.

Kill a black cat, take it to a graveyard at midnight, and rub it on the wart.

To Cure "Misery in de Back"

Dig up some pine roots in a road where there has never been any corpse, burn the roots, and then apply the "rosin" to your back.

CHAPTER VI

Reminiscence

TENNANT took me to River Falls; his father was a friend of our host's. As we drove out from Andalusia he said: "We might live here for weeks and never see him. He's always glad to have friends drop in and live with him a while. But if your hours don't gee with his—well, he goes his way and you go yours. When you want something you ask a nigger for it. That's all there is to living here."

We drove up to a big box-like frame house, covered on the outside with green shingles. Down to the left of us we could hear the screech and whine of the sawmills. At the right at a distance of a hundred yards or so was a long one-story building roughly thrown together, evidently some kind of barracks.

We went inside the house and wandered around. All the rooms were alike, upstairs and down. Each held a table, a few chairs, and a cot. On the wall hung a couple of shotguns of recent pattern. Under almost every table slept a hound dog. Now and then a negro servant passed us without showing any surprise or particular interest. Tennant spoke to one of them, a little misshapen black woman:

"When will he be back?"

"I dunno, sir. He ain't been in in a couple o' days. Reckon he's up to Montgomery."

"We'll have supper in one of the downstairs rooms at six o'clock."

"Yes, sir."

"And we'll sleep in this room and the next."

"Yes, sir."

"Breakfast at nine on the gallery."

"Yes, sir."

So we established ourselves in River Falls. Wearied by our drive through roads roughened by spring rains, we had taken off our shoes and coats and were dozing on our cots when I heard men's voices raised in sharp monosyllabic cries. There was a series of metallic clicks—unmistakably the sound of guns being broken, loaded, snapped back to readiness.

"What's that?" I said.

"Marchin' the convicts from the mills to the barracks," said Tennant.

"What convicts?"

"He hires 'em from the state."

I rose and looked out the front window. At the right of the house stood a long double line of negroes in striped uniforms. White men in gray flannel shirts and khaki breeches stood near them, each with a double-barreled shotgun in the crook of his arm. "Right *face!*" said one of them and the negroes turned slowly. "March!" and they shambled off in slow dispirited steps toward the long low barracks. Two of the white guards opened the doors and the long line gradually disappeared inside. As the last stripes were lost in the dark cavern of the entrance, the heavy doors were swung back into place and big wooden bars lifted against them. I saw that the windows held no glass and were intersected with iron bars.

"That's the end of them for today," said Tennant, "unless we want Philip to play his guitar for us later. He's the only one allowed to come out at night."

Three hours later we sat on the gallery of the ugly house. Philip on the lower step strummed his guitar. The chatter of the black convicts, shut up in their wooden prison, was a soft murmuring to our ears.

"Sing us about John Henry," said Tennant, "about that time he killed himself beatin' the steam drill."

"That was over to Leeds in Jefferson County," said Philip, still plucking the whispering strings, "my daddy seen 'im do it. I reckon John Henry could out-whop any man in the worl' an' any machine. He was a double-j'inted natural man an' he swung a twelve-poun' hammer in each han'. My daddy say his shaker could hardly get the drill turned halfway roun' 'fo' John Henry'd whop it agin. Nobody ever tetched that drill sence John Henry drapped dead. It's still stickin' in the hole at the mouth o' the tunnel 'twixt Donovan and Leeds."

"Sing us about it," said Tennant.

The whispering of the strings grew into a talking. Then Philip sang:

> When Jawn Henry wuz a baby,
> Sat on his granddaddy's knee;
> Said, "The Central o' Georgia railroad
> Gonna be the death o' me."
>
> Jawn Henry hammered in th' mountains,
> And blows from his shoulder did rain
> Hung his hammer on a little blue point,
> Sayin', "Lord, I'm a steel drivin' man."
>
> Jawn Henry hammered in the mountains,
> Hammer from his shoulder did rain,
> His hammer hung on a little blue point,
> Cried, "I b'lieve these mountains cavin' in."
>
> Cap'n said to Jawn Henry,
> "Gonna bring me a steam drill 'roun',
> Take that steam drill out on the job,
> Gonna whop that steel on down."
>
> Jawn Henry said to de Cap'n,
> "A man ain't nothin' but a man,

'Fore I iet yore steam drill beat me down,
I'd die wid m'hammer in m' han'."

Jawn Henry said to de Cap'n,
"A man ain't nothin' but a man,
If I let your steam drill beat me down,
Lay five hundred dollars in yo' han'."

Jawn Henry said to de Cap'n,
"Send me a twelve poun' hammer aroun',
Er twelve poun' hammer wid a fo' foot handle,
An' I beat yore steam drill down."

Jawn Henry said to his shaker,
"Nigger, why don' you sing?
I'm throwing twelve poun' fum my hips on down,
Jes lissen to de col' steel ring."

Jawn Henry went down d' railroad,
Wid er twelve poun' hammer by his side,
He walked down the track, but he didn't come back,
'Cause he laid down his hammer an' he died.

Jawn Henry hammered in de mountains,
The mountains were so high,
Th' las' words I heard d' pore boy say,
"Gimme a cool drink of water 'fore I die."

Jawn Henry had a little baby,
Hel' him in the pa'm uv his han'
An' the las' words I heard th' pore boy say,
"Son, yore gonna be a steel drivin' man."

Jawn Henry had er little woman,
Dress she wore wuz blue,
Las' word I heard de pore gal say,
"Jawn Henry, I been true to you."

Jawn Henry had er little woman,
Th'd dress she wore wuz brown,

Th' las' words I heard the pore gal say,
"I'm goin' whur m' man went down."

Jawn Henry had another woman,
Dress she wore wuz red,
Las' word I heard de pore gal say,
"I'm goin' whur m'man drapt dead."

Jawn Henry had er little woman,
Her name wuz Polly Ann,
On th' day Jawn Henry drapt dead,
Polly Ann hammered steel lak a man.

Where did you git dat dress,
Where'd you git t'ose shoes so fine?
"Got dat dress fum a railroad man,
An' shoes fum er driver in er mine."

"That's a good song, Philip," said Tennant. "You can go
back now. We're going to bed."

"I could sing you a lot more," said Philip. "I made up
some more verses about John Henry."

"Go back to the barracks," and Philip strolled away, the
strings whispering again.

"We'll ride in the morning," said Tennant. "You'll find
some sort o' clothes for it in every closet in the house—and I
want you to see the stables. Twelve thoroughbreds—all but
two of 'em ribbon snatchers."

"Horse shows in this country?"

"He ships 'em to Chicago. Keeps 'em here for his friends
to ride."

After a shady breakfast on the gallery the next morning we
strolled down beyond the mills where the saws were already
singing through the long pine trunks.

"Did you notice that mulatto girl that served us the bacon

and grits?" said Tennant. "She's in for life for killing her black baby. The father was a white man at that."

"Do you mean all those black servants at the house are convicts, too?"

"Sure—and all in for long stretches. That kind make the best servants."

"But suppose they cut your throat in the night?"

"They never have."

The stables were housed in a barn of more graceful proportions than the house. The big sliding door was open and as we entered we saw a stocky figure seated on a beautiful sorrel mare. Friendly. gray-blue eyes looked down on us from a strong weathered face.

"Well," he said, "glad to see you two. Heard you were somewhere around. Stay as long as you like and see that you're taken care of. John, get these gentlemen Lucy and Arrow. Sorry I can't ride with you but I'm on my way to town. What do you say to some music after supper?"

The sorrel moved forward—stopped suddenly. "Who left that stall open?" The gray-blue eyes were sharp and stern.

"I'll close it, boss," said black John running.

"No. I want the man who left it open—"

A spare, gangling figure appeared from the back of the stables running. As he came near I saw he was a white man—and frightened. His face was a greenish yellow. He closed the gate to the stall and stood by it breathing heavily.

"Don't let that happen again," said the man on the horse. He turned to us. "You might ride down by the river—the honeysuckle and wild azaleas are very thick there. You can ride for ten miles or so that way and not be off my land. I'll be seeing you tonight."

When he had ridden from sight Tennant and I walked our horses along the river trail.

"That second stableman is the only white man bossed by a nigger in the whole state, I reckon," said Tennant. "John is head stableboy, has been for years. He killed his wife's lover and was sent up for life. The white man is in for forty years for a bank robbery."

"What kind of music did the boss mean?" I said. "Will Philip play again?"

"There's just one room in the house that's locked," said Tennant. "That's just to the left as you go in. It holds a good phonograph and one of the most complete collections of opera records in the world. All the walls are lined with cabinets full of 'em. The whole thing sounds sort of medieval, doesn't it? Everything he wants—music, horses, food, guests, and a gang of murderers and cutthroats to do what he tells 'em to. I reckon you wouldn't find that in many other parts of the world right now."

We had ridden over a mile but the screeching song of the saws was still audible. I thought of the long line of uniformed men.

"I reckon you wouldn't," I said.

Now things are different at River Falls. The state doesn't rent convicts out to people any more. The mills are there but even the big house is different. It looks neater and prettier. The boss doesn't look as grim as he used to. He's married now and there is a gentle lady to welcome visitors to River Falls.

MOBILE *and the* BAYOU COUNTRY

CHAPTER I

Mobile

MOBILE stays in the heart, loveliest of cities. I have made many journeys down the Black Warrior and I have always found happiness at its mouth. And so I summarize my impressions rather than tell the story of a visit.

Few travelers "pass through" Mobile. The old city rests apart, remembering the five flags that have flown over her. Spain and France and England and the Old South, grown harmonious through the mellowing of time, are echoes in the streets. But since only people who "are going to Mobile" are her visitors, her charms have been less exploited than those of any of the other sea cities of the South.

Whether you come by train or by boat you arrive in the same part of town. There is a smell of hemp and tar about it. Long low two-story buildings, their intricate iron balconies interrupted here and there by signs—"Sailors' Supplies," "The Army and Navy Store," line the narrow streets. Sometimes the balcony overhangs the sidewalk and makes a roofed passage for pedestrians, ornate iron pillars supporting it at the street's edge. These buildings once housed a roistering assembly. The crews of ocean windjammers found liquor here in gilded saloons. They lined up at the mirrored bar with the bully-boys of North Alabama—keel-boatmen on the Black Warrior, planters' sons arrived by side-wheel steam packet from the wide estates on the Tombigbee, badman gamblers in extravagant apparel. One of these squalid doorways was the entrance to Madame Valerie's, where in chandeliered brilliance a soft-voiced Creole dowager conducted her salon of culture and lechery, her ladies advertised as educated, refined, charming; all sisters in profession, however, of the sloe-eyed ivory-colored quadroons in the "houses" nearer the water. The waterfront itself is no longer as picturesque as it was in the days of the clipper ships or the river packets. The gay welter of colorful types has disappeared. Where it once reveled you may sometimes meet a strange woman, ragged and unkempt—a small hat set on the top of her wide profusion of yellow hair. "Floating Island" the Mobilians call her and they will tell you she waits for a sailor lover who embarked fifty years ago and was drowned. Each day she looks out over the tossing horizon for signs of his returning boat—mumbling to herself.

Or, tottering along the cobbles on a sunny morning, Cudjo may greet you—a wizened black man who must be treated with respect. The boat that brought Cudjo to America was the last of the slavers to run the Federal Blockade. Hardly had he and his companions been delivered to the slave-dealers when the end of the war made them free men in an alien country. Huddling in a terrified group, they built their cabins close together—cabins that are now all empty save one—and in their little community they continued to use their native tongue. Cudjo is very old now. But he haunts the shores of the ocean over which he was brought, a frightened prisoner, so many years ago. He says he was the son of a king in Africa. Only a few words of the strange primitive language he once spoke so fluently remain in his memory. He repeats them slowly, knowing there is a reward. Where he stands all is businesslike that was once picturesque. The bustle of the quai has been supplanted by the silence of great warehouses. Above their dark massive screen white gulls circle and dip out of sight toward the waters of Mobile Bay.

It seems that almost any street of downtown Mobile will lead to Bienville Square—most revealing symbol of the city's

quality. With modern business buildings completely surrounding it, the gnarled old oaks spread grotesquely, making sharp
patterns of sunlight and shadow on this dreaming acre.

Business may be briskly American on one side of the street,
but the Mobilian need only look to the other to feel the serene
influence of time's passing over land and trees, in wind and sun
and rain. The events that Bienville Square has seen, moreover,
emanate a magic—a distilled essence of history which even the
ignorant cannot help but feel. De Soto was here, Bienville and
Iberville, General Andrew Jackson, Admiral Farragut.

It was near this square, the legend goes, that a German
colony settled a little over two hundred years ago. Among
them was a Russian woman whose beauty and prideful bearing
were such that all Mobile wondered. The town's curiosity was
soon satisfied. For with eyes flashing more brilliantly even than
the gorgeous jewels she wore, the lady stated that she was
wife of Alexis, son of Peter the Great. Her husband, she said,
had been so cruel to her that she had fled from him to the
refuge of a new world, and his pride had been so great that
he had announced that she was dead. The story aroused such
a storm of emotion in the breast of an aristocratic young French
officer that he offered his name to her, and there was a wedding
full of pomp and ceremony as befitted a princess and her noble
consort. They sailed for France soon and lived happily ever
after—so the story is told—even though it was later discovered
that she was only a servant to the princess she impersonated,
and had stolen the jewels. So Mobile provided America with
a mystery of a Russian princess long before the days of Anas-
tasia.

The air is soft in Mobile—filled with sea moisture. The
tropics reach toward the town from the south. Palms raise
straight trunks to the greening tufts that cap them. Fig trees
and oleanders, magnolias and Cape jasmine, Cherokee roses

and azaleas make the breezes heavy with sweet odor through the long warm season. It is a gentle air. Like the atmosphere that the people of Mobile create among themselves, it is friendly and easy-going. It folds with equal warmth about the white pillars lifted by a retired Black Belt planter and the wrought-iron patterns of a façade conceived by a French immigrant. Unlike the New Orleans Creoles, with their enclosed patios, Mobile's Latin colonists chose to build homes that looked out on the world. The lawns on which the French and Spanish houses rest have been green for almost two centuries. Outside the commercial streets down by the waterfront Mobile is a city of leisured space. The old part of the town is a honeycomb of exquisite design. Fleurs des lys in formal grace adorn a balcony that faces a wild profusion of grape clusters across the street. The bees of Napoleon, were they to take flight from their iron frame, might light upon the roses of Provence that clamber over the railings of both upper and lower galleries next door. At the city market, once the Spanish government buildings, the iron curves have a cleaner, freer sweep and they turn more delicately against the white stone.

Mobile has not always been a city on a byway. In the days of her glory the big-hatted, bright-waistcoated planter brought his wife and daughters down the Black Warrior for the theater, the horse racing, the shopping. Perhaps they embarked at Wetumpka on the famous *St. Nicholas,* its calliope tooting out *Life on the Ocean Wave* to the panic of negroes along the shore. Or they may have come from Gainesville down the Tombigbee on that gorgeous packet *Eliza Battle,* fated to be consumed in flame with a loss of forty lives. In a bayou up the Warrior, a few miles from Mobile, lie many of the sisters of these ships. In that graveyard of the steamboats few names are discernible now. Perhaps the *Southern Belle* rests there, and the *Orline St. John,* the *Ben Lee,* stern-wheeler, the *Allen*

Glover (named for her planter owner). An old riverman who knew them all might be able to tell which is the shell of that glory, *The Sunny South,* which the *Octavia, The Forest Monarch, Cherokee, Magnolia, Antoinette Douglas, Mary Clifton, A Fusilier, Empress, Selma, Eighth of January, Cremona, Fashion, Czar, Messenger.*

Paris gowns went back up the river. So did memories of Charlotte Cushman as Rosalind and Chanfran Booth as Shylock, of Parisian ballet, of Jenny Lind, of the race between the famous horses, Louisiana's *Ricardo* owned by W. S. Minor and Alabama's *Brown Dick* who belonged to Colonel Goldsby.

Though these days are memories now, the city has not forgotten. With all its outward semblance of calm, Mobile is gayest of American cities. Its free spirit, less commercialized than that of New Orleans, has kept its Gallic love of the fantastic and amusing. Behind the ornate balconies and long French windows that sedately face the streets live a people to whom carnival is a natural heritage.

While Mobile waited the coming of the new year, 1833, candles burning in the windows, the horses of dandies clopping daintily along the cobblestones of Dauphin Street, a band of young men in whom the liquors of many a bar rioted, descended upon a hardware store—accoutered themselves with rakes and cowbells—and turned the night into a bedlam. Thus the society of *Cowbellian de Rakian* was born. For a hundred years thereafter Mobile has had its mad, bad time of Carnival. Until the War Between the States, New Year's Eve witnessed its revels. Now the Cowbellians are no more; only the Strikers, a similar carnival organization, celebrate the birth of the year with a ball, and all the other social groups make merry on Shrove Tuesday at the annual Mardi Gras festival.

It is difficult for most residents of America to understand the social processes of a Southern coast city. The rigid formality that was once natural to the aristocratic émigré has now become a game that must be played as strictly according to the rules as bridge or chess. The Strikers' Ball given annually in Mobile at the old Battle House is a revelatory example of the quality that makes the survivals of social rituals in American life so charming. The Strikers are the oldest mystic society in Mobile. It is a popular fiction that no one knows who its members are though there is hardly a distinguished gentleman in the city who can truthfully deny membership. The origin of the name is explained variously. Some say that the first Strikers were markers of cotton bales; others that they were a group which broke away from the Cowbellian Society.

As New Year's Eve approaches an atmosphere of tension and mystery settles over the homes on Government Street and its environs. Débutantes look anxious, though they know that they at least will be present and be danced with. The hearts of post-débutantes and wives grow lighter when an envelope bearing the cherished "call-out" card, a masker's request for the honor of a dance, appears. The men of the house disappear frequently to attend unexplained "conferences" over costumes, favors, procedure. The younger men and the male visitors in town importantly make engagements for the "black-coat" dances that maskers unselfishly allow them.

The lobby of the old Battle House, as nine o'clock of New Year's Eve approaches, is filled with an excited crowd in full evening dress. They enter the ballroom to discover that curtains have been hung from the balcony to shut off the dance floor and the stage at the far end. Four or five rows of chairs, close to the curtains, are occupied by ladies, happy ladies who carry big bouquets of flowers, débutantes, sweethearts, wives who have received the "call-out" cards. Behind them sit the other guests of the Strikers.

At nine o'clock the band strikes up a march and the curtains are drawn. On the stage, grouped in striking tableau, stand the maskers. They may be in the laces and knee breeches of the court of Louis XIV, in the regimentals of the American Revolution, in the buckskin and beads of Indians, in the attire of any one of countless picturesque periods. Suddenly from the back of the stage the Captain of the Ball, in more elaborate dress than any other, leads out to the center of the tableau the girl who has been chosen by the Strikers as the princess of the night's revel. She wears a white gown and her arms are filled with red roses. There is a burst of applause as the two bow and then the Captain leads the girl down the center of the floor. Spotlights play on the couple from the balcony, sequins sparkle from their costumes, the applause grows deafening, almost drowning the blare of the band. Marching in single file the maskers follow the couple. At the end of the hall, while the Captain and his lady wait, they find their partners for the grand march—the first call-out. The Strikers' Ball has begun.

In the old days the guests were entertained at eleven o'clock with a champagne supper in the main dining room of the Battle House. The maskers had their supper in another room—a secret chamber where they might unmask without fear of being recognized. But prohibition brought the abandonment of a custom that may yet be revived.

Mardi Gras in Mobile is the most formal and elaborate function in modern America. Felix, Emperor of Joy, rules over the revels of this day of days. His identity and that of his queen are made known at a dinner in the Battle House on the preceding Saturday. They sit at the head of the central table. On Monday morning Felix proceeds once more to the Battle House wherein occurs a ritual entitled the Dressing of the King during which he and his knights attain at least a slight degree of alcoholic stimulation while he is being invested with the royal robes of his office. Thence the royal party is spirited by devious route to a government revenue cutter down the bay. The royal vessel, pennants fluttering, then moves up to the wharf at the foot of Government Street. Here King Felix makes his formal entry to the city, mounts his throne, and is borne through the streets in a vast procession of colorful and elaborate floats. In her pavilion before the Athelstan Club in Bienville Square the Queen awaits his coming. The throne float stops at the pavilion and a cupbearer brings His Majesty a silver flagon brimming with champagne. The King lifts it high in honor of the Queen, drinks, and the procession moves on through the crowds of merrymakers that line its path.

That evening at the municipal wharf the coronation ceremony takes place. Thousands crowd the vast building to its doors as the King and his court enter along a raised platform, over a hundred yards long, that runs down the center. Each participant in the ritual walks beneath a battery of spotlights the full length of this passage to the stage at the other end, on which the throne is reared.

After the coronation is over King and Queen and entire court in full costume appear at the ball of the Infant Mystics, their entrance heralded by massed trumpeters. This ceremonial visit at an end, they move on to other festivities throughout the city, ending their royal progress at a ball at the Athelstan Club where, regal robes discarded, they join in the dancing.

On the morning of the next day, Mardi Gras itself, the entire city is given over to masked merrymaking. Noon sees the parade of the Knights of Revelry and the Comic Cowboys, and the high float of the King sways through the streets again. The monarch's last appearance before the populace is in the flare of countless torches borne by strutting negroes to light the parade of the Order of Myths. That organization, founded in 1868 for the express purpose of dispelling the gloom brought about by the War Between the States, chose as its emblem the figure of Folly belaboring Death with colored bladders. The first float in its parade is always a representation of this emblem, and its annual ball on Mardi Gras night is always prefaced by Death's wild dash across the ballroom floor pursued by Folly who mercilessly whacks him with the resounding bladders. This ball, similar to the Strikers' in formal ceremonies, brings the day's revels to a close and the city enters the solemn Lenten period fortified by gay memories.

Mobile is a city of intimacies that have stood the test of time. On Government Street the houses shaded by magnolias and Cape jasmines shelter families whose grandfathers and great-grandfathers were friends. Along the azalea-strewn road to Spring Hill, the old Episcopal college, today as a hundred years ago, a black cook bears a gift of wine and jelly from her white folks' kitchen to the white folks next door. Affections are strong in this place, for they have been long depended on.

Even the heat of summer drives but few of the people of Mobile northward. Point Clear "across the bay" or Biloxi on the Gulf Coast a few miles away are pleasant enough for vacations. Country houses on the picturesque Dog River are usually filled with gay parties on week-ends throughout the year. At midday the city's homes are cool refuges and streets are empty. In the evening thousands of automobiles line Mobile Bay while a breeze from the moonlit waters blows inland and little sailboats scud about silhouetted against the shining surface.

It is easy to become adapted to the rhythm of this city. Acquaintances gradually become friends. The processes of earning a living are slow and comparatively unimportant to the living itself. Dignity and charm and gayety permeate life there. Mobile is a city of the lotos—bringing forgetfulness of everything except the pleasant passing of the hours.

Coq d'Inde

THE old shell road out of Mobile leads to a coast land of bayous. Bienville saw wild turkeys there and named an inlet Coq d'Inde. Coden it is now, lying beside Sans Souci and Bayou Labatre and Point aux Pins. Near these little towns wine-colored streams reflect Spanish moss hanging in long tatters from the water oaks, and bathe the roots of fragrant orange and lemon and oleander trees. Now the country is inhabited by fisherfolk and summer guests. Once its uncharted sinuous channels gave refuge to more dangerous residents, to robbers and pirates, even to Jean La Fitte.

That bane of British and Spanish commerce put into the Mississippi Sound one day between Isle aux Herbes and the mainland and found Coden. The legend is that he buried treasure there, knowing that his rich colony of marauders established at the Island of Grande Terre could not resist for long the forces of law and order. The Laurendines, the Girards, the Rabbis, descendants of the oldest French families in the region, know where he built his shack and they have speculated for generations now on the direction he and his men took when they went from it one midnight staggering under the weight of chests of gold. But the spades of treasure hunters have not yet uncovered the buried metal.

Knowing the ways of summer resorts, I gave this legend little credence when I first went to Coden. The faith of "Bud" Rabbi, fisherman, in its truth finally brought me to make inquiries as to its origin. My search led to the Moore family, early residents of the section, and to a correspondence which amazingly corroborated the legend of Coden's buccaneers.

In the late 1880's a daughter of the Moore household, which had migrated to Alabama from South Carolina early in the century, set down in family letters a number of her mother's reminiscences. From them I culled the following extracts:

" 'The first man I met of romantic interest,' I have heard my mother say, 'was an old gentleman named La Mas. He was one of the Black Flag men who sailed with La Fitte, the pirate captain. La Mas was an old man when I met him. He wore a long beard, high boots outside his trousers, and always carried, stuck beneath his belt, blunderbusses and knives of curious workmanship. He lived on a green knoll in a quaint wooden house which was fastened to the earth by chain-ropes of iron, for the tornadoes and gales at Coq d'Inde were often very severe.

" 'Las Mas was always ready with his tongue and his language was courtly. He had the manners of a gentleman of "the quality" and great admiration for his former leader. "Why, Lady Moore," he once said, "I have stood knee-deep in human blood on deck with La Fitte and yet he was a man of fascinating and unquestionable charm and finish." ' "

In another section of these epistolary chronicles their author writes that the remains of the shack built by La Fitte "are still standing, storm-blown, time-touched, crumbling under a gigantic chestnut tree. All about are blowing cowslips and English daisies. I can see the ruins from the window of Anatol Rabbi's stone dining room, set off from the rest of the house, where, under the orange trees, I am enjoying my breakfast of mullet, salt bread, and café noir served by a pretty Creole girl."

This odd tangent to the biography of the French pirate-hero of the Battle of New Orleans is not the only romance-laden tale of the Alabama bayou country. At Sans Souci shrimp fishers tell the story of a French buccaneer who discovered that his beautiful daughter was in love with a Spaniard and meeting him secretly. The father immediately killed the girl by cutting her throat and buried her beside the bayou, where her ghost appears nightly. And at Bayou Labatre there are many variations of the tale of a headless Indian who appears beside the dark copper-colored water just at sundown, moaning dismally of some forgotten crime.

Most beautiful of all the Gulf Coast legends, however, is that of the Sea-Maiden of the Biloxi. It has been told to me by the islanders of Dauphin and Isle aux Herbes, by trawlers in Bonsecours Bay and the shrimp fishers of Pascagoula which is across the Mississippi state line. Each narrator claimed that the spot where the wonder took place was in the waters within a few rods of his residence. Of the many versions, this one, told to me one moonlight night by Pierre Laurendine as we sat on the white sand beside Coden bay is most affecting:

"A long time ago a tribe of Indians, named the Biloxi, lived on this island. They believed themselves to be children of the sea and they worshiped a sea-maiden. But the Spaniards came and they forced the Indians to give up their belief and take the Christian religion. A Spanish priest went among them with his cross and bell and box and the Indians had to bow to him and his God. One night the priest was wakened by a sound of stirring waters. He looked out and saw dark waves risen into a trembling mound that almost reached the clouds. At its peak, close against the blue moon stood the sea-maiden. She sang:

> 'Come to me, children of the sea.
> Neither book, nor bell, nor cross
> Shall win you from your queen.'

Then, before the priest could interfere, he saw the natives fling themselves into the water and swim toward the maiden leaving behind them great streaks of fire. When they had circled the column of waves it burst with a great hissing roar, engulfing the whole tribe in the subsiding waters.

The churchman who saw this strange thing happen believed that it was due to the fact that he was not himself in a true state of grace. On his death-bed he said that if a priest would row to the spot where the music sounded and drop a cross into the water all the souls at the bottom would be redeemed though he himself would be instantly swallowed up by the waves.

No one has ransomed the souls of the Biloxi. The sad music that haunts the bay today, rising through the waters when the moon is out, comes from the sea-caves down below where they live."

CHAPTER III

Dauphin Island

IT is a short ride by the little channel steamer from Coden to Dauphin Island. I had not wearied of the salt breeze and the sunlight on the choppy waves before I could see the low-lying white sand banks that edge it. Iberville saw them in 1699, blown by a gulf-storm into the little harbor at the east end, in the lee of Pelican Island. He found there "burning heat, barren soil, and sand so white as to injure the eye." He found, too, a great shell mound, differing from those that dot the mainland around Coden only in that beneath the huge wind-twisted cedars that surmount it he saw hundreds of human skulls. And so he called the place Massacre Island, letting it take its name from an unknown tragedy. Eight years later French officialdom rechristened the island Dauphine, a name whose final *e* time and usage have obliterated.

When I stepped off the boat on the white, salt-bleached planks of the dock, John Sadinier, fisherman, small, weather-browned, taciturn, was there to greet me. He guided me across the hot blinding sands toward the little group of low frame houses in which the islanders live. His home was a glistening whitewashed shack—long and narrow, its shingled roof sloping down over a shallow porch to three scantling supports. The interior was dark and cool and we sat for a little while beside a rough-hewn table above which on a shelf stood a little holy group of plaster figures. Hot light from the open door struck inward like a shining knife and with its aid I made out a bunk in a corner, a tattered net hanging across one wall, a box stove

near the stone fireplace at one end, and a pair of oars leaning
against the doorframe.

Then a shadow cut across the shaft of light from the door.
A slim tall girl stood before us. Her face, with high cheek
bones, aquiline nose, strong chin, was angularly beautiful. Her
eyes were deep-set and black, her hair so black that it seemed
to have a purple tinge.

"This is Veronica Lachette," said John Sadinier simply. "She
talks more than I do."

"You have a pretty name," I said. "How do you come by
it?"

"My father was French," said Veronica, "and for a long,
long time almost every girl on this island is called Veronica.
My mother was Veronica, too."

"Was she French?"

"No, no," said Veronica with a vivacity that belied her apparent Indian heritage, "she was English. She came from
English parents far back—they were in the first colony and
got lost.

"I come from them, too," she added proudly, looking not
at all like a pink-cheeked, yellow-haired English immigrant,
"I come from the lost colony of Sir Walter Raleigh."

John Sadinier's eyes were twinkling.

"Maybe," he said to the girl, who flashed an indignant look
at him. "But this gentleman is here to see the island and we'd
better get started, and not stay here telling stories."

"But stories are what I came for, too," I protested, and
Veronica smiled, showing strong even teeth.

"They were all killed by the Indians except a few," she said.
"They took pity on my family and two or three others."

I did not tell her of the many other theories and claims that
center about the fated group of which she spoke with such
simple assurance. We three rose and went out into the pitiless

glare, wading through the sand toward the Shell Banks. No archæologist has yet plumbed the secrets of these great mounds of oyster shells built up hundreds of years ago by Indian tribes. The road-builders of the mainland have destroyed some of them around Coden, crushing the shells to make surfaces for the highways, disregarding surprising pieces of patterned Indian pottery. The largest mound on Dauphin Island rises to a height of fifty feet and it was obviously built in ten-foot layers.

"They say the Indians and the French had a big powwow here long time ago," said John Sadinier. "Twenty-four chiefs came and smoked the peace pipe with the new owners for two months. Some folks tell that this mound is just the shells of the oysters they ate—but I reckon even then nobody could eat *that* much."

"That was when they set out the figs," said Veronica. "You see those trees over there? Well, the oldest ones were planted at the peace meeting. Ever since any two people that eat off the same fig can never quarrel. Let's go and get some."

"I don't hold with that much," said John Sadinier.

"You wouldn't," said Veronica dangerously, "but I can remember my mother's sending me and my brother here when we were little because we fought so much. And we ate off a fig and now we never fight. When I get engaged the first thing I do is make the young man eat a fig with me—just like the other married folks here have always done."

"Never noticed it did much good," said John.

"You know perfectly well," said Veronica, "that story about Mr. Marcu's grandfather. He courted a Swiss girl in Mobile and brought her to the island to live. But they got so mad at each other they used to yell and swear and disturb everybody. One day all the islanders went to their house and grabbed them and took them to the fig trees and made them eat. They never quarreled after that and they had a lot of babies."

"Let's go over and see what's left of the old French town," said John.

We walked inland and were soon in the shade of wateroaks, bearded with Spanish moss.

"Some of the rich people from Mobile settled here for a while," said John, "until the harbor went out. They brought their own slaves and built big houses. See that foundation over there." I saw a stone wall, evidently the former support of a massive building. Near it a few lemon trees stood in vined imprisonment.

"The garden flowers used to bloom every year but they won't grow wild for long. There's a few crape myrtle left over there," said John, pointing to a riotous evidence of a life that had been much richer than his own.

"Show him where the church was," said Veronica mischievously.

"Wouldn't tell if I knew, not till I'd looked 'round a bit." He laughed. "They built a beautiful church here. They called it *Fort Belle Eglise*. It had a high tower on it and at the top of that was a big gold cross. Fishermen could see it when they were a good many miles out. One day a British pirate ship from Jamaica saw it and piled into the harbor here with the black flag flying. The people were scared and ran away and hid—all except the priest—Father Hivre his name was. He ran to his church and up the steps into the tower—then he climbed the rest of the way up to the cross and managed to get it loose. By that time the pirates were already in the town. There was a big wide well beside the church and Father Hivre jumped from the top of the tower carrying the gold cross with him right into it. Nobody has ever seen anything of either of them since. When the pirates couldn't find the cross they were so mad they burned the church, and the place where it stood has never been found. But we all look for it sometimes. Every boy on the island thinks he'll find that well."

"That and the pot of gold," said Veronica. "We ought to get Jimmie Mellon to tell you this story because it happened to him—but he's out fishing."

"And you want to tell it," said John.

"Captain Kidd used to bury his treasure on this island," said Veronica imperturbably, "and back in nineteen sixteen Jimmie Mellon found it. A storm washed away half the shell bank and uncovered a brick cistern underneath a lot of Indian stuff. Jimmie opened the cistern and there was a clay pot with the cover sealed up. Mr. Dewberry was in charge of the island then—he and some other rich folks were planning to develop it—so Jimmie closed up the cistern and sent for him. As soon as he came they both ran over to the spot and opened the cistern but the pot was gone. There was one old Spanish gold-piece at the bottom of the cistern. Nobody had left the island and nobody *could* leave for a while without bein' searched. But they never found anything. Jimmie says he bets the Mermaid took it."

"I know that story," I said. "They told me that over at Coden."

"They ought to be ashamed," said Veronica indignantly. "It happened here."

"A few years ago," said John, "a Pascagoula man shot one of us islanders for sayin' she belonged here. Said it happened right where the Pascagoula River empties into the Sound."

We turned away from the foundations of the old town and started back toward the sea.

"Why did all these people give up and go back to the mainland?" I asked.

"Bad luck," said John. "It all started, they say, 'round the year seventeen-forty. This harbor was better than the one at

Pensacola then, and all the big boats used to make it. Then one day the big sailing vessel *Bellona* was standing off waiting to take the governor, Bienville, to France. The weather was just as calm and clear as it is now. All of a sudden she sank—without any warning—sank and drowned half her crew. They say she just slipped straight down. A couple of weeks later come a twelve-day blow that just wiped out the harbor—took one arm right away. Nobody would stay here after that. The rich families all left and the houses and orchards rotted away. Spain didn't get much when she bought us from France. But if we could get some salvagers after the *Bellona* and bring her up, we'd get flush times again. Her sinkin' was what started it all."

CAJAN

CHAPTER I

Citronelle

IT was the hottest day I had known in Alabama, although I
had been living there six years. I had left Tuscaloosa—
perhaps for the last time—and I drove alone down a dusty
road. Lazy Lawrence danced in front of me shimmering between the rows of drooping trees that lined my path. I passed
the tobacco fields of a green little town, somehow contriving
to look fresh even in the heat. The name on the wall of the
railroad station was Cuba. A few more miles and there was a
worn sign on a tree, "Mississippi State Line." Then long, long
stretches of gravelly road—Meridian, Shubuta, Hiwannee,
Chicora, Bucatunna. In the afternoon it hardly seemed that I
could go on. Great waves of blistering air struck my face. My
hands were hot and dry with dust. No matter how often I
stopped to drink at roadside stores, I was thirsty. About five
o'clock I saw a post office labeled Yellow Pines and I knew I
was back in Alabama. The hours of intense heat had sickened
and wearied me. The wind still burned against my cheeks, my
mouth, my dry, aching eyes. At last I saw an arrow on a pine
tree that marked a fork in the road; "Citronelle" it read and
with a surge of relief I knew I was near journey's end.

I took the fork down which the arrow pointed. For a few
miles it provided a narrow passage through pine woods—then
it ceased to be a road. I stopped and left the steering wheel to
look. In front of me lay a white sandy surface covered with
shrubbery and scrub pine. Apparently other motorists had not
been daunted by this transformation, for I could see the tracks
of cars ahead of me. I returned to my seat and drove on. The

tracks curved, aimlessly it seemed to me, over the level waste of sand and brush. Once they passed over what had been the bed of a stream, now dry and stony, and once they stopped altogether as I almost ran into the trunk of a small pine that had blown across the way since the last car had passed. I drove around it and picked up the track again but I was growing more and more uncertain. Then the trail forked and I knew I was lost. Neither fork appeared the more traveled and I had to rely on a guess. I took the left, a little frightened at wandering alone in a barren strange country. A half-mile farther on I saw, about fifty yards to my left, a one-room weathered shack against which its owner had built a sort of lean-to. I called out "hello" several times and finally a woman in a faded blue dress appeared in the doorway and moved slowly toward me. Bent and listless, she heard me ask the way to Citronelle.

"This ain't it."

"But how can I reach it?"

"You go back and take the right fork. I don't know what you do after that. I ain't been in much. My husband goes in onct in a while."

"Whose place is this?" I said.

"My husband's."

"But what's his name?"

She looked at me and I saw that she was much younger than I had thought, and that she hated me.

"He's a Rivers," she said. "We're Cajans." She turned away and walked toward the shack.

"Thank you," I called after her and turned my car about.

A half-hour later I found myself on a broad pike with a reddish clay surface and suddenly the woods and the sand ended. The sunset threw a gold light on a luxuriant cornfield and as I passed it a sudden evening breeze set it tossing. I saw a house standing very white beside the red road and smoke was blowing from its chimney. A pine-needle smell was in the cooling air. The almost intolerable trial of heat and dust and loneliness was over. Citronelle was a promised land after exile in a grim unyielding wilderness.

I drove up to a small white hotel standing on a slope above the town. Friendly young people took my baggage to my room. My bath was ready. Dinner would be held for me another half-hour. Mr. Jernigan was expecting me and would drop in about nine. I could endure living—even enjoy it, maybe—by bed-time.

When Lyle Jernigan came on the hotel porch, tall and cool in white clothing, I had almost forgotten the black despair of the afternoon. There would be tennis for us tomorrow after-noon—and a men's fishing party on Saturday.

"But what," I said, "about the reason for my visit? I want to know about Cajans."

"I reckon you'll pick that up easy enough," said Lyle, smil-ing. "We can all tell you something. And you'd better see Dr. Thompson because he gets out among 'em more than the rest of us do. His boy, Paul, knew you at the university. He'll be over to see you tomorrow. Let's go down to my store and have some ice cream."

The next day, waiting in the store for Lyle to finish up and join me at tennis, I got another glimpse of the people I had come to see. A young man and a girl came in to buy ice-cream cones. They were both dark and tall, the man about six feet. Save for their height, they looked like Sicilians. The man's hair was curly, his cheek bones high, his features aquiline, his eyes large and gray. The girl was of olive complexion and her straight well-formed nose and generous mouth under a wealth of dark brown hair that was braided and caught up at the base of her neck gave her exotic beauty. Her loveliness was marred only when she smiled, for then her teeth showed dark and neglected. Her companion wore blue overalls and a gray flannel shirt, and she a shapeless dark gray dress. Both were barefoot.

As they left I said to Lyle:

"What's your theory of the origin of these people?"

"I can tell you as good a one as the next man. Which one do you want to hear?"

"Doesn't anybody know?"

"Try asking around, just for fun."

So, for two days, I asked around.

"Long time ago wasn't no folks on them sand flats," a "turpentine nigger" told me. "Couldn't even get niggers to live out there. Them Cajans sprung up right out'n the ground. Some say they come from animals—coons and foxes and suchlike—but that ain't right. Just sprung up out'n the ground."

"They get their name from the Louisiana Cajans," an old white man told me, "but they really came from pirates that used to have their headquarters along the east coast of Mobile Bay. They used to put in there after they had captured vessels and divide up the spoil—cargo, gold, women. The women were all kinds—Russian, Spanish, French, English, Nigger—and so were the pirates. I reckon they're the most mixed-up people there are."

I asked a Cajan—a fairly successful intelligent farmer named Byrd.

"All the real Cajans sprung from the Byrd family," he said. "Captain Red Byrd was a Mexican Indian and he come to Mobile County a long time ago and married a Louisiana Cajan— that's how the name happened. He had a band of wild men with him. They called him 'Daddy Lem' but everybody else called him Captain Red Byrd because he and the men stuck red feathers in the little caps they wore. They all dressed in animal skins and carried clubs to hunt with, and after they had killed a beast they ate his meat raw. Captain Red Byrd was eight feet tall and he had hair all over him and he was stronger than anybody."

A farmer who drove in from around Vinegar Bend to the north of Citronelle said: "They all come from Tibbi up near my country. 'Most a hundred year ago it was, a free Jamaica nigger by the name of Daniel Read come in there and he bought a bondwoman named Rose from General Gaines and made her his wife. He built a place that's still there called the Rose Read place. Folks goin' from Choctaw and north Washington County to Mobile to market with wagons o' cotton and such-like used to stop overnight there and it got to be a kind o' hotel. He had to build another house for the niggers to stay in. He had a big family o' sons and daughters an' they all looked white an' they all married white. Reckon one of 'em married French an' that was where the name Cajan come from."

Paul Thompson came to see me and took me to meet his father. The doctor was a sun-browned healthy man on whom physical facts had impressed a breadth and tolerance not known to his immediate neighbors. He said:

"I'm going out in Cajan country tomorrow morning. Would you like to come along? I'll be starting around five o'clock."

I went. We rode before sunrise over the flat sand, among the low pines and intermittent brush. I asked the doctor how he knew the way.

"They can tell me how to come, but, even knowing the country as well as I do, I get lost sometimes. There's a kind of legend, you know, that the Cajans don't live anywhere—they just come to town out of no place. There's an occasional stream to help me out on direction. You see that branch over there to the right. That means I turn left here," and he boldly struck off cross country.

In a few minutes he said:

"See that light in front of us to the right. They're wavin' a lantern at us."

We drove up to an unpainted dark-gray shack set up off the earth by four piles of small rocks. A woman stood in the doorway holding a lantern yellow in the gray light that precedes dawn.

"Better wait here a minute," said the doctor and left me.

The sun was beginning to streak the sky above the stubby pines when he called to me from the doorway:

"Come in for a minute."

I entered a house of shadows. The lantern turning in the woman's hand revealed a wooden bunk against the far wall and on it a recumbent blanketed figure. At the center of the room stood a crude table and beside it lay a box evidently meant to be sat upon. At the right against the wall were two wide saw-horses on which planks had been placed. On the planks slept three little children, all fully clothed, a boy and two girls. Above their heads hung a colored calendar depicting the idyllic rendezvous of a gorgeously feathered Indian brave and his sweetheart.

"He'll be all right now," the doctor said to the woman, "just a touch of malaria. Give him the medicine regular." He turned to go.

"This gentleman," he said, putting a hand on my arm, "has come a long way to find out about Cajans."

The woman said nothing. But she looked at me just as we left and I saw the same hatred in her face that I had seen in the eyes of the woman who had saved me from being lost on the day I came to Citronelle.

"We'll stop by a couple more places," said the doctor, "and then I want to take you to a Cajan school."

The next shack we visited seemed identical with the first and I remarked on it.

"They're pretty much alike," said the doctor. "They're all old houses built by their fathers or their grandfathers. They have a superstition that it's bad luck to move out of 'em, so they stay—no matter how rich they get or how many children they have; sort of ancestor worship, I reckon. You won't get a chance to come in this time—not if I can guess what's the matter with this fellow."

He was back in a half-hour.

"Gonorrhea. The woods are full of it. The lower class Cajans are a passionate, free and easy lot and once a venereal disease starts around here it spreads like smallpox. Makes it hard on some of these kids we're goin' to see."

The schoolhouse was a one-room frame structure which its builders had thought to dignify with an ecclesiastical-looking belfry—but had given up the idea when it was half realized. The doctor told me it was used as a church on Sundays. Beside it was a graveyard—a cluster of mounds with only an occasional headstone to distinguish one of them. Outlining each mound, though, were bits of broken china, electric light bulbs, lamps, glasses.

The stopping of an automobile outside seemed to be an automatic signal for temporary dismissal of school activities. The doctor had hardly turned off his engine when the children poured out of the door in a dense crowd of a score or more. Following them came a white girl of about eighteen, pleasant of face and friendly.

"How are you, doctor?" she said. "We're all glad to see you." The children stood in a wide semicircle about the car and stared at us.

"This gentleman," said the doctor, "has come a long way to see your children and your school. He wants to know a lot of things."

"We'll try to tell him," said the girl, smiling. "Perhaps

you'd like to see my roll-book so that you can know who all these children are."

We looked at it together and she pointed out the names of the larger families. Here were the Byrds, the Weavers, the Chestangs, the Riverses, the Sullivans, the Johnsons, and beside these names were Bedreau and La Soliallet, evidences, perhaps, of the long-lost link with the exiles from Grand Pré.

The children watched us solemnly as if in wonder and I gazed back quite as amazed to see among the curly-headed boys and girls of olive complexion a number of yellow-haired, blue-eyed blonds—as Nordic in appearance as Dakota Swedes. The teacher saw my look of surprise and laughed:

"Yellow and black hair often run in the same family. You Weaver girls stand out here with your brother."

Two little blonde misses sidled forward and a boy who, with his straight black hair, looked as Latin as a resident of southern Italy.

"Dave," said the teacher, "tell these gentlemen about the Cajan people. Where did they come from?"

"From French people that married Indians," said the boy, and then he added—a little belligerently, "and not from any niggers at all."

The children sang a school song for us and I noticed that they kept its rhythm with surprising accuracy—it was almost as if they were one voice. Then the teacher tried to get them to sing a song that they had learned at home—a Cajan folk-song—but only a few voices took it up and they died away as their companions grew restless.

"It's no use," said the teacher; "I've been trying to get them to sing that for me for months." She told her charges to go behind the school to play and gave her attention to me.

"You're fortunate to be here while our school is in session. We hardly ever have more than three months of it."

"These separate schools for the Cajans don't run as long as the others, then?" I said.

"No, even the negro schools run longer. They have more people interested, missions and so on."

"And how do you happen to be their teacher?"

"I'm earnin' my way through the university by teachin' in the summer. I've just finished my freshman year. The school board offered the Cajans a six months' school if they'd take a mulatto teacher that just graduated from Tuskegee but they wouldn't do it."

"And what about high school?"

She laughed. "These girls get married when they're sixteen and the boys go to work farmin' or in the turpentine woods— long before they're ready for high school. There's just one Cajan high school I've heard of. The Roman Catholics gave 'em that over at Chestang."

"I know of one Cajan who went through a college," said the doctor, "an Alabama college at that—but I reckon nobody but his parents and me knew about it. He was a smart boy and now he's some kind of rich engineer up north." He laughed. "Reckon we better be getting along."

The sound of our starting engine brought the children running. They stood about us as we backed into the road.

"Good-by, children," said the doctor.

There was a long, loud, quite ununderstandable chorus.

"What are they saying?" I asked.

The doctor chuckled. "That's the way a Cajan says good-by. 'Come go home with me.' Sort of nice and graceful, isn't it? They mean it, too. They're always visiting around and they're glad to share what they've got with each other. Time for my office hours already. You better just sit tight for a few minutes while I take us into town in a hurry. If you don't you may shake right out of this thing."

The Hell-Raisin'

LYLE JERNIGAN and I were driving back from a swim in Cedar Creek at the end of a hot day when we heard a long wavering cry that seemed to be coming out of the sunset. Lyle stopped his car.

"What in God's name is that?" I said.

"It's a Cajan yell, way they have of letting off steam; usually means some sort of hell-raising. Even when they're hoein' a field all of a sudden they'll let go like that. Sometimes drivin' home from Mobile late at night I've heard it comin' out of a swamp; gives you the creeps."

The sound came again from the west—piercing, terrifying, and the still country was suddenly filled with echoes.

"I thought so," said Lyle. "We'll just drive over that way. Maybe we can see somethin'."

We drove almost a mile before Lyle turned quickly in behind a screen of brush and stopped the engine. "There's the house," he said, pointing through the foliage in front of us.

It was a long low shack made of timbers weathered gray and set up in typical manner on four rock piles. The porch was deeper than those of most Cajan houses. On it, leaning back in a wicker rocker, sat a white-haired old man with a violin held in the curve of his arm. Notes cascaded from the strings. Before him a lanky, black-haired fellow stepped and sidestepped with a blonde thin girl. As we looked the man raised his hands to his mouth and the wild call rent the beginning twilight.

"This is the way their dances begin," said Lyle. "Sort of spontaneous combustion. They get all riled up inside and then

264

they bust loose. In a minute you'll see some more of 'em comin' to see if there's a chance for a shindy."

Sure enough, down the wagon tracks that led by the front of the house strolled a couple, tall, dark, slow. But when they reached the porch they were quickly assimilated into the swinging, circling dance. There was a sound of crackling brush near us and we saw a lithe young man carrying a green bag enter the clearing and stride toward the house.

"Another fiddler," said Lyle. "I don't mind stayin' here a while, but we better lay low and hope they don't see us. If they do I'm goin' to leave here on the jump, for I don't trust a Cajan full of corn."

"Do they make their own moonshine?"

"They do. And they can hit a revenuer with buckshot as far as they can see him. Revenuers don't do much but draw their salaries in the Cajan section if they want to keep healthy."

"Would they let us join the dance?"

"Sure they would. But one of those girls in there might like one of us. And neither of us yearns to carry a corpse back to town. Cajans get jealous quick and easy."

"We'll stay here," I said, "and you keep your foot on the starter."

Other couples were coming down the wagon track now and there was a clapping of hands to the rhythm of the fiddle. A great reddish moon was rising behind us and it made the woods almost as light as they had been before sunset. A lamp was burning inside the shack and we could see the hopping, whirling figures silhouetted against the doorway and the windows. The Cajan yells sounded again and again.

"They're gettin' pretty well liquored up," said Lyle. "He's playin' *I'd Like to See Louisa;* they like that fiddle-tune."

Now they were stamping their feet to add emphasis to their rhythmic clapping. A yell no sooner started than it was taken up by a dozen voices with such volume that it was almost deafening to us.

"I'd suggest," said Lyle, "that my mother's ice-box has cold chicken and cold tea. This blow-out will last until midnight but I don't believe we could. Besides, there's no knowing when they may discover us out here—maybe take us for revenuers."

"Step on the starter," I said.

CHAPTER III

Twilight of the Races

TWO days later Lyle Jernigan said to me: "I've fixed it up for you to call on the richest Cajan hereabouts. Go up there now if you like. It's about a mile. Just keep on the road around the hill and you'll see a bright blue house. That's where he lives."

The bright blue house was a rambling cottage built on the side of a hill. Green vines shaded its spacious veranda, affording a color contrast that was echoed by the sycamores and blue sky beyond. My host came to greet me, a sturdy man with sandy hair, reddish mustache and very blue eyes. We sat outdoors for a while looking down on the neat design of his fields.

"Yours is a good name in South Carolina," I said. "Did you come from there?"

"It's just as good a name here," he said simply. "Yes, my folks live in South Carolina now. But I came here and married a Cajan woman and that makes me a Cajan and all our children, too."

"That doesn't seem to have worked against you," I said. "You have a pleasant home—a fertile profitable farm. They tell me you have plenty of money in the bank."

He was silent for some time. Then, as if he had been making up his mind, he spoke determinedly:

"My farm and my money don't make other farmers friendly. And they can't buy my children a decent education. I don't so much care for myself or my wife—we get along. But I've tried hard to help my children. They're as white as you or me—and I put 'em in a white school. Soon as the teacher found out who they were, she sent 'em back. So I went to law about it, spent a lot of money putting up a big fight. They couldn't prove my wife wasn't white but they decided that technically my children were the same as niggers. They could go to the miserable Cajan schools or to nigger schools but they couldn't go to school with other white children."

I had not expected such an outburst and I was a little embarrassed. Probably, I thought, I am the first disinterested person this fellow has had a chance to talk to about his life—and a man needs to let off steam once in a while.

While we sat there mulling it over silently, a bright-eyed woman appeared in the doorway bearing two cups of steaming coffee. She wore a checked blue and white apron over a blue dress figured in yellow. Her straight black hair, parted in the middle and knotted at the back, was flecked with gray, and her sun-browned face showed many interlaced delicate lines.

"My wife."

"Howdy," she said. "Here's your before-dinner coffee. The rest'll be on the table by the time you finish."

"But I mustn't," I said.

"We've been expectin' you," said my host. "We'd like to have somebody from outside the state for our guest."

I could see that they really wanted me; I was glad to stay. While we sipped our coffee a bell rang at the back of the house. In a few moments two boys in blue overalls appeared on the veranda. "This one is Jack," said their father, pointing to the taller of the two—a tow-headed blue-eyed youngster of about fourteen; "and that's Tom," indicating a small edition of Jack, possibly two years younger.

We four went in to sit at a long plank table for dinner and while the menfolks ate, the wife and little ten-year-old Catherine, who looked like her mother, brought them salt pork and collards and turnips and bread and molasses. I looked about the room that apparently served both dining and general living purposes. Aside from the table at which we sat the furniture was store-bought, including a "mission" divan. There was a large framed photograph on the wall—probably of a South Carolina relative. On a small corner table was a portable phonograph.

We sat outdoors again after dinner, and I tried to get the boys to talk to me, aided by their proud father. At first they were very shy—but they got excited when I spoke of baseball and said I had seen Babe Ruth hit a home run. Their questions came thick and fast and their eyes sparkled. Their minds seemed quite as quick as their active squirming bodies. Finally their father said: "Better get your hoes on down to that lower forty if we're goin' to have a corn crop," and they left us.

When I rose to go a few moments later the richest of the Cajans took my hand.

"I'm proud to know you," he said, "and I wish if you're goin' to write a book, like you say, I wish you'd put somethin' in it about people like me that want their children educated but don't get a chance."

"I'll do the best I can," I said.

AFTERWORD

IT is hard for me to believe that I lived in Alabama for six
years. The period since I left my home there seems much
longer. Now I remember my life in Tuscaloosa as an unreality
stumbled upon long ago—and as suddenly ended. Like a character in imaginative fiction, I feel that I stepped into a past that
lives and is concurrent with today. But, unlike persons who
have been under a spell which, once exorcised, may never return, I know that the witchment does not end. I know that since
I left them little has changed beneath those incomplete heavens
from which the stars fell. On the high plateau of Sand Mountain at noonday smoke and the smell of mash still rise from
secret places in the quiet woods; and at night a chorus of guitar
notes twangs upward. A letter from Mary Louise has just arrived saying that Antimo is in high glee over having cooled
down a revival meeting of negroes screaming, "Can't nothin'
hurt me 'caze I'se a chile o' God, I'se holy sanctified," by
standing up on a bench and waving his bandanna handkerchief
and shouting: "Look here, niggers, maybe you *is* holy sanctified, an' maybe nothin' can never hurt yuh no mo', but I won't
believe it till one of yuh takes dis here red bandanner out in
Marse Jesse's pasture where dem Jersey bulls is an' comes out
o' dere alive." Mary Louise writes that Antimo says to tell me
he's still got his bandanna. Ida Carter, I am informed, has
raised her prices on May Water and John the Conquerer Root
because, as she says, in hard times people need good luck just
that much more. Two-Toe Tom is still a crawling menace, last
heard of near Andalusia, so Tennant told me on a recent visit

270

to New York. He says Gilmore keeps on whipping lazy black boys and can offer plenty of arguments in support of the practice.

And in my old home, the river-bordered town of Tuscaloosa, dreaming most of its days away beneath the shade of elms and live oaks and magnolias, the fateful compulsion is at work again. As I write this, news comes that a mob of a thousand men has surrounded the dingy yellow courthouse. A machine gun mounted on the steps looks bleakly down on them. I can picture them milling about on the lawn of the Snow place next door, talking in excited groups near the Baptist church across the street. There will be dark doings soon. The men in khaki uniforms who serve the machine gun and stand guard with their rifles at the doors look nervous and uncomfortable. The mob is made up of their friends. But the guardsmen have seen the glint in the eyes out there. They know that the old irresistible urge is upon the shifting crowd. No ties will hold them when that madness lowers. The spell cast in the "year the stars fell" is not yet broken.

Fiddlers' Tunes

The following list contains the names of over a hundred tunes. These were selected as the more picturesque titles out of a catalogue of about four hundred which I compiled from the repertories of a dozen or so fiddlers as told to me by them.

Alabama Coon Jigger
Alabama Gals
Arkansas Traveller
Baby Bend
Back Side of Albany
Bacon and Collards
Barlow Knife
Bile the Cabbage Down
Bill Silvy
Billy in the Low Ground
Bird in the Cage, He Can't Get Out
Black Bess (referring to the train)
Blackberry Blossom
Blue Tail Fly
Bobbed-Tail Buzzard

Bran' New Nigger
Buck-eye Jim
Bucking Mule
Bung Your Eye
Boatman's Dance
Cackling Hen
Chaw Roast Beef
Chicken in the Bread Tray, Scratchin' Out Dough
Circus Rider
Clucking Hen
Cotton Choppin Dick
Cotton-eyed Joe
Cross-eyed Charlie
Corn Shucking
Daddy's Pack of Hounds

Danny in the Cotton Patch
Dead up the Stump
Devil's Hiccough
Diamond Joe
Dog and Gun
Double Headed Train
Down the Road
Devil's Dream
The Drunkard's Hiccough
Fire in the Mountains, Run Boys Run
Flat Woods
Fly in the Buttermilk, Shoo! Fly Shoo!
Goin' Down the Road Feelin' Bad
Gonna Raise a Rookus Tonight
Granny's Cock-eyed Cat
Half Moon Dance
Happy Times in Butler
Hawk's Nest
Hell After Yearling
Hop Light Ladies
Hog Eye
Horse Shoeing
I'll Never Get Drunk Any More
Indian Squaw
Jim Along Josy
Jim Crack Crow
Johnny Sand
Leather Breeches
Lost Child
Lost John
Methodist Preacher
Mississippi Sawyer
Mister Chicken
Money Musk
Mountain-top Cabin

Mustard Plaster Hurts
My Mule, Aunt Nell
Nigger Heel
Nigger in the Wood Pile
Nigger Preacher
Oh Susanna
Old Aunt Peggy, Won't You Set 'Em Up Again?
Old Cow Died in the Forks of the Branch
Old Dog River
Old Joe Clark
Old Molly Hare, What You Doing There?
Old Time Sorghum Mill
Old Water Wheel
Old Zip Coon
One-eyed Goose
Peanut Gal
Pop Goes the Weasel
Rabbit Plowed the Possum
Rakin' Up Hay
River Bridge
Rocky Hollow Hard Times
Rum Has Made a Fool Out-a Me
Rye Straw
Sandy Loves Taters
Set My Trap in the Old Straw Field
She's Comin' Around the Mountain
Shortnin' Bread
Shout Lula
Stealing Chickens
Stick Out Your Nigger Foot
Such a-Getting Upstairs
Sugar in the Coffee
Sugar in the Gourd

Syrup Pudding
Thaddy You Gander
That Big Black B'ar Will Get You, Honey
Third Party
Three Nights in the Piney Woods
Throw My Fiddle Over the Fence
Two-faced Devil
Two Little Niggers
Turkey in the Straw
Uncle Wash Has Washed His Corn

Up in the Hills and Down the Straight
Waggoner
Went Down to the New Ground
Whole Hog or None
Who's Been Here Since I Been Gone? A Pretty Girl With a Red Dress On
Wild Goose
Wild Horse in the Canebrake
Wildcat Whiskey
Wooden Leg Diana
Wolves A-howlin'

Quilt Patterns

This is the list of Mattie Sue's quilt-names as she gave it to me.

Garden of Eden
Star of Bethlehem
Tree of Paradise
The Cross
Wonder of the World
Love Rose
Lover's Links
Lincoln's Platform
Radical Rose
Hobson's Kiss
Old Maid's Puzzle
Churn Dash
Sugar Loaf
All Tangled Up
Hearts & Gizzards
Crosses and Losses
Odds and Ends

Circle Saw
Golden Gates
Solomon's Temple
Forbidden Fruit Tree
Air Castle
Charm
True Lovers' Knot
Wedding Knot
Harrison's Rose
Whig Rose
Widower's Choice
Baseball
Log Cabin
Old Bachelor's Puzzle
The Road to California
Tangled Garters
Bed Time
Economy

Joseph's Coat
Solomon's Crown
Art Square
Lady of the Lake
Wheel of Fortune
Friendship Quilt
Old Tippecanoe
Democrat Rose
Handy Andy
Joseph's Necktie
Necktie
Ice Cream Bowl
Drunkard's Path
Hairpin Catcher
Aunt Sulky's Patch
Swinging Corners
Devil's Claws

All-Day Singing

The United Sacred Harp Musical Association is said to have between twenty and fifty thousand members—the largest singing society in the world.

Among the sketches I later found in the Sacred Harp Song Book I found the following: "Amariah Hall was a farmer, manufactured straw bonnets, kept a hotel, and taught singing schools. With him music was only an avocation."

"R. E. Brown was a Baptist minister and ventriloquest."

"Professor T. B. Newton of Georgia has a fine voice and sings every time opportunity presents itself."

"Mrs. Dana Shindler of South Carolina and

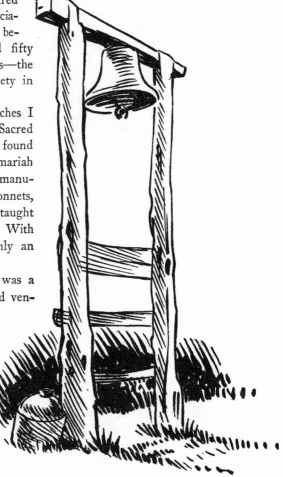

PLANTATION BELL AT THORN HILL

Texas, first married Mr. Dana and afterward became Mrs. Shindler. She wrote on the death of her husband, 'I am a Pilgrim and a Stranger.'"

"To Lowell Mason of Georgia the music came naturally on reading the poetry. It flashed through his mind like lightning and he wrote and composed the music as if by magic. Mr. Mason said that he made no effort at all in this composition."

"During Jeremiah Ingalls's travels as a singing teacher, he stopped at a tavern in the town of Northfield for dinner. His dinner was very slow in coming. He kept thinking 'how long?' He fell into the rhythm of Watts' sacred lines ('How long, dear Savior, O how long, Shall this bright hour delay?') and the tune came with it. He named the tune *Northfield*."

"*Sawyer's Exit* was composed by Mr. Sawyer on the day of his death and was set to music which in its Secular form was called 'Old Rosen the Bow.'" (A tune well known to many generations of country fiddlers.)

Mountain Superstitions

While I visited Henry and Mattie Sue I persuaded them and their friends to tell me the superstitions that are prevalent in the Alabama Mountain Country. Some of the more picturesque are presented here:

If one finds a baby pacifier, there is going to be an addition to the family.

If a baby teethes early, it is making way for a new baby.

If you cut off a baby's finger nails, it will die before it is six months old.

Putting a hat on a baby's head will cause bad teething.

Letting a baby look in a mirror will cause bad teething.

If you see a buzzard flying through the air, make a wish. If he does not flap his wings before he flies out of sight, the wish will come true.

If anyone sweeps in front of you, you will not be married.

If you drop your dishcloth, your sweetheart is coming.

Throw a love vine on a bush; if it grows, your sweetheart loves you.

If you shiver without apparent cause, someone is walking over your grave (the ground where your grave will be).

If you plant a cypress vine on your house, some members of the family will die.

A mad-stone, a stone-like substance sometimes found in the body of a deer, will prevent the bite of a mad dog from producing hydrophobia.

To cure bone felon, catch a live frog, split open its back, taking care not to inflict instant death, and place the space over the affected part.

The frog is bound and kept there till it dies, and the inflammation is said to pass into the frog's body.

To stop a flow of blood, read a certain passage in the Bible. This verse is known to only a few people. When there is a bad case of bleeding the name and age of the unfortunate person is carried to the one having this power. He or she will retire to a room with the Bible. After reading the verse and chanting a few magic words, the conjurer will claim that the flow has stopped.

Tie a frog around a child's neck to make it teethe easily.

If your children wear a little bag of asafetida around their necks, they will not catch whooping cough.

A buckeye is very potent as a preventive of headache.

Bend a horseshoe nail into a ring to avert rheumatism.

Warts are caused by touching frogs and may be obliterated; by applying to them three times at intervals "stump water," that is, water which has been concentrated or partly evaporated through exposure to sunlight when held cupped in a rotten stump. This is a sure cure.

Stepping on ants brings rain.

Stepping on a spider brings rain.

The cry of a rain crow after a drought is a sure sign of rain.

If you sit on a featherbed, lightning will not strike you.

If you put your feet in a bowl of water during a storm, lightning will not strike you.

A turtle or crawfish will not let go until it thunders.

If you sew on Sunday you will have to pick out each stitch with your nose.

Animals can talk at midnight on Christmas Eve.

A cat can cause the death of a sleeping person by sucking the breath.

To keep a dog at home, cut off the tip of his tail and put it under the doorstep.

Feed a dog gunpowder and raw meat to make him savage.

If you kill a toad your cow will go dry.

A whippoorwill's singing near a house means a death in the family.

Butterbean bulls must not be burned or fed to cattle or hogs but thrown into the road in order to insure the fertility of fields, cattle, hogs, and wife.

When the stars begin to huddle
The earth will soon become a puddle.

If the November goose bone be thick, so will the winter weather be,
If the November goose bone be thin, so will be winter weather be.

Curls that kink, and cords that bind
Signs of rain and heavy wind.

If a cat washes herself in the usual fashion, the weather will be fair, but it will be bad if she licks her fur the wrong way or washes above her ears, or sits with her tail toward the fire.

Whooping cough can be prevented by swallowing three small living minnows.

Measles may be avoided by swallowing three buckshot each day until nine have been taken.

To cure "sore mouth" among children, give them seven sips of water from a heel of a shoe that has been worn by one who was born after their father died.

If one dreams of crossing muddy water some of the family will soon die.

Rub rabbit brains, still warm, on his gums and the baby will cut teeth easily.

Whatever one dreams while sleeping under a new quilt will come true.

Whoever plants a cedar tree that lives will not live long.

Sun beds on Monday
Have the doctor before Sunday.

If a dove flies over the house a sad message is coming.

If you point your finger at a grave, you will be the next one to be buried in the cemetery.

If a mouse cuts a hole in a house, someone who is not related to the owner must patch it. If anyone in the family patches it, he will have bad luck.

A couple will never prosper until the wedding clothes are worn out.

If you hear a turtledove call in the morning, you will move in that direction soon.

If a butterfly comes into the house, someone will come that day wearing a dress the color of the butterfly.

Break green gourds over a dog's head to make him bark up a tree.

If clothes are washed on New Year's Day the one who washes them will wash for a corpse before the year is gone.

If the ashes are carried out of the house on New Year's Day, there will be a death in the family before the year is over.

> If the milk gets wrong and will not turn,
> Put a piece of silver in the churn.

If a chicken crows after it goes to roost, it must be killed that night or some member of the family will die.

Keep a horseshoe in the fire to keep the hawks from catching the chickens.

When an owl hoots at night put the shovel in the fire, tie a knot in the corner of a sheet, or turn all of your pockets wrong side out to make it hush.

Cook peas on New Year's Day and you will be blessed with plenty all the year.

When a cow gets sick through losing her cud, wind a ball of wool thread tightly and fry it in hot lard and make her swallow it.

When the baby takes thrash (sore mouth), brew tea of nine saw bugs and make him drink it; if this fails to cure, send for an old granny woman who will cross two sticks in his mouth while talking in an unknown tongue.

GAINESWOOD

Big House

In the days before the War Between the States, an abolitionist preacher from Boston decided to come south and investigate slavery first hand. He appeared in Demopolis where he met Mr. Williamson Glover, owner of Rosemount Plantation, who invited him to come to his home and study the question. As a result of this visit the preacher wrote a book called *The Conversion of an Abolitionist* in which he described everyday life on a plantation.

He tells how the negro girls were trained, some as cooks, some to weave, others for housework and sewing. Children had their duties looking after the chickens and eggs and running errands. When the plantation bell rang, the men assembled every morning to receive their instructions for farm work from Mr. Glover, who then could sit at ease upon the top of the house, and with his spyglass check up on all those who were loafing in the field. When reprimanded, they never suspected how he knew.

A cabin was set aside for the sick and Mrs. Glover visited the sick constantly and frequently sat up all night with the more serious cases. He found all the slaves well fed, in excellent health, and devoted to their master and mistress.

Judge Bernard Harwood of Tuscaloosa gave me this information. He read the book when he was a boy clerking in a country store near Eutaw.

SLAVE CABIN AT THORN HILL

Negro Superstitions

From the negro servants of Thorn Hill, Rosemount and a few other of the oldest plantations I culled a wide variety of superstitions that are still earnestly believed. These are a few of the more interesting:

To wrap tightly a small bunch of a child's hair will raise his palate.

To take the rings off one's finger will bring on heart trouble.

If you hear a dove cry and it is the first one you have heard, take off your shoe and stocking, and on the inside of the foot of your stocking you will find a hair the color of the man's hair that you are to marry.

If you are the first person a cat looks at after he has "licked hisself," you are going to be married.

If you put a kitten under the cover of your bed and leave it until it crawls out by itself, it will never leave home.

If you walk through a place where a horse wallows, you will have a headache.

If a woodpecker raps on the house, someone is going to die.

286

If an owl screeches, turn the pocket of your apron inside out, tie a knot in your apron string, and he will stop.

If a rabbit runs across the road in front of you, to the left, it is a sign of bad luck; if it goes to the right, it is a sign of good luck.

If you cut a child's finger nails before it is a year old, it will steal when it grows up.

If a cow lows early at night, or a whippoorwill cries at midnight, someone is going to die.

If you put your hand on the head of a dead man, you will never worry about him, he will never haunt you, and you will never fear death.

If the pictures are not turned toward the wall after a death, some other member of the family will die.

If you see a dead man in the mirror, you will be unlucky the rest of your life.

To stop the clock after someone has died will keep away bad luck.

If a man's nose bleeds after he is dead, it is a sign he has been killed.

If a dead body does not get stiff at once, some other member of the family is going to die.

If a grave is dug the day before the dead is to be buried another death will be sure to take place, because an open grave at night causes death.

If a piece of the dead man's hair is put in a certain spot, you will always know where his spirit is, and if you remove the hair, you will be haunted.

If you walk backwards nine steps and then dig in the ground, you will find a hair the color of that of your husband-to-be.

If you roll three times toward the call of the first dove you hear, your backache will be cured.

If you hold a mirror over a well at twelve o'clock on the first day of May, you will see reflected the image of your future husband. If a casket is reflected, it means death.

When you shiver when you aren't cold, it is a sign you are in love.

If you lose a finger through an accident, and the finger is buried instead of burned, the place will still hurt until the buried finger takes root.

If, after you have taken a splinter from your hand, you run the splinter through your hair, the place will not hurt any more.

If you find a hairpin and hang it on a pine tree, you will surely have a letter by the next mail.

Unless your bed is pushed straight against the wall, you will have bad luck.

If you sneeze before you get out of bed, someone is coming. If you sneeze while eating, you must rinse out your mouth or there will be a death in the family.

If you cut a baby's hair before it is a year old, it will become "weak-backed" and will die.

Rubbing a baby's knees with greasy dishwater will make it walk early.

To prevent death from a rattlesnake bite, split open a frog or young chicken and put it on the bite. (The chicken must be put on hot.) When it turns green put on another.

For earache, find a cockroach, take off its head, split it in half, press the juice in the ear, and put cotton in the ear to keep the juice in it.

This will also cure an abscess in the ear.

Wear a match in your hair to keep from having headache.

To cure rheumatism, tie a dried rattlesnake skin about the affected part.

A narrow leather strap worn on the wrist prevents cramps; a copper wire band will prevent rheumatism.

To relieve sore throat, coughing, and to cure an enlarged palate, a small bit of hair in the center of the head is raised and a cotton scrap tied close up to the head, stretching the hair. (A piece of cloth rather than a string must be used, and when it is tied it is wrapped the entire length of the hair. This is called "tying up the palate." So long as it is left this way the palate will stay off the tongue, relieving the sore throat and gradually healing.

Many negroes will not burn the wood of a tree that has been struck by lightning for fear that their houses will burn or be struck by lightning.

It is bad luck to burn sassafras wood in the house; it may be burned in the yard under the wash-kettle.

A blue-gum negro is a bad negro.

Never sweep under the bed of a sick person, or he will surely die.

Never clean the finger nails after dark.

Vine and Olive Colony

In France recently a historian discovered a piece of old wall paper on which is printed a picture of Eaglesville as it looked in the early days of the colony. The Alabama State Department of Archives hopes to acquire it some day.

The Sims War

I own a copy of *The Veil Is Rent,* "A Journal created to show the 'Truth of God as it is written': And its perversion by the devil's Iscariots who 'Sop in the dish' with Jesus Christ." It was published at Womack Hill, Alabama, in May, 1891, just a few weeks before the Sims family was hanged. The following is a characteristic passage:

But where is liberty? gone. Compare our grievance with theirs. Instead of liberty the same cause that revolted the fathers are today revolting us. The foreign tyrants are resurrected in our own country, and the valiant blood that the fathers poured out for the freedom of their posterity is again coursing the veins of a nation of slaves. One consolation remains: the spirit of the fathers which sustained the Declaration of Independence is also resurrected.

Liberty! It is one of the fundamental principles for which the constitution of the United States was ordained. It is written on their flag, stamped on their coins. Yet Satan's ministering angels (lawmakers) prohibit the laborers from converting their wasting products into spirits, which would cheer their hearts and invigorate their tired bodies. The little liberty the laborers get, they have to steal it while the tyrants sleep, like poor Gideon when he threshed his wheat (Judges 6:11). After the laborers steal enough liberty to convert their wasting produce into useful spirits, they are not permitted to sell, give nor lend any of it to anybody. Laborers are not allowed to carry pistols and dirks like the devil's angels who go about on tax money hunting distilleries, harassing people, destroying their property. Liberty! Where? Not even permitted to give a boy a cigar, nor a girl a box of snuff! a leading commodity in all the civilized world.

Brer Rabbit Multiplies

"Centennial, I want to hear some more stories. I want to write some in a book like Mr. Harris did."

"If you want 'em writ in a book I can git 'em for yuh. My niece over to Eutaw kin write an' she knows a lot on 'em. I'll send word over for her to write 'em down and send 'em to yuh."

The following tales are printed as received:

BRER RABBIT AND BRER DOG

One cold morning Brer Rabbit was going down the road and he met brer dog and brer dog asked brer rabbit was he foots coal and brer rabbit say yas, and they both walked along togather and talked for some distance after while brer rabbit ask brer dog whar he git sich good sho from and brer dog tole him he git dem fum de cheny store so brer dog took pity fer de rabbit and told him to try on one of his shoe so de rabbit put on one and went up the road a little piece and cum back and asked to try two shu so brer dog being good nature he let the rabbit the Secon Shoe the rabbit com back and said the two front shu too high infrunt so the dog let him have two hind shoes and the rabbit ran off with the dog shoe and the dog ran after him holling wait dar, wait dar, and ever sence dat day dog have been running rabbits just to git his *shoes fum him*.

BRER FOX CAUGHT UNDER A ROCK

Soon one morning brother rabbit was gathering he self sum hucaberries and looked over the bank of rock and saw brer fox under a rock and grunting very loud so he ran where the fox was and raised the rock off the fox and as soon as he did so the fox grabb'd the rabbit and said you are so sharp until no one can catch you, so the rabbit beg and told him in he country when a man do a good deed as he had done there is nothing to harm him so both argued for some time and at last they agreed to let the brer tarpin settle the matter so they both went down and called the Tarpin out and he said good monin boys and the both spoke so brer rabbit told how he helped brer fox, and then brer fox wanted to eat him up so brer Tarpin said you have to show me jest how you both were before you help brer fox so the three went to the place, and brer Tarpin said what was you brer fox and brer fox went down the hill and brer rabbit raised the rock as before and brer fox laid under it and the rabbit let it down on him as before so then brother Tarpin told bro rabbit show me what you was doing when you saw brer fox and where you was standing brer rabbit said I was rite up here and—hurry! hurry! hurry! cried brer fox this rock is heavy. Now boys said bro Tarpin I shall settle this matter the best I can fur—hurry! hurry! hurry! please—cried bro fox Well bro rabbit brer fox is not starving so you had better let him alone for an gone home, and every sence then the foxes don't built their caves in the ground. You will find them in stumps and hollow logs.

BRER RABBIT'S HORSE

Brer rabbit and brer fox was coating the same gal and the rabbit was so small and the fox would joak him before the guirls so he decided to get even with him, so he slipped to see the gals by he self while he was dare he tole them that brer fox was his saddle horse and that he would ride him over that very night to see dem so he went back and told brer fox that dey both muss call on de gals tonight so they both got ready and the rabbit said to the fox, suspose we ride. The fox say brer rabbit you studie the plan for us so the rabbit said I will get a bridle and saddle and you ride me half de way and I will ride you de other half so they started to see the gals, brer fox jumped on de rabbit and rode him over half de way so the rabbit was very tired brer rabbit put the bridle and saddle on the fox and just as he got to the gate brer rabbit spurred the fox in his short ribs and the fox ran in the house where the guirls was and the rabbit jumped off and said to the guirls I told you that brer fox was my saddle hosse every sence that day the rabbit and the fox have never visit together again.

THE FOX AND THE RABBIT

The rabbit and the fox were buddies. They always had a farm together. The rabbit say, "Brer Fox, what will we plant this year?"

Brer Fox say "we will plant peas, Brer Rabbit."

Brer Rabbit say "I will take the top this year and give you the bottom an' nex' year I'll take the bottom an give you the top."

When the nex year come round Brer Fox ax Brer Rabbit what we will plant this year. Brer Rabbit say "we will plant peanuts this year an I get the bottom an you get the top."

When nex year come round Brer Fox say, "What we plant this year, Brer Rabbit?" Brer Rabbit say, "Wel plant corn this year, Brer Fox, an' I gits the top." Brer Fox say all right. When the nex year come round Brer Fox say, "What we plant this year, Brer Rabbit?"

Brer Rabbit say, "I get the bottom this year so I guess we plant taters." An so the fox never got nothing to eat and Brer Rabbit got it all.